DEPRESSION

First published in 1983 when it won the MIND book of the year award, this best-selling book has helped thousands of people leave the prison of depression. Dorothy Rowe gives people a way of understanding their depression which matches their experience and which enables them to take charge of their life and change it. She shows that depression is not an illness or a mental disorder but a defence against pain and fear, which we can use whenever we suffer a disaster that our life is not what we thought it was.

Depression is an unwanted consequence of how we see ourselves and the world. By understanding how we have interpreted events in our life we can choose to change our interpretations and thus create for ourselves a happier, more fulfilling life.

Depression: The way out of your prison is for depressed people, their family and friends, and for all professionals and non-professionals who work with depressed people.

6 X 8/05

DEPRESSION
The way out of your prison

Third Edition

Dorothy Rowe

BR Brunner-Routledge
Taylor & Francis Group

HOVE AND NEW YORK

First edition published 1983 by Routledge and Kegan Paul
Second edition published 1996 by Routledge
Third edition published 2003
by Brunner-Routledge
27 Church Road, Hove, East Sussex, BN3 2FA

Simultaneously published in the USA and Canada
by Brunner-Routledge
29 West 35th Street, New York, NY 10001

Brunner-Routledge is an imprint of the Taylor & Francis Group

Typeset in New Century Schoolbook by
RefineCatch Limited, Bungay, Suffolk
Printed and bound in the UK by
TJ International Ltd, Padstow, Cornwall

Cover design by Lisa Dynan

British Library Cataloguing in Publication Data
A catalogue record for this book is available from
the British Library

Library of Congress Cataloging-in-Publication Data
Rowe, Dorothy.
   Depression : the way out of your prison / Dorothy Rowe.—3rd ed.
     p.   cm.
Includes bibliographical references and index.
   ISBN 1–58391–286–X (pbk. : alk. paper)
   1. Depression, Mental.   I. Title.
RC537 .R66   2003
616.85′27—dc21   2002151126

ISBN 1–58391–286–X

CONTENTS

PREFACE

Depression is as old as the human race, and rare is the person who has not felt its touch. Sometimes, suddenly, without apparent reason we feel unbearably sad. The world turns grey, and we taste a bitterness in our mouth. We hear an echo of the bell that tolls our passing, and we reach out for a comforting hand, but find ourselves alone. For some of us this experience is no more than a fleeting moment, or something we can dispel with common-sense thoughts and practical actions. But for some of us this experience becomes a ghost whose unbidden presence mars every feast, or, worse, a prison whose walls, though invisible, are quite impenetrable.

Depression, in this century, [the twentieth] has been called an illness and treated with pills and electroconvulsive therapy (ECT). Some people are greatly helped by this treatment. Their depression vanishes, never to return. However, for some people, pills and ECT bring only temporary relief or no change at all. For these people something more is needed, and this is not surprising, since being depressed is something more than being ill.

If we have measles or a broken leg, we may feel miserable and inconvenienced, but, unless we feel we are so ill that we might die, we do not spend our time worrying about our sins, or contemplating the futility of existence. Yet if we are depressed this is what we do. In our own way and in our own terms we think about, agonise about, the issues of life and death – which are about what purpose life has, what faith we can live by, whether our life ends in death or whether something lies beyond death, what we have done and our feelings of shame and guilt, fear and courage, forgiveness and revenge, anger, jealousy, hate and love. For some of us, out of this period of painful turmoil comes a measure of peace and wisdom; for others, the confusion continues.

Depression is so common in all cultures and throughout history that it seems to be more than just a painful illness. It seems to be a universal experience, a period of unhappy withdrawal, an uncomfortable hibernation where the person comes to realise that something has gone wrong with his life and that something needs to be put right. Why is it, then, that some people going through this experience do discover what it is that needs to be put right, while others go on and on in miserable confusion?

Over the past twelve years I have had long conversations with people whose depression has persisted despite all the best medical treatment. I have also had long conversations with people who have had their fair share of problems but nevertheless still cope. People who cope and people who get depressed see the issues of life and death in very different terms.

Some of the depressed people I have talked with have found their way out of their depression. Others still get depressed from time to time, but they now have some idea why this happens. Depression is a prison which we build for ourselves. Just as we build it, so we can unlock the door and let ourselves out.

Dorothy Rowe
Eagle, Lincolnshire, 1983

PREFACE TO THE SECOND EDITION

When in 1983 I was writing this book I never anticipated that it would still be being read a decade or more later. In that time my life changed, as did the National Health Service. The substance of the book remains as valid as ever, but there are some things which I now know are important but which were not in the first edition. Many people have told me that they have been greatly helped by this book, but depression remains as common as ever because we fail to understand ourselves. The cure for depression is not pills but wisdom.

Dorothy Rowe
London, 1995

PREFACE TO THE THIRD EDITION

Ideas permeate throughout society slowly. When this book was first published in 1983 an idea held by very few people was that depression could be understood and dealt with solely in terms of how we live our life. Nineteen years later it is a far from rare idea, although it still causes controversy.

Some ideas permeate society from the top down. Fashion idols such as the famous Beckhams start a fashion and others follow. Scientists invent a theory, create new jargon, and gradually the whole world starts to talk of holes in the ozone layer, global warming and greenhouse gases. Some ideas begin at the bottom and permeate up. People discover from their own personal experience that what those at the top, the 'experts', say is not right. When someone like me, an unknown psychologist, puts what they have discovered into an accessible book they are delighted, and they tell their friends.

It is this word-of-mouth, grassroots publicity which has ensured the longevity of this book. I have not been showered with recognition and honours by my psychologist colleagues and certainly not by psychiatrists. But what has happened, time and time again, some complete stranger has written to me or accosted me after a lecture with the words, 'You wrote that book about me.'

When ideas develop at grassroots level they flow around and we ingest them, often without knowing that we do. We produce the idea and feel that we have invented it. When we know that we got the idea from someone else we acknowledge this at first but then we stop doing this and pass the idea off as our own. An idea which is central to this book, that depression can be our response to the discovery that there is a serious discrepancy between what we thought our life was and what it actually is, I got from Phillip Hodson, now Fellow of the British Association for Counselling and Psychotherapy. In the first few months of talking about this idea I used to acknowledge Phillip as its author, but, as I once told him, I stopped doing this. Phillip did not mind because, like me, he sees his ideas as children. You create them, and then you have to let them go. If they go out into the world and do good, you can feel happy, even though you cannot take the credit.

Often grassroots ideas inspire people, who otherwise would have lived quietly, to do brave things. One such person is Terry Lynch, an Irish GP. Psychiatry in Ireland is still very traditional, and this is the kind of psychiatry which Terry Lynch would have learnt in his training. As a GP he could have enjoyed a hard-working but quiet life, tending the physically ill and sending those with troubled minds to the psychiatrists, but he found that what the psychiatrists did did not accord with his experience. So he encouraged his troubled patients to talk to him, and out of these talks he wrote his book *Beyond Prozac: Healing Mental Suffering without Drugs*, a book which he knew would not please his psychiatrist colleagues. In this he said,

I now believe that depression is not a 'psychiatric illness'. Depression is a coping mechanism, a withdrawal within oneself when reaching out to others has become too painful, too risky. Depression is an unhappy place to be, but for the person who suffers with it, depression is the lesser of two evils. . . .

Doctors believe that depression serves no purpose. We have had 'Fight Depression' and 'Defeat Depression' campaigns, as if depression were an enemy to be exterminated. These campaigns have received great publicity. But they have made little impression, either on depression or on the suicide rate. I believe that even the most severe depressions make sense, and are

understandable in the context of the life that person has
lived and experienced.[1]

In his book Terry Lynch told the story of Jean whom
psychiatrists had diagnosed as having a severe anxiety disorder. They had spent no time listening to her and trying to
understand her story. Terry Lynch wrote,

Had they focussed on the real issue – her total lack of
inner safety and security – they might have got
somewhere. Jean's anxiety was not her problem – quite
the opposite: it was her protector. Feeling constantly
unsafe and under threat, her anxiety protected Jean from
taking risks which would have left her open to further
hurt. Even simple things like going for a walk had
become very threatening to her. While becoming a
recluse was painful to her, it was less painful than taking
any risks.[2]

That depression and anxiety, and other mental disorders, are defences, not illness, is an idea that is spreading
gradually.[3] Different people in different places can come to
the same conclusions. While Terry Lynch was dealing with
the pregnancies and births in his practice, Paula Nicolson
at Sheffield University was researching the problem of
postnatal depression and writing an excellent book for
mothers and fathers, essential reading for any family where
postnatal depression is, or could be, an issue.[4] They both
came to the same conclusion. Terry Lynch wrote,

What women with post-natal depression need is social,
emotional and psychological support. Post-natal
depression is not a 'mental illness'. It is an understandable
human response to one of the most challenging human
experiences of all – becoming a mother. Why do we need
psychiatric reasons when there is a perfectly adequate
human explanation?[5]

The Welsh poet Gwyneth Lewis told me that she had not
read any of my work until after she had gone through a long
depression, emerged from it, and then written what is
undoubtedly the best book I have ever read about one per-

son's experience of depression. It is *Sunbathing in the Rain: A Cheerful Book about Depression.* Gwyneth wrote,

We are all the artists of our own lives. We shape them, as best we can, using our experience and intuition as guides. But we're also natural liars and we get things wrong. It's so easy for the internal commentary that forms how we live to become a forgery. Approached in a certain way, depression is a lie detector of last resort. By knocking you out for a while, it allows you to ditch the out-of-date ideas by which you've been living and to grasp a more accurate description of the terrain. It doesn't have to come to this, of course, and most people are able to discern their own truths perfectly well without needing to be pushed by an illness. But my imagination is strong and it takes some people longer than others to sort out pleasing fancies from delusions.

If you can cope with the internal nuclear winter of depression and come through it without committing suicide – the disease's most serious side effect – then, in my experience, depression can be a great friend. It says the way you've been living is unbearable, it's not for you. And it teaches you slowly how to live in a way that suits you infinitely better. If you don't listen, of course, it comes back and knocks you out even harder the next time, until you get the point.

Over twenty years I've discovered that my depression isn't a random chemical event but has an emotional logic which makes it a very accurate guide for me. It kicks in when I'm not listening to what I really know, when I'm being wilful and harming myself. Much as I hate going through it, I've learned that depression is an important gift, an early warning system I ignore at my peril.[6]

When you become depressed you have a choice. You can choose to make your depression a lifelong prison from which you get rare glimpses of sunlight, or you can make it a tough school which teaches you wisdom. If you choose the tough school you will find this book to be a useful textbook.

Dorothy Rowe
London, July 2002

ACKNOWLEDGEMENTS

The author and publisher are grateful to the following for their permission to reproduce passages from copyright material as follows: Fleur Adcock for 'Things' from *The Inner Harbour* by Fleur Adcock (published by Bloodaxe Books); Connie Bensley for extracts from her poems 'April', 'Technique' and 'Willpower' in *Central Reservations* (published by Bloodaxe Books, 1990); Alan Brien for extracts from *In the Name of Love* by Jill Tweedie (1979); Faber & Faber for quotations from T.S. Eliot (*The Elder Statesman*, 1958 and 'Little Gidding' in *Four Quartets*, 1974), D.H. Lawrence ('The Hands of God' in *The Ships of Death & Other Poems*, 1950), Robert Lowell (*Day by Day*, 1978) and Louis MacNeice (*Collected Works*, 1966); Farrar, Straus & Giroux Inc. for quotations from 'Day by Day' by Robert Lowell and 'The Elder Statesman' by T.S. Eliot; Harcourt Brace Jovanovich Inc. for a quotation from 'Little Gidding' from *Four Quartets* by T.S. Eliot; HarperCollins Publishers Ltd, for extracts from *Part of a Journey* by Philip Toynbee, © Philip Toynbee, 1981; HarperCollins Publishers Ltd for extracts from *Sunbathing in the Rain* by Gwyneth Lewis, © Gwyneth Lewis, 2002; Dr Terry Lynch for extracts from *Beyond Prozac: Healing Mental Suffering Without Drugs* (published by Mercier Press, 2001); 'For Wolf Graf von Kalckreuth' from *Requiem and Other Poems* by Rainer Maria Rilke, translated by J.B. Leishman, published by Hogarth Press (1957), used by permission of the Random House Group Limited; Shambala Books Inc for extracts from *Tao Te Ching* by Lao Tzu, translated by Gia-Fu and Jane English.

Chapter 1

THE PRISON

What is the difference between being depressed and being unhappy? There is a difference, and when you have experienced both you know what this difference is.

When you are unhappy, even if you have suffered the most grievous blow, you are able to seek comfort and let that comfort come through to you to ease the pain. You can seek out and obtain another's sympathy and loving concern; you can be kind and comfort yourself. But in depression neither the sympathy and concern of others nor the gentle love of oneself is available. Other people may be there, offering all the love, sympathy and concern any person could want, but none of this compassion can pierce the wall that separates you from them, while inside the wall you not only refuse yourself the smallest ease and comfort but you also punish yourself by words and deeds. Depression is a prison where you are both the suffering prisoner and the cruel jailer.

It is this peculiar isolation which distinguishes depression from common unhappiness.[1] It is not simply loneliness, although in the prison of depression you are pitifully alone. It is an isolation which changes even your perception of your environment. Intellectually you know that you are sharing a space with other people, that you are talking to them and they are hearing you. But their words come to you as if across a bottomless chasm, and even though you can reach out and touch another person, or that person touches you, nothing is transmitted to you in that touch. No human contact crosses the barrier. Even objects around you seem further away, although you know it is not so, and while you are aware that the sun is shining and the birds are singing, you know, even more poignantly, that the colour has drained from the sky and the birds are silent.

How can you describe this experience and convey its meaning, to someone else? Saying that you are depressed, or really down, or fed-up, can mean to another person no more than the Monday morning blues, or something you could snap out of if you really tried. But you know that it is not a passing mood or something that will vanish if you try to 'pull yourself together'. The turmoil of your feelings is so great that it is impossible to know where to begin to describe them. So it is better to remain silent.

Yet there is a way of conveying what you are experiencing. If you were an artist or a film-maker, you would be able to create an image which would convey at least something of what you are experiencing. It is for this reason that I always ask my depressed clients, usually at our first meeting, this question. *If you could paint a picture of what you are feeling, what sort of picture would you paint?*

Some people answer immediately and describe their image, often in a complex way. Some people are rather shy to answer and fumble for words, sketching their image in very simple terms. But no matter whom I ask, it seems that a person's image of being depressed will be one of the following kinds.

First, there are the images of the person alone in a fog. The fog may be grey, or black, or a tangle of violent colours. The fog may be swirling round the person or still and thick like cotton wool. The person may be trying to find his way out of it, or he may be frozen in fright and hopelessness.

Next, there are the images of empty landscapes, waterless deserts or frozen wastes, or images of boundless oceans. The person sees himself trudging alone towards an empty horizon or caught in a violent storm, or sitting helplessly immobile on a burning rock or a melting ice floe.

Then, there are the images of the person, alone in a space, wrapped tightly in something or pressed down by some heavy weight. The wrapping may be a shroud, or a thick black cloth, or some encasing garment. The weight may be a crushingly heavy box, or a stone lodged over one's heart, or a bird like a heavy black owl which perches on one's shoulders. Andrew Solomon saw his depression as a heavy vine that wraps itself around an oak tree and sucks out its life, 'a sucking thing that wrapped itself around me, ugly and more alive than I.'[2]

The most elaborate images are those where the person finds himself trapped. He may be travelling along an endless black tunnel, or clinging to the sides of a bottomless pit, or grovelling in the crater of a burnt-out volcano, or locked in a cold dungeon, or sealed in a metal sphere or a black balloon. Cages come in many shapes and forms. A person may see himself alone in a diving bell deep in the waters of the cold North Sea, or abandoned high on a Ferris wheel in an empty fairground, or crouched in a small cage which is suspended by a fraying rope over a bottomless abyss.

All the images are terrible. Some contain a modicum of hope. Perhaps you could find your way through a swirling grey fog, or lift a weight from your shoulders. Help might come from outside – a friendly Eskimo might chance along or someone arrive with the key of the Ferris wheel. Perhaps you could gain the strength to help yourself – to clamber out of the pit or unwrap the heavy cloth. But, however the image is expressed, all the images have one thing in common. You are enduring a terrible isolation.

You are alone in a prison.

Chapter 2

INSIDE THE PRISON

'When I wake up in the morning,' said Rose, 'I'm too scared to get out of bed. I've lived in that house for twenty years and I've slept in that bed for just as long, and I'm too scared to get out of it and walk across the room and open my bedroom door. So I lie there and I think the most terrible, terrible thoughts and I get so frightened, I want to get up and rush around doing something so I'll be thinking of something else, but I'm too scared to get out of bed. So I just stay there getting more and more frightened.'

John gets up and goes to work. He feels safe in his small office, but when his boss comes in, first to criticise his work and then to tell him he has to attend a meeting at the factory the next day, John breaks out in a sweat and feels sick. At lunch-time he goes home, gets into bed and pulls the blankets over his head. His wife finds him there, but neither her sympathy nor her abuse can make him move. 'You're just selfish,' she cries as she goes out, slamming the door.

'Selfish' is right. Inside the prison of depression you are very selfish. But then, aren't we all selfish when we are fighting for our lives? Feeling the terror of imminent death, we strive to save ourselves. To the outside observer the depressed person does not seem to be in danger of dying, but inside the prison of depression you feel a fear as great as that of death. If you told people how frightened you are they would think you are mad. Perhaps you are mad. The thought of this makes you more frightened. The fear is so great that death might be welcome as peace, a cessation of the fear. But what if after death there is something worse than here? Or death may bring peace, but dying is so painful. There must be a reason for feeling so frightened. Perhaps you are dying – that pain in your chest – is it a heart-attack – or cancer?

But words like 'death', 'madness', 'heart-attack', 'cancer' do not convey the totality of fear that you feel when the totality of your very existence is threatened. If you are a Christian you can call it damnation.

That awful and sickening endless sinking, sinking through
    the slow, corruptive levels of disintegrative knowledge
when the self has fallen from the hands of God and sinks,
    seething and sinking, corrupt
and sinking still, in depth after depth of disintegrative
    consciousness
sinking in the endless undoing, the awful katabolism into
    the abyss.[1]

If you tell your friends that you are damned, they will hasten to tell you that you are not, that the idea of damnation is silly, that God is not like that, that you are a good person, really. If you tell your friends that you are frightened because you cannot do your job properly, you are not a good mother, that the world is a terrible place and everything is going to get worse, they will say don't be silly, your boss really appreciates you, you're a wonderful mother, don't look on the black side, it'll never happen, worse things happen at sea. They do not know what it is like in the small hours of the morning.

There are worse things than having behaved foolishly in
    public.
there are worse things than these miniature betrayals,
    committed or endured or suspected; there are worse
    things
than not being able to sleep for thinking about them. It is
    5 am. All the worse things come stalking in
and stand icily about the bed looking worse and worse and
    worse.[2]

The fear permeates your life, undermining your confidence, until the smallest decision, 'What tie shall I wear?', 'What shall I have for lunch?', becomes an impossibly difficult task. Sometimes the fear comes raw and brutal as fear; sometimes it comes in the special guise of guilt.

You have become an expert in guilt. Every action or every omission of an action you can interpret as a cause for guilt. You have failed yourself and failed other people. You have not lived up to your expectations of yourself. You have not ensured the total happiness of the people around you. You review the stupidities and failures of your life and punish yourself for crimes known and unknown, while all the time you beg yourself for peace.

> My own heart let me more have pity on; let
> Me live to my sad self hereafter kind,
> Charitable; not live this tormented mind
> With this tormented mind tormenting yet[3]

You feel guilty about being depressed and you know you deserve the punishment of depression – and worse.

> Depression is like a dark mist lurking in the corners of the
> room, always there, always ready to come surging forward
> and rising up to envelop you. It is blackness, it is
> emptiness, it is meaninglessness and total inner despair.
> Others may think you are fortunate, but you know it is all
> an empty fraud, and that one day the hollow balloon will
> burst, you will be found out and your crime exposed. What
> crime? You don't know; you only know you are guilty; and
> you can hear them coming down the corridor to get you.
> The penalty, of course, is Death and you might as well be
> your own executioner.[4]

You long for death to bring you peace and you fear death for it may bring you something worse than life. Death may bring peace, but it will take away the hope that one day the terrible grief you bear will be recompensed, that your heart will be lightened. You tell no one of this grief, since a sensible person would say, 'You should be over that by now', or 'What a stupid thing to grieve over.'

The grief might be one from childhood when a parent died or deserted the family – or deserted you. How can you describe what that meant or still means? How small and weak you were, how vast and dark and terrifying was the world. No one could understand or comfort you. 'Children soon get over it,' you heard people say. You stopped crying, but you didn't get over it. And sometimes, even now, when you remember that terrible day, you wonder, 'Was it my fault?'

The loss might be more recent, when the person you depended on, or a child you should have protected, died, or when a loved and hated parent left this life without a word of reconciliation. How can you show how guilty you are at your failure, how angry at being deserted, how desolate at being left alone, abandoned, never to make recompense, never to be reconciled, never to be approved of and receive absolute, unconditional love?

Perhaps the loved one has not died but has gone away and loves another. 'Find someone else,' say your friends, but how can you do that when the defection of the loved one proves that you are unlovable? And how can anyone else know how important the unfaithful one was to you? You can well understand the epitaph to the trooper killed at El Alamein.

To the world he was a soldier,
to me he was the world.[5]

How can you go on living when your world has ended and everyone else's world is tawdry and dull?

You can grieve over the loss of more than just people. What about grieving over the loss of childhood, and so fearing to grow up? What about grieving over the loss of youth, of beauty and virility, and so seeing yourself no longer desirable, while dreaded old age approaches? Or do you look back to when your children needed you, or you were the man in charge, the leader in your field, and now no one needs you, no one admires or respects you? You fear becoming dependent on others and having them pity you. Or are you mourning a dream, something that was once bright and splendid but now unrealisable in this hard, cruel and sordid world? There will be no promised land, no happy ending. Such losses are hard to name and even harder to mourn.

Griefs like these bring hopelessness. Things will never change, or if they do they will only get worse. What is the use of hoping or striving? Once you were ambitious; now you are bitterly resigned to your awful fate and cannot fight against it. You are filled with grey and heavy indifference, even towards people who were once important to you. Love has fled, leaving only an awareness of an absence of love. Once you were concerned about other people and yearned to right other people's wrongs. Now other people's tragedies do not impinge on you, or only serve as further proof, if further proof were needed, that the world is in a perilous state.

You do not love, but you are filled with bitterness and jealousy. Bitter that your life has gone awry and jealous that other people, quite undeserving, have such easy lives and do not suffer as you do. You hate yourself for feeling such horrible jealousy, just as you hate yourself for being unable to love. You get so angry, angry with yourself and angry with the world. Why isn't the world the way you know it ought to be? You try and try to make the world, life, people, what they ought to be, and you get nowhere. You feel futile, frustrated, and very, very angry.

> Loved ones – my wife Sally and the children – all agree I'm less impatient than I used to be. And that was no minor failing. An intolerant, and intolerable, demand that things happen, people act, just when I wanted them to happen and act. I never really thought that the whole line of traffic in the jam ahead should immediately get on to the verge and let us pass; but I spoke and behaved as if I did think this. Possessed by a noxious demon of furious impatience. The rampant, tumescent self.
>
> Not that I'm now a model of saintly patience; far from that. I doubt if I've even reached the average level. But now, when held up on the road, I get out my rosary and repeat my mantra – 'The Peace of God' – and nearly always manage to keep my mouth shut – instead of taking it out on poor Sally. (Though at bad times the beads get rough treatment and the unspoken mantra sounds more like a curse than a blessing.)[6]

Irritable and miserable, you push people away from you, and then get scared that they will go and leave you all alone. So you pretend that everything is all right. You try and smile and to be ordinary, but the pretence is so wearying and inside you are silently screaming.

'When I walk down the street with my friend,' said Jackie, 'I feel there's a glass wall between us. I feel I'm alone. I want to scream and shout out. I try to break the glass but its like plastic. It bends but it doesn't break.' One day, despairing that those around her would ever understand what was happening to her, she wrote the following account and gave it to her doctor. He passed it on to me.

Four years ago next January I gave birth to a little boy, it was one of the most happy times of my life. We were told we'd never have children, so you can imagine I'd never felt so happy and elated. Although I'm the eldest girl of seven and thought I knew a lot, little things happened every day to prove me wrong, but I coped with everything and enjoyed it immensely. When Neil was three months old we were posted to Holtby, from then everything in my life seems to have changed (mainly me). I became very lonely, no friends, no-one to chat with, started taking it out on my husband Ron. Neil was not a sleeper, caused a lot of trouble at nights, I became over the next few months very nervous, depressed, aggressive with Ron, I remember feeling very low at the time, I went to the doctors with it but couldn't talk about it, couldn't talk to Ron about it, couldn't talk to friends, couldn't talk to Mum as she's the kind of person who says 'I've had seven kids I never felt anything like this, so it doesn't exist.' I started to feel all sorts was wrong with me, I remember getting an awful lot of pain in my right breast, I was so frightened. I stopped making love out of fear, couldn't bear him to touch me, I became lower and lower. Finally I went to the doctor but it took me months to be convinced it was muscular.

I felt so badly depressed that if I read in a paper someone had this disease or that disease in my mind over the next few weeks I would have it, but no matter how I tried I just kept getting lower and lower. The doctor after a while sent me to see the psychiatrist who treated me with anti-depressants, but I couldn't talk to him. I wouldn't take the pills he prescribed me 'cause all the time I could hear mum's voice saying this isn't real, you don't get like this, so I became more fearful of trying to tell anyone. I became worse and our marriage was beginning to show strain. I dreaded getting out of bed in a morning to start another day.

I went to see the doctor again and whilst we were chatting he asked to take some blood tests as I'd had little dots come up under my eyes and he said it could be caused by a higher fat level. I was petrified waiting for the results. When they came back he said yes, your fat is too high so he put me on a special diet, I tried to talk to mum about everything I'd felt but she said I was silly. That was the last time I talked to anyone. The doctors told me not to worry about having a higher fat level, with the proper diet I could keep it under control and bring it down even.

At this time my dad seemed to be ill a lot, always dizzy and off colour, he was put on blood pressure pills and I noticed that he got the spots under his eye too, so my mind put two and two together and trouble really started then. I stopped sleeping, stopped eating and just started living in a full time nightmare world. I was so closed in my own frightened world there just didn't seem to be a way out. Ron had a lot of patience with me but he got so mad and frustrated with me because I couldn't talk. I got pregnant again and I was told I was having twins. For a while other things didn't matter although deep down the thoughts never left me, but I was so intent on looking after myself so the babies would be okay that I felt different for a couple of months, but as soon as they were born everything started again. I didn't know how to cope. I was so tired all the time. We went home for Xmas. At Boxing Day tea time dad had a stroke, my world fell apart. He was in hospital a week then came home. I was convinced then it'd happen to me. Two weeks later he died. My God, I was so full of grief it was like I'd lost a part of my body, but from then I've become even more down and depressed and still couldn't talk to anyone, until one day I thought I'd explode, I thought I'd really gone demented, that's when I called Mrs Bates, the health visitor, in and got taken into the psychiatric hospital.

Now I don't seem to have a life. There's always some fear to take over the next one. I don't sleep, I'm frightened all day of the night to come because I know that I'll get restless and tensed up, won't be able to breathe, won't be able to swallow, will start feeling numb and petrified – all the time I drum into myself that I've got to snap out of it. There's far more going on in my head than what's on this paper, I just feel all the time there is a way to unjumble it all please somebody help me find it. I'm twenty-seven with three lovely children, a good husband, I can't bear the thought of living another day like I've lived the last four. I've been shaking and nervous whilst I've written this but I feel calmer now please somebody help me get rid of everything in my mind.

Chapter 3

HOW TO BUILD YOUR PRISON

Depression is not a genetic fault or a mysterious illness which descends on us. It is something which we create for ourselves, and just as we create it, so we can dismantle it.

If you have talked to a GP or psychiatrist about being depressed you might have been told that the depression results from a 'chemical imbalance' in your brain. You might also have been told that the antidepressant drug you were prescribed would restore the chemical balance of your brain. Words such as 'low serotonin levels' and '5-HT neurotransmission' might also have been used, so that, even though you might not understand the doctor's explanation, it sounded like real medical science. You were not to know that what you were listening to was what David Healy calls 'biobabble'.[1]

David Healy is a psychiatrist internationally renowned for his research on the drugs used in psychiatry. In writing about the latest group of antidepressant drugs, the selective serotonin reuptake inhibitors (SSRIs) he pointed out that 'There is no correlation between how effective these drugs are at blocking serotonin reuptake and how effectively or quickly they cure depression. The reason why so many of these compounds are being produced has probably more to do with marketing and legal issues than with "science".'[2]

David Healy is not alone among psychiatrists in rejecting the idea that depression can be explained as a chemical imbalance. In an editorial in the *British Journal of Psychiatry*, Dr P.J. Cowen, reviewing the research on the chemical changes in the brain while a person is depressed, wrote,

What we do not know is why these changes are associated with the development of depressive disorders in some people but not in others. At the root of this problem lies the need to understand individual differences in response to stress and adversity. Only models providing an integration of biological, personal and social factors are likely to have sufficient explanatory power for this task.[3]

That is, to understand why some people get depressed and others do not, we need to understand how different individuals interpret stressful and adverse situations, and to relate this, not just to physiological events, but to the individual's life and the world he lives in.

Many people do not want to think about their life and the world they live in. They want to see their depression as being nothing more than an outcome of the biochemistry of their brain. Andrew Solomon pointed out that saying, ' "I'm depressed but it's just chemical," is a sentence equivalent to, "I'm murderous but it's just chemical." Everything about a person is just chemical if one wants to think in those terms.'[4]

Understanding depression in this way is a complex, difficult task. This is what I have set out to do. I try to write as simply as possible, but, nevertheless, to follow what I write the reader has to think, and thinking is the hardest work in the world. No wonder many doctors prefer to talk vaguely about 'chemical imbalance'. They rely on the fact that depressed people tend to be well-behaved, at least in public, and that they will not ask difficult questions such as, 'Where are the test results that show I have a chemical imbalance?' There can be no test results because there are no physical tests for depression, or any of the states which psychiatrists call mental disorders.[5]

Of course there are physical changes when we are depressed. Every emotion, pleasant or unpleasant, is accompanied by physical changes which become more profound the longer the emotions persist. Being depressed is a profound emotional experience, and this upsets the body's functioning. Depressed people are very prone to catching colds or flu, and, sadly, some go on to develop cancer or heart disease. Happiness keeps us healthy.

Some people have found that they become depressed after a bout of flu, and some women find that they get depressed or become more depressed in the week before menstruation. However, this is not to say that influenza or premenstrual tension causes depression. Not everyone gets depressed after a bout of flu and not all women endure a monthly depression. When we are physically ill we feel miserable, which means that we tap into our store of miserable thoughts. If these are the kind of thoughts which lay the foundation for the prison of depression, then the flu or the onset of menstruation can be the pathway into the prison of depression.

Whenever we become aware of some change in our body's functioning we have to interpret it in some way, just as we have to interpret or find a meaning for everything that happens to us. (When we say we cannot understand something or we find something to be meaningless we are still interpreting that thing as being not understandable or as being meaningless.) Suppose we trip over a carpet, fall down a flight of stairs and break a leg. How shall we interpret what has happened? We can see the physical reasons for the leg breaking – the carpet, the fall, the way we landed. But there are other reasons as well. Some of us would immediately see the cause as being in ourselves – we were stupid, we should have looked where we were going and been more careful. Others of us would locate the cause in other people – the person who left the carpet like that, switched the light off, designed that flight of stairs, told you to go down those stairs. Some of us would find a deeper reason – it was God's way of punishing me, teaching me a lesson; the Devil or malign Fate is out to get me; this is the second disaster in a week – there will soon be a third. After that, the treatment for our broken leg can be interpreted in so many ways – we can have faith in our wonderful doctors and nurses or know that they are all incompetent, especially if they are foreign. We can feel pleased that we are making use of all the money we have paid towards our health care, or we can worry about how much it is all going to cost, all the extra expense of being off work or needing help in the house. We can choose to enjoy a rest in hospital or to fret over what is happening at home or at work. We can feel sure that the bone will knit properly and the leg soon be as good as new, or else we can know that the doctor really is not telling us the truth and that we shall be maimed for life. (Convinced and practised pessimists can think of far worse eventualities than these!)

Such a simple event, and yet no two of us would, when it happens to us, interpret it in exactly the same way. No two people ever see anything in exactly the same way. We all know this, just as we know how there are some things which we see differently now from the way we once did. Everyone has different opinions, and opinions can change.

Yet, even though we know this, we can still believe that the world *is* the way we see it and we *are* the way we are and we cannot change. In fact, we see the world the way we have learned to see it. How we see depth and distance, shapes and movement, what we see as important and what we ignore depend on our past experience. Your picture of the world is something you have created. In the same way your picture of yourself is something which you have created out of your experience. You might think that you inherited your father's bad temper and nasty nature, but you think that because as far back as you can remember that was what your mother said about you, especially when she had been upset by your father and she was taking her bad feelings out on you.[6]

Alas, if we grow up believing that the world *is* the way we see it and we *are* the way we are, then sooner or later we will get into trouble for the simple reason that everything changes. You might think that your bad temper and nasty nature are immutable, but you find that when you leave home and get a wonderful job and some equally wonderful friends your bad temper and nasty nature disappear because you are no longer constantly frustrated and made to feel bad. If, however, you do not see what has actually happened and go on believing that you are basically, unchangeably, a horrible person, then you will not believe anyone who says they love you, and so you destroy your chance of a happy, fulfilling life.

Similarly, if you believe that the world *is* the way you see it then when the world changes you feel frightened and lost. In Northern Ireland there are many people who believe that the world is the way they see it, divided into Catholics and

Protestants, eternal, unchanging enemies. To such people the Peace Process is utterly frightening, and so they do what they can to destroy it. They prefer the security of the misery they have always known to the uncertainties of happiness.

Thinking like this, people come to believe that their opinions represent the Real and Absolute Truth about the world and that anyone who does not agree with them is either mad or bad. If we believe this, we make life very difficult for ourselves and the people around us. We get angry (and frightened) because life does not always conform to our Truth, and other people do not always see the error of their ways and accept our Truth as their Truth. Our lives and the lives of the people around us can become exceedingly unhappy because we have ignored the observation of that wise ancient Greek philosopher, Epictetus. He said,

It is not things in themselves which trouble us, but the opinions we have about these things.

This book is about our opinions and how we can change them.

Nothing in life is so simple that it has one single cause. Everything that happens emerges out of a whole network of causes, and so to understand why something happens we have to bear in mind a number of different things.

To become depressed you have to have acquired over the years a complex set of interlinked opinions which relate to the particular circumstances of your life. When two people meet together in the process of psychotherapy it can take a long time to unravel these opinions and to choose whether or not to change them. Even where two people hold similar opinions, each will express the particular opinion differently. One person might say, 'My marriage is very important to me', while the other says, 'I always think of myself as part of a couple.' There are some people who hold opinions about everything under the sun, and some people who ignore most of what goes on in the world and have few opinions. However, there are some things in life that no one can ignore and about which each of us must have an opinion. It is the set of opinions we hold about these aspects of life which determines whether or not we become depressed.

So, if you want to build for yourself the prison of depression this is what you must do.

Hold as if they were Real, Absolute and Immutable Truths the six following opinions.

1. *No matter how good and acceptable I appear to be, I am really bad, evil, valueless, unacceptable to myself and other people.*
2. *Other people are such that I must fear, hate and envy them.*
3. *Life is terrible and death is worse.*
4. *Only bad things happened to me in the past and only bad things will happen to me in the future.*
5. *It is wrong to get angry.*
6. *I must never forgive anyone, least of all myself.*

Now let us see what it means to our life when we hold such opinions.

1. No matter how good and acceptable I appear to be, I am really bad, evil, valueless, unacceptable to myself and other people

'I've never thought much of myself,' said Jackie.

Helen said, 'I am not worth loving.'[7]

Joan said, 'If someone doesn't like me it must be my fault.'[8]

Mary said, 'If someone gets angry with me it must be my fault.'[9]

John said, 'If I am on my own I cease to exist.'[10]

Peter said, 'If I could construct a model of me, inside it would be something in the form of a bucket which was full of broken glass which was being rattled about rather violently, and bits fly off and this is rather dangerous.'[11]

Siegfried said that a child comes into the world 'a complete savage . . . I think that at an early age I saw this badness (in myself), unpleasantness, nastier features, and by accident or by luck I disliked them. Difficult to change one's mind after fifty or sixty years, isn't it?'[12]

Carol put her opinion of herself in a poem.

What is this self, this me?
Why do I want to change me?
Why can't I accept me?
I just don't like me, why?
Others seem to accept themselves
Why can't I? Am I so different?
Questions, questions, where are the answers?
Why do I swing so fiercely from a too high mood
Down to the miserable depths?
Why can't I be the happy medium?
When in a high mood I'm told
'That's better, more like your old self.'
Horrors. I Don't Want to Be My Old Self.
Little do they know what lay behind the 'Old Self'.
Misery, bewilderment, anxiety, unrest,
Disappointment, all hidden behind a mask,
Which is still put on even now
To face the outside world.[13]

The feeling that you are essentially bad can be expressed in many different ways. It can be felt in many different ways. Some people, like Peter, believe that inside them is something so corrupt and evil that they are a danger to other people. Some people, like Siegfried, are not so much frightened that their evil will corrupt or injure other people as proud that they have identified this evil in themselves. Some people, like Helen, would not so much see themselves as evil as simply and devastatingly dislikeable. They dislike themselves and so expect other people to dislike them. Like Mary, they always take the blame for other people's anger. Some people see themselves not so much evil or dislikeable as simply inadequate, unable to cope, to do things properly. Sometimes the sense of inadequacy becomes so overwhelming that the person, like John, feels as if he does not exist and has to have people around all the time to confirm that he does exist.

A common experience for many of us is that we think of ourselves as basically good people, but then something terrible happens that makes us feel there must be something wrong or evil inside us. Accidents or illnesses may lead us to believe that God is punishing us for sins of which we were unaware; betrayed or cruelly used by someone we thought loved us, we come to think of ourselves as soiled or unlovable or disgusting and horrible. As time goes by we may allow our friends and our common sense to convince us that, despite what has happened, we are good and lovable. But if you are convinced that you are bad and evil, then you resist all evidence to the contrary. Anyone who tells you that you are good and lovable is either too stupid to see what you are really like or is lying and wanting to deceive you, either because he pities you (which you hate) or because he wants to use or to hurt you. When professional people like doctors or nurses or psychotherapists say that they like you, you know they do not mean it. They're just paid to say that.

Knowing that you are bad you must constantly struggle to be good, to present an acceptable face to the world. Like Carol, you need 'a mask ... to face the outside world'. You can never be yourself, since if people knew what you are really like they would reject you. You might have been wearing a mask or playing a role for so long that, even if you wanted to, you could not be yourself because you do not know who you are or what you are really like and you dare not take the risk of finding out. To know how to behave you have to rely on other people's opinions, and so you live under the tyranny of *'they'*. 'What will *they* think?' is the thought that accompanies every action and determines every decision.

When I worked in Lincolnshire many of my clients were depressed housewives and mothers. Often our conversation turned to the worries and stresses of housework, and I formed the impression that there must be a book of rules of housekeeping which was handed down to Moses at the same time as the Ten Commandments, and, while it is possible to break all the Ten Commandments and still be forgiven by God, infringements of the Heavenly Housekeeping Book are Absolutely Unforgivable either in this world or the next. The Heavenly Housekeeping Book contains a large number of rules and regulations, all aspects of the one Universal Law – YOUR HOME MUST BE PERFECTLY CLEAN AND TIDY AT ALL TIMES.

Thus your life must be spent in keeping this rule and in

getting your family to keep it as well. God sends his inspec-tors in the form of your mother (alive or dead) and the woman down the street whose house is always spotless, who has children who put their things away, who always looks beautiful and can easily cope with a full-time job and a large family. Even if these inspectors cannot see everything, God knows if it is over two weeks since you tidied the linen cupboard or turned out the spare room.

I often laugh at this kind of keeping up of appearances, but I do know what it means to have the rules of the Heav-enly Housekeeping Book branded into your flesh. I know the terrible despair you can feel when keeping the house clean is just beyond your strength, or, when your life is going badly awry, you obsessively clean and tidy your house since this is the only part of your life that you can control and keep in order. Now younger generations of women might scorn the idea of the Heavenly Housekeeping Book but they have their own set of Immutable and Absolute Rules for Being a Woman. These are that you must have a very successful career as well as several brilliant, ambitious, beautiful chil-dren, all well-behaved but each an individual. You must be a superlatively good cook and hostess. You must have an attractive personality, always smiling, always happy, and you must be slim and dressed in the latest fashions. You do have one choice. You can be very happily married to a tall, hand-some, successful man or you can be a sophisticated single leading a glamorous life, but, whichever you choose, you must be a very accomplished and successful lover, never rejected but always under siege from dozens of desirable suitors. Fail to keep ALL of these rules and you are a Complete and Utter Failure. However, even if you do manage to keep all these rules you must never admit that you have done so. You must always insist that you are a failure.

Women not only inflict these punitive ideas on them-selves, they inflict them on other women and so create what the journalist Julie Burchill called 'the Culture of Cringe'.

Earlier this year, the actress Zoë Wanamaker said quite an extraordinary thing. Talking about her quirky looks, she then added: 'But then I don't know any woman who is happy with her looks. I certainly wouldn't want to be friends with anyone who was.' I thought this last sentence was the most extraordinary thing I had read in ages, and sat back waiting for it to turn up as a prime piece of loonyspeak in all those loose-talk titbit columns that most of the broadsheets have. But the weeks passed and not a whisper of this wacky twittering came to light. And then I realised that I, not Miss Wanamaker, was the one out of step. And that the Culture of Cringe among successful women was a club that practically everyone but me had a key-card to.[14]

When a woman takes part in the Culture of Cringe she is either lying, because she actually values herself but pretends that she does not, or she is telling the truth and thus allowing the Culture of Cringe to deplete her minimal self-confidence even further.

Men have an equally silly obsession. To deny this badness they must constantly be involved in competing with other men in every situation which might be remotely construed as being a competition. When I was writing my book *Friends and Enemies* my friend the novelist Tim Lott and I compared notes on how men and women conducted friendships. Tim's first novel *White City Blue*[15] concerned four men who believed that they had been friends from schooldays. Certainly they had met one another at school but, as the story unfolded, it became clear that what held this group together were not the hallmarks of friendship – trust and loyalty – but endless competition. Neither in his novel nor in his talks with me did Tim deplore such competition. To him this was what men did. Competition for men was as natural as breathing. This is all very well if the man is self-confident and does not feel destroyed if he loses. But, as Tim showed in *White City Blue*, these four men were competing in order to hide from others and from themselves what they each saw as their contemptible weakness. Two of them came to be destroyed by their self-deception. The other two, by acknowledging their weakness as their own truth, became strong, and thus were able to enjoy the trust and loyalty of true friendship.

Alas, not many men achieve such self-understanding. Rather than reveal their weakness, their badness, by, as they see it, losing a competition or even compromising on some group decision, some men are prepared to sabotage the institution they work for, or to neglect and reject their wives and families, or to undermine their own health and strength. Not all such men are aiming at great riches and power. All some might want is to compete well enough so as not to be wiped out by the men they see as strong. Such men are scared of everyone they see as being in a position of power, and so they have to work extremely hard to avoid criticism and rebuke. They cannot risk appearing lazy, or less than keen, or insufficiently prepared. Like the women who try to present themselves as being perfect in every way, they fear being found out.

Many men use alcohol to hide from others what they see as their despicable weakness, and to hide from themselves their fear and despair. For forty years the American writer William Styron drank to excess. He saw alcohol as 'the magic conduit to fantasy and euphoria, and to the enhancement of imagination.'[16] Eventually his liver rebelled and he found he could no longer tolerate the smallest amount of alcohol. He discovered that, in fact, he had used alcohol 'as a means to calm anxiety and incipient dread I had hidden away for so long in the dungeons of my spirit.'[17]

Women too can use alcohol in this way. At one point in her life Gwyneth Lewis used alcohol to hide from herself. She wrote, 'My great fear was that I'd never be able to write sober because I'd now become too dull and boring. I was making a common mistake among writers – confusing chaos with creativity. Of course you can manage the odd piece of good work in the midst of a crisis – a fluke – but this is the exception rather than the rule. The truth is, it's far easier to lead a colourful, "poetic" life than actually write poems. The former requires a good liver and seedy friends, the latter all the discipline of a civil servant.'[18] It is not just writing that requires the discipline of a civil servant. If you want to do any job well you have to be sober.

When we lie to ourselves about the truth of our feelings we cannot simply be ourselves. We force ourselves to play a role, indeed, to play many roles. All these roles serve to deny to ourselves who we actually are.

Playing a role, you have to be very careful of your appearance. If you experience the badness within you as filth then you have to become extremely clean. You have to devote a great deal of time and effort in keeping your body clean. If you experience the badness within you as some dangerous force to be kept under control then you will expend a lot of effort in keeping your hair neat and your clothes regular and tidy as a uniform AND you keep your feelings under control. You might devote much time to painting on a face with which to face the world, or buy extravagant, eye-catching clothes to distract the observer from the sham within, or you dress shabbily because you do not want to attract attention and you do not deserve anything better. Some people try to appear good by denying themselves all but the bare necessities of life while others try to obliterate their sense of weakness and inferiority by the acquisition of many objects.

If you experience yourself as bad then you can come to feel that you have no right to exist, to walk upon this planet and to breathe the same air as other people. So you either have to disappear or do something to justify your existence. What can you do? You can look after other people. You can be needed. If you feel that your partner and children would reject you if they discovered how bad you really are, then you can shower (and control) them with such unselfish, loving devotion that only people much wickeder than you would dare to reject you. If you feel that as a child you were deprived of loving care, you can try to make up this deficiency by caring for others (victims like you) in the way you would wish to be cared for. Thus you can devote yourself to your family and give them more care and attention than they could ever need or want. Or you can show up your family and friends for the selfish, self-indulgent people that they are by devoting yourself to Good Works. Fortunately our world never lacks the necessity for Good Works, so if you put your mind to it you can find something which allows you to support your prejudices, to annoy your enemies, to ennoble your appearance and to punish yourself. And it is at punishing yourself that you excel. You cannot merely take simple pride and pleasure in keeping your home nice, in doing your job well, in enjoying games and sport and friendly banter, in dressing in a way that suits you, in owning some things that you like, or in helping other people. Everything you do is aimed at hiding the badness within you and at punishing yourself for being bad.

It is the idea of *punishment* that gives us the clue about where the sense of badness comes from. The Bible may teach that each newborn baby carries the burden of Original Sin, but babies do not know whether they are good or bad any more than it knows whether they are boys or girls. Children learn these things from the adults around them. If you have parents, aunts and uncles, grandparents, older siblings who generally define you as good ('Who's the most gorgeous baby in the world?', 'This is daddy's darling little girl', 'Isn't he the cleverest boy you've ever seen?', 'That was a silly thing to do, dear. You won't do it again, will you?'), then there is a fair chance you will believe them, just as you believe what they tell you about how old you are and what your name is. If you have parents, aunts and uncles, grandparents, older siblings who generally define you as bad ('What a pity it's another girl', 'Mummy doesn't love a bad boy', 'You're stupid', 'You're a disgusting, wicked girl') then there is a fair chance you will believe them, especially if your childhood contains more punishments, disappointments and loneliness than rewards, security and love.

Some parents believe that a child's upbringing should prepare him for adult life in a harsh world and so a child should not be 'spoilt' by being indulged and petted. Some parents want their children to be a credit to them and, although they love their children, the children never know that they are loved because the parents are always trying to force the children to be what the parents want them to be. Some parents love their children but are so beset by their own worries and needs that the child never feels the warmth of his parents' love. Some parents do not love their children. Most parents mean well but make mistakes. Whatever the reason, every child, sooner or later, finds himself suffering and he has to explain to himself why this has happened. Is it his fault or his parents'? But if it is his parents' fault then that means that those people on whom his security depends are not looking after him properly. This thought terrifies him because he knows that he cannot look after himself. The only way out of this dilemma is for the child to re-define his situation. He decides that he is bad and is being justly punished by his good parents. The American cartoonist Jules Feiffer showed this process of reasoning in a cartoon of a little girl talking to herself. She said, 'I used to believe I was a good girl until I lost my doll and found it wasn't lost. My big sister stole it. And my mother told me she was taking me to the zoo, only it wasn't the zoo, it was school, and my father told me he was taking me to the circus, only it wasn't the circus, it was the dentist. So that's how I found out I wasn't good. Because if I was good, why would all these people want to punish me?'[19]

So, to preserve your parents as good you have sacrificed your own essential goodness, and this first act of sacrifice has begot a million others. Even today you dare not contemplate the possibility that your parents were less than perfect and that they did things to you which harmed you. Even just to think such a wicked thing about your parents shows what a wicked person you are. You try to forget the pain of childhood, sometimes by blotting out your childhood so completely that your remembered life starts when you are sixteen or seventeen. But some things are hard to forget, such as being beaten by your father or your schoolteacher. You cannot forget the pain of that, but you can do something about the pain of knowing that your suffering was being inflicted by the person who ought to be looking after you. You can protect yourself from the memory of this second terrible pain by deciding that it was right that you should have been beaten. Not only did you deserve the punishment because you were wicked, but also the person beating you was doing you good by punishing you.

In many cases the harsh punishments are inflicted so frequently that the child finds it hard to think of the punisher as being good, so he insists to himself that the punisher is good by deciding that, 'I am bad and deserve to be punished, and when I grow up I'll punish bad people in the way I was punished.' Thus the skill of being cruel gets handed down from one generation to the next.

Children who are beaten and who tell themselves that they deserved to be beaten are likely to grow up to be adults who declare, 'I was beaten as a child and it never did me any harm.' Such people do not realise that the harm the harsh punishment did them was to be unaware of the harm that was done to them. As a result they have no sympathy for themselves. They cannot empathise with the child they once were. If we cannot empathise with ourselves we cannot empathise with other people. Empathy is the skill of imagination which allows us to bridge the gulf between ourselves and other people. Empathy joins us to other people. It overcomes the aloneness of our human condition. It is a skill we are all born with, but harsh treatment in childhood can lead us to lose that skill.

One very striking feature of people who get depressed and stay depressed is the lack of love and empathy they have for the child they once were. On many, many occasions, when a depressed client told me about his or her childhood, my face revealed my shock and pain in response to this story of suffering, humiliation and cruelty endured in childhood. My client's response to my reaction was always to say something like, 'I was a bad child and I deserved my punishment. Don't get me wrong, Dorothy. My parents were wonderful people.' Such clients might express great concern for little refugee children and children who tragically die, but they cannot weep for the child each of them once was.

Alas, if they cannot weep for themselves as a child they will remain depressed. Being depressed is, in effect, a refusal to mourn for the child you once were and for the irreparable losses you have suffered. But to be able to mourn you have to be able to look at your parents and the events in your childhood with an adult eye. Adults observe critically, but you dare not criticise your parents. You may not remember the exact words of the Fifth Commandment but you dare not disobey it. The Fifth Commandment states, *Honour thy father and mother so that your days be long in the land.* Criticise your parents and you're dead.

If you listen to what people say in ordinary conversation

you will often hear them protecting their parents whenever there is some suggestion that their childhood was less than happy. When, on BBC television, Michael Parkinson interviewed the actor Martin Clunes he suggested that Martin Clunes may have been less than happy when he was sent away to boarding school following the death of his father. Martin Clunes at first demurred, saying that he had accepted it in the way that all children accept what happens to them, but then he realised that he could not honestly maintain that he had been happy. Rather than say anything critical about his family, he drew attention to the universal experience children have of adults. 'When you're a child,' he said, 'they line up to be horrible to you.'[20]

Many people will say that they had a happy childhood and, as they remember it, they did. However, there are two kinds of happy childhood.

The first is a childhood where the parents love the child simply because the child exists. Their love is unconditional and totally accepting. They do not criticise or chastise or discipline the child but instead they listen to the child, they encourage and praise, not indiscriminately but in ways which help the child to become aware that every action has consequences, and that consequences must be taken into account in making decisions. Provided that no chance disaster strikes the family bringing hardship and loss, the child in such a family is very likely to be happy, a happiness emanating from a strong sense of self-confidence and worth.

The second kind of happy childhood is one where the child very quickly identifies what will please the parents and becomes proficient in producing that kind of behaviour, and the parents consistently reward the child for being good. (Some children learn what the parents call good behaviour and produce it regularly but the parents' rewards are only intermittent and their punishments harsh. Such children do not enjoy a happy childhood.)

Knowing what pleases his parents usually enables the child to identify what will please his teachers, and so the queue of adults lining up to be horrible to him is relatively short. However, happiness based on being good is not secure. In childhood being able to please parents and teachers by being good is very simple compared to the impossible task in adulthood of pleasing family, friends, colleagues, society and God by being good. Then every day becomes a struggle to be good enough. Sooner or later disaster strikes, and it can be a hard lesson to learn that no amount of goodness prevents disaster. Only good people get depressed, and people stay depressed because they cannot accept that they need to make fewer demands upon themselves in order to satisfy themselves that they are good.

Andrew Solomon described his childhood as 'reasonably happy'.[21] In his book on depression there is a constant theme about the necessity of being good, but he did not make a clear link between striving to be good and being depressed. He described his life in some detail but he seemed not to be aware of the consequences of his interpretations of what happened to him. As a small child he sensed that his beloved mother was not happy. He wrote, 'My greatest happiness when I was a little boy came from making my mother happy. I was good at it, and it was not easy to do.'[22] Taking responsibility for his mother's happiness was an enormous task for a child. It was also an impossible task because his mother held ideas which ensured that she would be unhappy. As her son described, she believed in order and structure, something which is extremely difficult to impose on a family. He could not remember any occasion when his mother broke a promise or was late for an appointment, an achievement which comes only from enormous self-discipline, something which is not conducive to happiness. He saw in his mother a reservoir of loneliness which went back to her childhood. How could a son possibly make such a mother happy?

He tried, and no doubt she saw him trying and loved him for that. She would tell him what would make her happy, and he would try to carry out this task. Then came the day when she told him that what would make her happy was for him to kill her.

He was trapped. Whatever he did would place his sense of being a person in peril. He had built his sense of being a person on being good by pleasing his mother, so to refuse her request would mean that he was bad. How could a good son kill his mother? Moreover, he was someone whose absolute top priority in life was relationships, and the one relationship which maintained his sense of being a person was that with his mother. 'We sat in the kitchen and talked, from the time I was five until her death when I was twenty-seven.'[23]

His mother had terminal cancer and felt she could no longer endure the suffering. Other people were involved in her decision to commit suicide – her husband and her younger son. Her husband and sons agreed to carry out her request and she died with quiet dignity.

Afterwards Andrew Solomon was, as he said, devastated. Immediately he blamed himself for failing her all her life, for publishing a novel of which his mother might not have approved, for the breakdown in a romantic relationship in which 'I had invested all my faith and hope.'[24] Blaming himself for all these disasters, he became depressed.

More depressions followed, not surprisingly because he continued to strive to be good. 'Being good,' he wrote, 'is a constant struggle.'[25] His book is a paean of praise for his parents. Never once did he question whether a parent should allow a child to take responsibility for the parent's happiness. He protected his parents and thus made it impossible for himself to understand why he had become depressed. He dealt with his depression by researching the topic diligently and so his book is a vast compendium of most of the ideas that have been held about depression, of the results of scientific research on depression, and, at considerable length, of his own experience of depression. However, never once did he question how he learned to be good. He dared not break the Fifth Commandment.

So it is that fear keeps you believing that you are bad and unacceptable. So does the pride you take in knowing that you are bad and unacceptable. There are many advantages in believing this.

When I asked Jackie what advantage she got out of thinking so little of herself she was surprised at my question and said she could not think of any possible advantage.

I outlined some of the advantages that people do find. If you see yourself as weak and always in need of protection then you do not have to take responsibility for yourself. You can blame others when things go wrong in your life. If you are unwise enough to see yourself as having ability you are then under the obligation of trying to put your ability to use, of striving towards something and so running the risk of failing. You can avoid all this danger by seeing yourself as having no ability. If you want to keep a little personal pride you can say to yourself that you could have been the greatest but you are the sort of person who attracts bad luck or other people's envy and spite.

None of these advantages struck Jackie as being applicable to her. So we went on talking about other things, which led to Jackie telling me how, although she loved her husband and children dearly, running a home left her feeling unsatisfied. She knew there was something wrong with her for feeling like this and she felt very guilty when people pointed out how lucky she was to have such a good husband and lovely children. Other women were satisfied with their lives. Why wasn't she? She had grown up expecting to get married and have a family. 'It was always expected that my sister and I would leave school as soon as we were old enough and get a job – any job – until we got married,' she said. It was her parents who had expected her to leave school. There had never been any chance that she could stay on at school. I made some remarks along the lines that a woman of her (to my mind) undoubted ability would find housework and three young children exhausting and time-consuming but unsatisfying and that it was a pity her mother had prevented her from staying on at school and perhaps going on to art college.

'Oh, I wouldn't have had the ability to do that,' said Jackie, sounding as if I had just suggested that she take over as head of the World Bank.

'Yes you have,' I said.

'No I haven't – and I can't blame my mother for not letting me stay on at school. It makes me feel too guilty if I think that about her. I'd rather think that I haven't got any ability.'

'There,' I said in triumph, 'that's the advantage in thinking so little of yourself.'

Living is very often a matter of making the best of a bad job, and so if you are taught early in life to see yourself as bad, evil, valueless, unacceptable to yourself and other people then there might be sense in finding some advantages in this. But, if these advantages become very important to you, you may never inspect your opinion of yourself to discover that it is merely an opinion and not an immutable Truth and that you are free to change it. The advantages of seeing yourself as essentially bad may blind you to the fact that the opinions we hold about ourselves form the basis of our assessment of everything else in our lives and every decision we make, and if we make the opinion 'I am a bad person' the foundation of our world then the cost of our world will prove to be excessively dear.

2. Other people are such that I must fear, hate and envy them

Everything that is fine, beautiful and worthwhile has something to do with the experience of love. When we are entranced by the waves dashing against the rocks or the delicate tracery of black branches against a pale evening sky we experience the love which binds us to our splendid cosmos. When we are enraptured by music, or a painting, or a poem, or a story, or thrilled by the brilliance of the people in a play or a sport, we experience the love which binds us to our fellows. When we create something which we know is good, be it a symphony or a batch of scones, we experience the love which is the joy of creation. When we snuggle into our parent's arms, or hold our beloved in ecstatic union, or cradle our baby on our lap, or share a sympathetic joke with a friend, we partake of an experience which is at the one time ordinary yet mysterious. It is ordinary because loving relationships between people are common and to be expected. It is mysterious because it is a quality we are all born with, a quality which is an essential part of being human. Without love for others and the wondrous world we live in we shrivel up and slowly die. For human beings to survive they need air, water, food, shelter and the opportunity to love and be loved.

Yet how can you love and be loved when you are certain that at your core you are bad, evil, valueless, unacceptable to yourself and to others? You may be able to love others, but when they return your love you know that you do not deserve it and that sooner or later those you love will find you out and then reject you. Sometimes, even, the strain of waiting to be rejected is too great and so you reject your loved ones or behave badly so as to force them to reject you. Better the pain of rejection than the anxiety of waiting.

So love to you means not happiness but desolation, fear and guilt. No wonder you fear the people who are the source of this pain, just as you fear the people who, you are certain, dislike you, who criticise and belittle you, who seek to do you down in every competition. Your fear of people extends beyond individuals to whole groups of people. Middle-aged women (just like your mother) or middle-aged men (just like your father) may terrify you. As a man you may fear all women whom you see as powerful and destructive beings, or as a woman you may fear all men whom you see as insensitive and cruel. You may fear all people in authority and be reduced to speechless terror by a policeman or a doctor's receptionist. You may fear all Catholics or all Muslims, or everyone with a skin different from yours, or the rich who make you feel inferior or the poor who are scheming to rob you of all you own. Your fear of other people may be so great that you hesitate to venture beyond your own front door. You prefer not to invite strangers into your home and prefer, as you often say, to keep yourself to yourself. Even if you would like to go out more, to do different things, when you fear other people and see yourself so inadequate and valueless you lack the confidence to mix with other people. It would be easier to jump off a precipice than to walk into a room full of people.

Of course it is very difficult to like people who do not like us and even more difficult to love people who do not love us. We can, if we choose, remain indifferent to the people who dislike us, but, if we fear them, we soon find that the experience of fear is so painful that we come to hate the people whom we see as the cause of this pain. We can, if we wish, deny that we are afraid and instead claim some virtue in hating our enemies. By then we have forgotten that, as George Bernard Shaw said, 'Hatred is the coward's revenge for being intimidated.'[26]

You can be sure that people dislike you because you are

such a bad person that no one could possibly like you, but you may be uncertain as to whether other people are basically good or basically bad. Neither alternative gives you much comfort. If other people are good through and through then they will despise you when they find you out. Their mere presence makes you feel inferior. If other people are like you, basically bad but pretending to be good, then you have every reason to fear them since their words and actions have meanings which are unknown to you but which may harm you. Some people, you observe, are self-confident and appear to approve of themselves, and so you envy them so much you come to hate them, and then you get frightened that, if inadvertently you reveal your envy and hate, these people will attack you.

Moreover, you can, like Siegfried, feel superior to those self-confident people because they have failed to recognise their own essential badness, but, while you have bolstered your pride, you have not resolved your resentment that these self-confident people are happy and you are not. In fact, you find that you envy other people just as much as you hate and fear them. In your heart of hearts you know that, although some people might appear to have big problems, anyone who does not have your problems really has no problems at all. You look at your relatives, your neighbours and colleagues and you see them coping with their lives and enjoying themselves. You may hate yourself for being so wildly jealous but you stay jealous just the same.

Fearing, hating and envying others robs you of what little self-confidence you might otherwise have, but lacking self-confidence makes you dependent on people in whom you have little trust. No matter how much your loved ones try to impress on you that they are everlastingly devoted to you, you suspect that they are secretly planning to leave you, and even before this happens the disaster which you know is inevitable will overtake them and leave you alone in a dangerous world. So you insist that your parents must never ever leave you; or you demand that your husband must come straight home from work and spend all his free time with you; or you refuse promotion because that would mean spending nights away from home, fearing that on your return you would find your family gone. Such lack of trust you know is preventing your growing up, or is destroying your marriage, or is ruining your career, but you feel powerless to do anything about it. However, you may not have entered into your marriage with any great hopes and if the truth were told it would be that to some extent you despise your partner. When you were young you dreamed of someone wonderful (and still do) but because you thought so little of yourself you married someone who was not as good as you wanted but as good as you deserved. You cannot help but see your marriage as a disappointment, and, while you hate yourself for being unkind to someone who cares for you, you cannot stop yourself from being crabby, fault-finding and ungrateful.

When we hate ourselves and fear and despise other people it is impossible to behave towards others in any frank, easy, kind and loving way. It is impossible then to achieve a happy life by following the Golden Rule, 'Do unto others as you would have them do unto you.' If you fear, hate and envy other people your life becomes yet another proof of the dictum which my father was very fond of quoting, *You only get back what you give away.* If you give away love and kindness you get love and kindness back (though the returning love and kindness does not always come from the source and in the form that you particularly desire). If you give away fear, hate, envy, resentment, coldness and distrust, even though you may try to hide these under the guise of love and kindness, such bad feelings will be returned to you, not only by mere acquaintances but by those whom you love and on whom you depend.

You fear others but you may not appreciate how much others fear you. A person may pride himself on the high standards he sets for himself and other people, but as Goethe said, 'He is a man who is impossible to please, because he is never pleased with himself.' You view your own imperfections and demand perfection of yourself, and fail to achieve it. You demand perfection of your family and when they, mere fallible human beings, fail to achieve it you get very angry, just as you get so angry with the world in general which falls so short of your expectations. Your family have learned to be frightened of your anger. They know that the smallest thing – a missing button, an unmade bed, a loud noise – can provoke in you a rage quite out of proportion to the provocation. They know that the simplest action, an unguarded remark, can bring your response of punishing silence which can last for days, weeks or even years. They know that your good humour cannot be relied upon since your mood can change with frightening, unpredictable suddenness. No matter how much they love you, their fear makes them retreat from you. The rule which governs your family might be that nothing should be done or said which upsets you, but, while this rule makes you very powerful it also makes you very lonely. Your family live their lives elsewhere and they do not confide in you. You doubt their love and indeed all their intentions.

We fear other people because we see them as wishing to harm us. Sometimes the other person's intentions are quite clear – someone coming at us with a knife or a gun or an upraised fist can quite rightly be interpreted as someone to fear. But when anger and aggression are not so clear we can make mistakes. A friend may sound rather abrupt on the phone and we can think, 'She doesn't like me,' when in fact our friend is ill or tired or distracted by worries that have nothing to do with us. We need to understand the other person to be able to judge accurately what that person's wishes, needs, worries, angers, loves and fears are at any particular time. But, if you fear other people, understanding others is not easy. If we want to understand another person we need to be able to get close to that person. We can never come to understand a person whom we have always feared, and, when we have always feared everyone, we can never develop our ability to empathise with others and thus understand how another person experiences himself and his world. In fact our understanding of others can be so limited that we do not realise how little we understand and we may even pride ourselves on being good judges of character. Our understanding of other people develops from birth onwards[27] just as other skills develop, partly through physical maturation and partly through having had the right experiences at the right time. Unfortunately, if we do not have the right experiences, our ability to understand other people may be more like a child's than an adult's.

Initially we do not understand that other people have perceptions, feelings, needs and desires. They are simply figures in our landscape. As the people around us start to make demands on us, expecting us to behave in certain ways, rewarding us when we do and punishing us when we do not, we begin to see other people in terms of our own self-interest. (Grandmother can be relied on to be rewarding no matter what you do, but woe betide you if you do not obey your father.) As we get older and go to school we begin to see people in terms of the roles they fill – mother, teacher, policeman, school friend. We can carry this mode of thinking into adult life and judge other people according to the categories in which we place them. ('All Scotsmen are mean', 'Of course he's unreliable – he's Irish', 'Fat people are always jolly', 'Once a thief, always a thief', 'All of Jack's family are like that', 'Any woman who doesn't want to be a wife and mother is unnatural', 'All men are rapists at heart', 'I don't know what the youth of today are coming to. In my day we respected our parents.')

The immature understanding of other people is where we see other people only in relation to ourselves. In fact we can look at the entire cosmos only in relation to ourselves. The sun shines solely for the purpose of warming us while the malicious wind blows only to chill us. We cannot enjoy a landscape for the beauty in itself, but we see it only as a backdrop to a drama in which we are the central character. Surroundings which do not lend themselves to our personal drama hold no interest, while people whose existence does not enhance our own we ignore or find boring. We do not object if nature is cruel and other people dangerous so long as people and nature do not ignore us. We do not like to think that the world has any concerns where we are not the focus of interest.

But of course it does. Nature takes no account of the existence of the whole human race, much less of one person, and we, as an individual, can be of importance to only a minute portion of the millions of human beings on earth. To understand how other people think and feel we have to be able to see the world they inhabit through their own eyes and not through our own. We have to be able to see ourselves in ways which add nothing to our vanity. We have to be able to accept that other people have opinions, attitudes and feelings which are appropriate for the world they live in but which are different from our own. To understand other people we have to be able to take many different points of view and to accept that our own view of the world is not the Absolute, Real and Eternal Truth.

Where other people are concerned we are often ignorant of the fact that we are ignorant. We can be aware that we do not know anything about nuclear physics or the game of chess, but we can be unaware that the thoughts and feelings of the person who shares our bed or who gave birth to us are a complete mystery to us. In therapy one of the processes is the gradual discovery by the client of how little he really knows of his nearest and dearest. One method of aiding this process is the writing of 'scripts'. I used this with one woman whose fear of other people kept her depressed and lonely in her own home, unable to venture out of her door unaccompanied. Her husband would bring her to see me when he could and at other times she would telephone me. Her conversation was full of complaints about her husband – how insensitive he was, how demanding, irritable with her and the children, unable to appreciate how she suffered, how he would leave her alone in the evening to go out drinking, how under his mother's thumb he was and so on. I did not doubt that he was no angel, but from the incidental information she gave me about his childhood, his family and his job I guessed that he was under considerable strain. Attempts by me to get her to view a particular situation as he might view it led to her either changing the subject to something of greater interest to her, or accusing me of siding with him against her. Since she enjoyed writing and had already provided me with a long autobiography, I suggested that she write a script which was an account of her husband's life. This account was to be in the form of an autobiography where her husband told his own story and described his own attitudes and feelings. She was most enthusiastic about this project, but the next time I saw her she had to report that she had not written the script. When she tried to write it, she came to realise that, while she knew about the main events in her husband's life, she knew nothing of his attitudes and feelings. She did not know how he felt about his mother's illness or being sacked from his first job or even how he felt about her. She was so taken up with her own concerns she had not spared the time to understand him, and now when she attempted to do so she discovered that she did not know how to begin.

Understanding others is a skill we have to acquire if we are to live comfortably with other people. If we do not learn this skill we are always making mistakes in our dealing with other people. We find ourselves always saying or doing something which upsets the other person and we do not know why. We act with the best of intentions, and lo and behold, the person gets angry, or refuses to talk to us. ('I just asked Jimmy what he wanted for breakfast and he slammed out of the house and never spoke to me', 'My wife's always on at me to finish painting the kitchen cupboards. I'll get round to it when I've got time, but she will go on and on', 'I never shop at large stores. The assistants there are so snooty.') If we are not afraid of other people, such mistakes do not bother us, but if you are afraid, especially when you are sure that the other person is angry with you, then you worry about these experiences even for years after. You try to get along with other people by being pleasant and doing things for them, but so often you find, as Tacitus observed a long time ago, 'More faults are often committed while we are trying to oblige than while we are giving offence.' You want to show your love, but when you try to do this the loved one does not respond in the way you want, and so you withdraw, hurt.

The disadvantages of fearing, hating and envying other people are so immense and widespread that it would hardly seem likely that there are any advantages in doing so. But there are advantages, ones that you may be reluctant to relinquish. Indeed, when I was writing *Friends and Enemies* I drew up a list of all the advantages of having an enemy. In the end this ran to some twenty-five advantages.[28] All these advantages come from the fact that hatred is a defence which we can use when we fear someone but feel weak and vulnerable.

Hating others can make us feel more secure in our own virtue. More than that, our hatred can become the measure by which we define ourselves. We can define the very meaning of our existence as residing in our being anti-Catholic or anti-Muslim or anti-white or anti-men or anti-the youth of today. If we gave up our hatred of this other group we would feel quite bereft. Hating others fills in a great deal of our time and provides us with plenty of things to complain about. If you know that you are quite incompetent, you can enjoy the pleasures of complaining without feeling any necessity to put to rights the matters about which you complain. (One good reason for not attempting to right the world's wrongs is that if you do try to do so you are in danger of discovering that the world does not conform to the picture that you have of it. You will discover that human problems are quite complicated and that other people have different points of view.)

Another advantage of fearing, hating and envying other people is that you can see other people as the source of all your misery. You are as you are because of your childhood or your family or society and there is nothing that you can do about it. Thus you are able to avoid the responsibility for changing the situation in which you find yourself. You would do something about it but *they* are against you.

Hatred is simple. Love, real love, is much more complicated. The problem about love is that it is inextricably linked with freedom. Love is spontaneous. We cannot love on demand. We cannot order someone to love us. Psychoanalysts may say that we love someone because he or she reminds us of our mother, and behaviourists may say that we love someone because we have been conditioned to regard that kind of person as a positive reinforcement, and there is some truth in what psychoanalysts and behaviourists say, but we all know that the mystery and wonder of love lies in the fact that it cannot be commanded and it can only be freely given. I cannot love you just because I feel I ought to or because you want me to. The fondness we feel for people, who give us things in the hope, perhaps, that we shall love them, we call 'cupboard love' and know it is not the real thing. We do not love someone just because that person is generous to us and does things for our benefit.

We may like to think that all children love their parents and that all parents love their children, but we know it is not so. Some mothers love their child from the moment it stirs in the womb while others feel no more than a mild benign interest in the child for its entire life. Some fathers would lay down their lives for their children while others can desert the family home without a backward glance. Some children can never in their whole lives think of their parents without feeling a warming of their hearts, while others cling to their parents only as a means of satisfying a need and discard their parents as soon as a more satisfying source becomes available. Some adults think that they love their parents, but their fear of their parents has driven out their love. What they feel for their parents is guilt and a wistful longing for the loving, accepting parents they never had. The passion we can feel for someone who meets our deepest needs and who promises the fulfilment of our secret fantasies we often call love, romantic love, but such a passion has more to do with possession than with love. If we do not come to love the object of our passion then, when the object ceases to meet our needs and demands, as he or she must as time goes by, we are left with a stranger who at best bores us and at worst repels us. This is the point where marriages come apart or turn into the cold routine of acquaintances who have to share a house.

But love is a risky business. It means getting to know another person. It means loving a person as that person is and *not as we want that person to be*. Just because we love someone does not mean that that person will love us or, even loving us, behave in the ways that we desire. Some people think that they can control their loved ones by threatening to turn their love on and off like a tap. ('Daddy doesn't love you when you do that', 'I don't see how you can expect me to love you when you prefer to spend your evenings in the pub rather than at home with me') but such behaviour rarely inspires everlasting love, rather the feeling of being unloved, used and manipulated. Some people believe that, if they show their love, the loved ones will take advantage of their 'softness' or in some way become 'spoilt'. Such people expect that their loved ones will interpret their sternness as proof of love, but usually the loved ones experience only a lack of love. One of the recurring tragedies in families is that children grow up thinking that their parents do not love them when in fact the parents do. Parents need to do more than just love their children. It is not enough to say at frequent intervals, 'Love you, darling.' Parents need to show their love in what they do.

Real love cannot be used as a weapon to control others. It can only be freely given, and, as a gift, it can be rejected. Loving is a very risky business. We risk rejection, and, if we are not rejected, we have to risk opening our innermost self to another person. That is risky enough if you feel quite good about yourself but, if you fear and distrust your innermost being, letting someone close to you can be too dangerous to try. Better to keep up a wall of fear, even though you, in some sense, know that while the opposite of fear is courage, the opposite of fear is also love.[29]

3. Life is terrible and death is worse

My apprehensions come in crowds;
I dread the rustling of the grass;
The very shadows of the clouds
Have power to shake me as they pass;
I question things and do not find
One that will answer to my mind,
And all the world appears unkind.[30]

Feeling as you do about yourself and other people, you cannot help but find that life is terrible. The thought of death does not comfort you since, though sometimes you dream of peaceful oblivion, you wonder, like Hamlet,

For in that sleep of death what dreams may come.

Far outweighing your fear of death can be your fear of dying and the pain and suffering that can entail. You become aware of every ache and pain and any unusual sensation in your body, and each of these you can become convinced is a symptom of a fatal disease – a failing heart or the dreaded cancer. You recall the members of your family who have died and the diseases they died from, and feel sure that you have inherited the fatal complaint. You may keep these worries to yourself or you may hasten to your doctor. When he assures you that you are perfectly well and good for many decades yet, you feel a fool, regard his prognosis of a long life as a curse and not a blessing, and suspect that he is not telling you the truth.

Some people say they never think of death. This may be because they live such busy, pleasant lives they do not give much time to meditating on their future, or it may be that death terrifies them so much that they dare not think of it. But if we do think what our own death means to us, each of us can say what we believe it will be – not the particular circumstances of our death (though we do fantasise about these) but what will happen to us at death. There are only two possibilities. Either death is the end of my identity or it is a doorway to another life. Some people say they can imagine both alternatives applying to them, but when they are asked which alternative they would bet on, they have no doubt on which one they would place their money. We all know whether we see our identity vanishing with our death or our identity in some form passing to another life, since it is this choice which has determined what we see as the purpose of our life. If we see death as the end of our identity then we have the task of making this, our only life, in some way satisfactory; if we see our death as a doorway to another life then we have the task of living this life according to the rules of entry to the next life. We can define 'satisfactory' life or 'rules of entry' in many different ways, but, whatever definitions we choose, we know when we are not meeting the standards we have set. Feeling that life is terrible and death is worse means that, if you see death as the end, you see your life as a failure and death as no recompense. If you see death as a doorway to another life, you know that you have not lived up to the standards required. You believe that when you die you will be forgotten by those you leave behind you, or that you will be consigned to hell or limbo or to an even worse life on earth than your present one, or left a lonely, wandering ghost. You know you are damned without hope.

When I first began talking with people who were depressed in order to examine how they saw themselves and their world we would talk about immediate realities – relationships, work, and the person's tumult of feelings. As I got better at understanding what I was being told the sooner we began talking about death, not just the losses the person was suffering ('My mother died when I was a child. I know it's silly but I still feel it was my fault', 'My son died four years ago. People tell me I should be over it by now and I feel guilty because I'm not', 'My father died last year I never got on well with him. I didn't know he was dying. The family kept it from me because they didn't want me to be upset'), but how the person felt about his own death. This would often lead on to a discussion of the person's religious beliefs. And here was a great problem.

British people are not great churchgoers when compared with people in some other countries, but whenever surveys are taken of religious beliefs a large percentage of British people say that they believe in God and an afterlife.[31] Similar surveys in the USA give even higher percentages of believers.[32] Such percentages would seem to suggest that religious beliefs are normal and important, but to a great many psychiatrists and psychologists the possession of a religious belief is, at best, evidence that the person is naive or stupid and, at worst, neurotic or even psychotic.[33] Whenever I ask a group of clinical psychologists whether they believe in an afterlife most of them say they do not, and when I advise them that in therapy with a depressed person it is a good idea to discover what that person's religious beliefs are, many of my colleagues look at me strangely and think that I have ceased to be a rational person, having discovered religion in my old age. I have been shocked to find that some of my colleagues, whom I have always regarded as the most open-minded of people, have shown themselves to be so against religion that they refuse to take seriously the religious beliefs of other people. They do not realise that, if a psychologist believes (and does not say) that the purpose of therapy is to help the client live a happy and successful life, and, if the client believes, or hopes (but does not say), that therapy will help him be a better person and to make his peace with God, then the therapeutic enterprise must fail, since the therapist and the client are travelling on different paths and not hand-in-hand. The therapist needs to understand that when you are in the business of saving your soul, happiness is irrelevant. However, that psychology is a science and science is opposed to religion is the justification of such attitudes by psychologists. Moreover, Freud stated authoritatively that the possession of religious beliefs was evidence of a neurosis and that religion was a universal neurosis. Jung opposed Freud in this, but it was Freud's views, not Jung's, along with the scientific attitudes to religion which influenced British psychiatry. As a result, a basic textbook, *Clinical Psychiatry* by Slater and Roth, carries only one reference to religious belief.

> Jung is probably right in holding that some neurotic subjects seeking help are really groping for some system of religious *belief* which will provide them with a source of strength and render their lives meaningful. These probably include the individual whose problems were in former times dealt with by the priest, the confessor or the head of the family; the hesitant, the guilt-ridden, the excessively timid, those lacking clear convictions with which to face life.[34]

So it is that if you tell a psychiatrist that the worst part of your misery is that you are shut out from God and that you dread life and death because you know you are damned, he is likely to nod sympathetically and note that you are exhibiting one of the symptoms of a depressive illness. Your statement carries the same significance as the red spots in measles.

However, such an experience is more than a symptom of an illness, and you feel angry and hurt when it is dismissed as such. Once in a letter to Gerald Priestland, then the Religious Affairs Correspondent for the BBC, I made a flippant comment about choosing one's religious beliefs. He shot back at me, 'The experience of damnation can be as compelling as the experience of salvation. You must figure that out for yourself, but unless you understand it your work among depressives is in vain.'[35] Alas, it is not just the atheistic psychologists and psychiatrists who fail to understand this experience but also many ministers of religion, committed Christians and those who declare themselves to be attuned to 'the spiritual.'[36] If you are unfortunate enough to take your problems to such a person you find that their platitudes about the certainty of God's forgiveness or the all-encompassing balm of the spiritual do nothing but cast you further into the darkness. Better to remain silent.

No one can live his life using only rational beliefs. Even the most scientifically minded person must hold, if not religious beliefs, beliefs which cannot be proved but only taken on trust. Believing that life ends in death is just as metaphysical a belief as believing that death is a doorway to another life, since neither can be proved in the way that Brand X washing powder can be shown to wash better than Brand Y. Philosophers have had a lot to say about the differences between rational and metaphysical beliefs, more than I wish to mention here. The difference I want to stress is that where our metaphysical beliefs are concerned, proof is irrelevant. If you believe that life ends in death, no account of the joys of salvation and eternal life will change your belief. If you believe that Jesus was the Son of God who died and was resurrected, no argument backed by the best of historical studies will prove to you that Jesus, if He existed at all, was only a man. Of course, sometimes people do change their religious beliefs quite dramatically, being either converted to a religion or losing their faith altogether, but such changes usually occur not so much through reasoned argument as through the profound emotions created by a significant crisis point in the person's life where such a change in belief brings some sort of solution to his problems.

Over the past few years I have spent a great deal of time talking to people about their metaphysical beliefs. Some of these people were my clients who were living lives of great misery; some were friends, acquaintances or colleagues who, despite many problems, not only cope with their lives but enjoy them. The group of people altogether included atheists, committed Christians, vaguely Christian humanists,

Jews, some people who believed in a form of reincarnation with or without a mixture of Hinduism and Buddhism, and some people whose beliefs were more mystical and magical than religious. The variety of possible beliefs amazed me. But, whatever the beliefs, they fell into one of two categories. Either they gave the person who held them courage and optimism or else they rendered the person who held them fearful and pessimistic. The first category were the beliefs of the people who coped with their lives; the second were the beliefs held by my clients.[37] People who cope with their lives hold metaphysical beliefs which liberate or at least do not impede them. People who do not cope have beliefs which serve to trap them in a life of misery, like this woman who, in the debate about shelters for battered wives, wrote to the *Observer*,

Why has nobody yet mentioned the part religion plays in the endurance by women of physical violence from their husbands?

Although the fact that I had no money and no place to take my young children were contributory reasons for my remaining with my uncontrollably violent husband, the main reason was that, having been brought up in a religious home, I believed that my marriage vows were binding and that 'for better for worse' really meant what it said.

Indeed, the greater the misery, the more I believed God was putting me on trial. It took me 10 years – during which I sought in vain for help from my parson, my doctor, a lawyer and the police (all of them, incidentally, men) – before I managed to shake off the religious teachings of my upbringing sufficiently to seek a divorce.[38]

Despite the wide variety of beliefs, there is no belief which, if held, will ensure complete happiness and security. Every belief has good and bad implications. The most popular metaphysical belief is that we live in a Just World, where goodness is rewarded and badness punished. This is what all religions teach, although they differ on what they call goodness and badness, rewards and punishments. Many people who would describe themselves as not at all religious still say that they believe that somehow, in the end, good people are rewarded and bad people punished. Within each religion there is a range of opinion about how the system of justice actually works in the Just World. Some people talk vaguely and soothingly about the necessity of trusting God's wisdom which we cannot understand and of God's unfailing forgiveness. Others put the principle of the Just World much more simply. Rabbi Shaul Rosenblatt, writing in the *London Jewish News* said, 'Judaism believes that nothing is random. If something bad happens in your life, there is a reason. You are doing something wrong. You can know the reason and, if you correct the wrong, you can get rid of the problem.'[39] This particular belief results in great cruelty being inflicted on many innocent, good people, but it is a basic tenet of the evangelical or fundamentalist movements in Christianity, Judaism and Islam.

If this is a Just World then nothing can happen by chance. The basic rule is simple. If you are good you are rewarded. If you are bad you are punished. There are two great advantages of believing in the Just World. It means that, if you are good, nothing bad can happen to you. If you are good, you and your loved ones are safe. The belief also saves you from the pain of pity. When you see others suffering you can know that they brought their suffering on themselves. ('If she hadn't been dressed like that she wouldn't have been raped.' 'If they hadn't supported the Taliban they wouldn't be refugees now.')

However, if you believe in the Just World and you suffer a disaster the only way you cannot explain this disaster by saying, 'It happened by chance.' If you have been good and a disaster happens to you it means that either the system of justice has failed you or that you deserve what has happened to you. You can rail against God and feel betrayed by the divine system of justice, or you can blame yourself. A friend of mine, a young man, killed himself. A few weeks later I visited his parents to sort out some of my friend's possessions. His father said, 'We always felt that our children did better at school and university than the children of the people we know. We were so proud of them. Our son's death is our punishment for being so proud.'

Loving parents whose child commits suicide berate themselves endlessly for what they had done and what they had failed to do. To compound this torture by saying that the death is the parents' punishment not only adds to the parents' pain but also denigrates the child who is defined as being nothing more than an instrument of God's justice. Believing that their child's death is the punishment they deserve saves the parents from having to inquire about what it was that the child thought and felt that led him to take his own life. My friend had never indicated to me that he knew his parents were proud of him. He felt that he had never lived up to the standards they had set him.

Many of us are taught about the Just World in child-hood but when we grow up and see the randomness with which life hands out rewards and punishments we leave the belief the Just World behind – or so we think. When we encounter a disaster we can find ourselves asking, 'Why me? What have I done to deserve this?' We can even try bargaining with the divine system of justice. When Cathy Comerford discovered a lump in her breast she had to wait twenty-five days before she would find out whether or not the lump was cancerous. By Day 11, she recorded, 'I have started the old childish practice of doing a deal with God. If this is all OK, I will never worry again about work or relationships. I will be so grateful for my health that I will not let anything else capture my attention. I really mean it.' She did not record whether, when the lump proved to be benign, she kept her bargain with God.[40]

Before I began asking people about their religious beliefs I had assumed that when we were children we might believe in God whom we saw as an old man with a long beard who kept a benevolent eye on the world, but as we got older we might realise that this was just a myth, just like Santa Claus, since no benevolent God would ever allow such hor-rors as our world contains. I was quite shaken by what my clients told me. Some of them, like Elizabeth,[41] had been told that gentle Jesus looked after little children, but painful events soon showed them that this was not so. Elizabeth prayed that Jesus would make her well when she was sent home from school for being ill. She knew her mother would

be angry. Jesus did not answer her prayer and she was punished by her mother. Later she asked her teacher, 'What if
one sparrow He missed, or one child?' She was told that the
child or the sparrow must have met with His disapproval.
Elizabeth may have given up believing in Jesus, but not
before she took these events as further proof of her essential
badness.

I discovered that some people do not give up their belief
in God when they suffer grievous blows. They simply give up
their belief in a benevolent God. Their faith in God is
unshaken, but God for them is an evil God. Siegfried told me
that if God exists, 'He's a shit . . . He couldn't intentionally
and with the ability to do something about it, run the world
like this, surely. How can He tolerate man being intolerable
to man? What end can possibly be served by Auschwitz, the
IRA, this wretched business we read about this morning? I
could do better than this.'[42] Tony said, 'I have a great fear of
the Christian God – He must be a bastard, what a bloody sick
joke creating this world. There must be some gods up there,
sitting around, and He's a baby God among the bigger
immortals, and the baby's been given the world to play with,
stirring things around in the world, seeing what havoc can
be caused. If there is a God, then this God is some sort of
holy maniac, an evil maniac. Evil because He allows enough
food to keep the dream going. It's the biggest con trick ever
played – the dream that you're getting somewhere.'[43] You can
hardly feel safe, at home and at peace in a world created and
managed by an evil God.

When the wife of C.S. Lewis died of cancer he kept a
diary through the period of intense grief and later anony-
mously published some of his thoughts. He had discovered
that

> You never really know how much you really believe
> anything until its truth or falsehood becomes a matter of
> life and death for you . . . not that I am (I think) in much
> danger of ceasing to believe in God. The real danger is in
> coming to believe such dreadful things about Him. The
> conclusion I dread is not 'So there's no God at all', but 'So
> this is what God's really like. Deceive yourself no longer.'

Friends tried to console him with the assurance that his wife was in God's hands. However, he could only wonder,

> But if so, she was in God's hands all the time, and I have seen what they did to her here. Do they suddenly become gentler to us the moment we are out of the body? And if so, why? If God's goodness is inconsistent with hurting us, then either God is not good or there is no God, for in the only life we know He hurts us beyond our worst fears and beyond all we can imagine. If it is consistent with hurting us, then He may hurt us after death as unendurably as before it.[44]

Trying not to see your God as evil and malevolent causes you great conflict and pain, and, like Gerard Manley Hopkins, the Jesuit priest whose experience of depression brought forth the most poignant of poems, you might argue with God and plead,

> Thou are indeed just, Lord, if I contend
> With thee; but, see, so what I plead is just.
> Why do sinners' ways prosper? and why must
> Disappointment all I endeavour end?
>   Wert thou my enemy, O thou my friend,
> How wouldst thou worse, I wonder, than thou dost
> Defeat, thwart me? . . .
>
> . . .
>
> . . . birds build – but not I build; no, but strain,
>
> Time's eunuch, and not breed one work that wakes.
>
> Mine, O thou lord of life, send my roots rain.[45]

We can go through life untroubled by the pain and misery of our fellows, but once we allow the knowledge of this suffering to penetrate the cocoon of our well-being we have to face the problem of evil. (When I wrote this five days before Christmas 1981, sixteen people were drowned as a ship and a lifeboat were wrecked off the Cornish coast,[46] in 1996 in the space of one day forty thousand children were dying of starvation,[47] and in 2002 nearly three thousand people had died when the World Trade Centre collapsed and within three months a greater, but unknown, number of Afghanis had died in America's war against terrorism.) When the suffering is personal, our loss and our pain, the question of why this has happened to me and mine demands an answer. In the Christmas of 1981 my friend Margaret Templeton, whom I had met when we did a phone-in on depression for BBC Radio Sheffield in 1978 and who had gone on to organise self-help groups for people in Sheffield, phoned to tell me that her youngest son, aged ten, had been knocked down by a car and killed. 'I didn't know he was outside,' she said. 'A child came to the door and said he'd had an accident. I tried to hurry.' (She wore a spinal corset.) 'I had to crawl up the bank to reach him. They'd thrown a blanket over him. I lay down on the road beside him. Someone said he was just unconscious. I didn't know he was dead. The car had gone right over him. I tried to wipe the gravel off his face. He was always such a happy boy – my baby. I feel I've lost part of me.' A good Christian woman. Why?

How can we account for evil? If we do not believe in God we have to account for evil in terms of the unpredictable ways of nature (floods, fires, earthquakes, blizzards, typhoons, the deadly virus, the burgeoning cancer cells, the blood clot) and the cruelty and stupidity of human beings. People who cope with life and who do not believe in God accept with some degree of equanimity the randomness of nature, regard scientific knowledge as largely beneficial and exciting, and see the cruelty and stupidity of people not so much as evidence of their inherent badness as of their poor education. Faith in man's capacity to learn from his mistakes gives hope of improvement.[48] But if you fear the randomness of nature, regard scientific knowledge as dangerous and frightening,[49] and believe that most, if not all, people are inherently evil and through wilfulness or stupidity refuse to learn from their mistakes, then you have no hope that life on this earth will improve.

If we do believe in God we have to ask why God allows evil to exist. If you believe that God inflicts suffering to punish the guilty and to show them the error of their ways, when you suffer a grievous blow you can interpret this as evidence of your essential badness. You can interpret the misery you feel, your state of depression, as the punishment you deserve for being so evil. If you believe in the justice of this punishment you will resist having your depression taken from you in case worse punishment will follow. If you were not such a bad person your mother would not have died, or your child would not have been born handicapped, or your husband's heart wear out before its time. Even as you accept this as proof of your badness you have to ask, 'Why should the innocent suffer? Why should they be made to pay for the sins of the guilty?' And not all people appear to suffer. Indeed, evil, as ever, seems to flourish like the green bay tree. In 2002 the wicked bosses of the multinational company Enron enriched themselves by many millions and then walked away from the debacle that they engineered, while the good people who worked for Enron lost all of their savings.

The ways of God are indeed mysterious. If He is all-powerful He hardly seems to be all-good; and if He is all-good, He cannot be all-powerful. At the very least He is inefficient. If you try to discuss these problems with members of your clergy you are likely to be told that you have to take God on trust. Now this is something you find impossible to do. You know quite well that you cannot trust other people. You are always being disappointed in other people. They are always letting you down, even your nearest and dearest whose behaviour you can usually predict. How can you trust God who is likely to come up with anything?

Trusting means accepting uncertainty, and that is one thing you are not prepared to accept. One way to be certain about God is to decide that He is harsh and cruel, if not malevolent, and that He is more likely to inflict suffering rather than to create happiness, and when He does create happiness He always follows it by pain. Another way of being certain is to see God as entirely good but not omnipotent. He is in battle with the source of evil, the Devil.

Many people believe in the Devil as a potent force in the world.[50] Belief in the Devil certainly makes the world appear as a dark and dangerous place, especially when you see the Devil as more powerful than God. Sometimes God and the

Devil are seen as personages locked in combat; sometimes God and the Devil appear as the Force of Good and the Force of Evil. Felicity said to me, 'I can remember as a child trying to think, "How did the world begin in the first place and if it was made in seven days, and this is a God sitting up there, well, where did that God come from? Where did the space come from?" You could go mad thinking about that.' She came to an answer when she got older. 'It's some kind of good and evil forces which are at war with one another, and I can only think that the evil forces are winning because certainly the world is not improving, is it?'[51]

Whether we believe in God or not, we all find it difficult to conceive of the complete and absolute end of our identity at death. All of us would agree that what we fear about dying is that this will involve great pain, but if we are asked, 'What is so terrible about passing from life to death?', each of us would talk about what we fear most in life. In this we divide into two groups. For one group, the people I call extraverts, their greatest fear is to be left completely and absolutely alone. This group spend their life keeping people around them, but, no matter if friends and family are gathered at your deathbed, you have to go into death alone. For the second group, whom I call introverts, their greatest fear is losing all control over their life and falling into chaos. This group plan and organise their life in order to keep everything under control, but death takes away this control and brings what is unknown, unplanned, and beyond our control. For all of us what we fear the most is what we see as threatening to annihilate our sense of being a person.

Our sense of being a person is what we call 'I', 'me', 'myself'. It is easy to imagine our sense of being a person continuing on after death. The problem is to decide what this post-death existence will be. Will it be the same for all of us? If we feel that one of the greatest imperfections of this world is the way virtue is not always rewarded and vice not always punished, we may look to the afterlife for the justice denied in this world. We can believe that the good (including the sinners who repent) go to heaven and the unrepentant bad go to hell, or that the good are reincarnated to a better life and the bad to a worse. Such beliefs may satisfy our need for justice, but they create an ever-present anxiety that we may fail to qualify for heaven or a better life. If we see ourselves as basically good with a few, not-too-terrible faults and if we set ourselves standards of goodness which are not too difficult to meet, then our anxiety is not very great. But, if you see yourself as basically bad with none or only a few minor virtues and if you set yourself standards of perfection which are impossible to meet, then your anxiety is great. Heaven or a better life may not be for you.

Just as great a sense of hopelessness and failure can pervade the lives of those who do not believe in a life after death. If you see yourself as essentially bad and if you set yourself standards of perfection, then you can never be the person you think you ought to be or achieve the things you feel you ought to achieve. You can never be the perfect child of perfect parents, the perfect housewife, mother, and career woman, the perfect and brilliantly successful man, husband, son, lover, father. You have been cheated of your birthright, badly used, wasted your talents and opportunities, disappointed those who love you, behaved badly, selfishly, foolishly. You may believe that your luck has run out[52] or that you are the helpless victim of a terrible Fate. You will leave behind no work that you will be remembered by; your virtues will not be extolled by your relatives and friends; you leave no children behind you to revere you, or if you do have children they are no credit to you. When you die you will be forgotten. It will be as if you never existed.

Whether we believe that our identity ends in death or that we go to another form of existence, we all like to believe that we shall leave some trace of ourselves behind on earth, through our works or in the loving memories of our children and friends. Some people's passionate ambitions are not simply to obtain an enormous share of the world's goods but to leave some permanent mark upon the world. Some people enter politics not only to make their country, in their terms, a better place but to enter the history books as well. Some people want to have children not just for the delight of having children but to secure the immortality of one generation succeeding another. Some people are kind to their fellow men not just because they love them but because they want to be remembered and praised. For such people the failure of their enterprise is not just the failure to become rich, or to receive acclaim as an artist, or to be elected to high office, or to beget children, or to win friends and influence people, it is the failure to achieve a kind of eternal life, and it is felt as keenly as the failure to enter the Kingdom of Heaven.

When we imagine our own death we summon up a scene where we are both the central participant and an observer. We are there seeing ourselves die. I rather fancy the death-bed scene favoured by the Hollywood movies of the forties, where I die beautifully and gracefully, without pain or discomfort, murmuring a few memorable last words, surrounded by my loved ones who, while regretting my leaving, are not too painfully distressed since I have reached a Great Age and had a Good Life. I do not fancy one of those deaths which are recorded in the funeral notice as 'after a long illness bravely borne', and I hope that no one is so dependent on me that my death will leave that person bereft. Not everyone has such faith in a Hollywood ending. If you have written a scenario for yourself which includes much pain and suffering, or circumstances which produce a terrible death scene, then this scene can take on a strange reality and haunt all your waking and sleeping moments.

When we imagine our death we consider not just the circumstances of our death but the kind of funeral that we want. I have discovered that people who do not believe in life after death can feel most passionate about their funeral, and the simple question, 'Do you want to be buried or cremated?' can produce a fierce argument.[53] Our preference can be based on positive reasons stemming from how we see ourselves in relation to life in general. We may want to be buried so we can become part of the life cycle or we may want to be cremated because we see burial as using up the scarce land resources. Or our preference can be based on fear and mistrust. If we cannot trust other people's judgement we may fear that we shall be placed in our coffin not dead but unconscious and awake to find ourselves being – well, which is preferable, being buried alive or burnt alive? For many people this is not an idle question.

John was referred to me because, since the death of his

closest friend from cancer, he had been depressed and extremely panicky. I wrote of him,

> John had a recurring nightmare about Paul's cremation. 'It starts where the coffin is just coming in. Then it sort of builds up from there. The noise gets louder and louder. The shouting is in the background, then it seems to build up and – it's really unbearable. It's like the shouting in the panic attack, but I can make out the words in this one because Paul's mother kept on saying, "Bury him, bury him". The voice gets louder and louder and then suddenly I'm awake.' . . . I asked John to imagine what would happen in the dream if he had not woken at that point.
> Reluctantly he thought about this. 'I think I would see the burning – all I can imagine is that he is still alive, you see.' I asked him to imagine that he was the person in the coffin. He said that he would be fighting to get out but would not be able to do this because it would be too late . . . John was against cremation, 'because there's nothing there. Nothing to show respect to. You can go back to a grave. You can carry on the love side, the respect. Whereas with the cremation it's final. There's not anything left.'[54]

Rose was terrified of being buried since it made her feel 'as though I was going to be suffocated. I dread being shut up.'[55] Mary accepted burial but expected that her grave would be neglected. She said, 'I'm frightened of being on my own when I wake up in heaven . . . When I'm depressed I often wish I was dead myself, though I don't know what good it would do. I feel everybody would be better off without me.' She pictured her husband and parents 'carrying on without me . . . I can imagine my grave being overrun with weeds and people not remembering – I can't imagine Robert at a funeral, not even mine. I can imagine him laughing and cheerful. He hates people crying all over the place. . . . I imagine them carrying on as usual – I suppose they would. It's as if I'd never existed at all. As if I'm completely forgotten.' To me it seemed unlikely that her family would forget her, but she had a good reason for wanting this. If her family remembered her, mourned her, and kept her grave tidy, this would mean that she, through her death, had upset them, and, as she said, 'I don't want to hurt anyone's feelings – I'm always frightened of upsetting anybody and anything. Even if I don't like them I shouldn't want to hurt them.' Rather than upset other people she would be a lonely ghost.[56]

It is the fantasies that you have about death that determine whether you will commit suicide when you are depressed. You think about death a great deal. It both terrifies and charms you. It may look attractive because it would be the end to your misery, but if you cannot bear to cause your loved ones suffering or if you fear an afterlife which is more terrible than your present life, suicide is no solution. But if you welcome death as an end without waking, a complete ceasing to be, an end to pain, or, if you are indifferent to the feelings of those you leave behind, or see your death as a triumphant vindication of your life, or as a means of a kind of rebirth, a second chance, or as a way of making the world a better place, or as a way of harming your enemies, then suicide can hold a promise which you may find hard to resist.

Jacky Gillott wrote about her years of depression in an article for *Cosmopolitan*. She said,

Depression is suffered by people who see no reason to like themselves at all. Depression is a state of self-hate. It is the horror of feeling oneself inescapably bound within the body of someone you fear, loathe and despise. Depression is a state of mind that inevitably invites paranoia; if you find yourself loathsome, you expect the rest of the world to find you loathsome too. What's more, you feel you have no business infecting other people's existence with your unpleasant presence . . . Because I have this loony belief that I am somehow contagious, and that those who might catch whatever it is hate me anyway, I become hysterically frightened of other people. I ignore the phone and hide if someone knocks at the door. If I have to go to the bank or the shops I will either walk miles the long way round to avoid people I know, or travel to another town where I can be fairly sure of going unrecognised . . . Many depressives commit suicide, I'm sure, as the last act of unselfishness . . . I'm convinced that many of the neat, quiet, unexpected suicides are committed by depressives who quite simply wish not to be a nuisance any longer . . . I find it quite easy when I'm at my lowest to present a logical case for my removal. It would, for instance, be infinitely kinder to my family. Hours are spent working out which would be the least inconvenient moment to lay my head in the gas oven. There never is a convenient moment, of course, because I've learnt over the years to crowd my schedule with certain unavoidable commitments . . . I always make sure I'm permanently in debt because I would feel it rather disgraceful to go leaving other people to pay my bills.[57]

Unfortunately for those of us left behind, in 1980 Jacky paid her debts and found a convenient time to take a lethal dose of tablets.

Taking an overdose of drugs is a popular way of committing or attempting suicide since it seems to offer a fulfilment of that desire for peace and the cessation of struggle which every depressed person feels at some time or other. Val expressed this in a poem which she wrote when she was very depressed. She imagined leaping off a cliff into the sea.

I am heaved from crest to crest,
Between wallowing in the gaping troughs.

The effects of exposure take their toll.
The clammy coldness slowly destroys me,
Until a salvage job seems worthless.
Now I look for an end to the tempest.
I long to sink deeper and deeper,
I yearn for the cool, calming caress of gentle ebb and flow,
To surrender to the peace it offers.

That is the desire. The actuality is different. Whether a person quietly takes an overdose or dramatically plunges from the top of a cliff, it is a violent act of self-murder. Suicide is an act of violence against that part of ourselves that wants to go on living. If every part of us, body and soul, wants to die, or, if we are totally convinced that death is inevitable, then we die without having to inflict any violence upon ourselves. An Australian aborigine who has been expelled from his tribe, no matter how strong and healthy he is, will die within days of being expelled, as will an Azande who knows himself to be the recipient of bad magic. Many old people give up and die. Traudl Junge was Hitler's secretary from 1942 to 1945, and she was with him when he died. After the war ended she lived in obscurity until she was eighty-one when she wrote her memoirs and took part in a documentary about her life. Her book was published and at the same time the documentary was shown at the Berlin Film Festival of 2002. A few days later she died. Othmar Schmiderer, the producer of the documentary, was one of the last people to see her alive. She said to him, 'Now that I've let go of my story, I can let go of my life.' [58]

If you have to do violence to yourself in order to die, then somewhere in you is hope and the desire to go on living. A large part of you wants to go on living. You should stay with that part of yourself.

Suicide is not about letting go and dying. It is about deciding to preserve the sense of being a person by killing the body. Living means surviving as a body, that is, physically, and as a person. We maintain the survival of our body by protecting ourselves from injury, and we maintain the survival of our sense of being a person by standing up to those who try to humiliate, belittle or treat us as an object of no importance, and by protesting when someone insists that we are something we know we are not. If you think of yourself as being honest and truthful, you protest when someone says you are dishonest and untruthful. If you think of yourself as being generous and kind, you protest when someone says you are mean and cruel.

Most of the time our situation is such that surviving as a person and as a body go along together. However, we can find ourselves in a situation where to survive as a body we cannot continue to be the person we want to think of ourselves as being. You might think of yourself as being someone who is competent and caring and looks after people weaker than yourself. One day your neighbour's house catches fire. You see two little faces pressed against an upstairs window. Without a thought of your own safety, you enter the house to save the children. Others try to hold you back, but you go, even though you might die. Later, when others commend you for your courage, you say, 'If I hadn't tried to save those children I wouldn't have been able to live with myself again.' That is, you have to be the person you want to think of yourself as being, even though that could mean that you will die.

This way of thinking is what leads young men and women to strap a bomb to their body, go among their enemies, and detonate the bomb. Their enemies have denigrated and humiliated them. These young men and women feel that to live in humiliation means that they are not the person they want to know themselves to be. Better die as a hero than live as a dog.

It is this same way of thinking which leads individuals to commit suicide. They feel that their situation does not allow them to be the person that they want to think of themselves as being and that they have no power to change their situation other than to die.

When Tim Lott first began his inquiry into the causes of his own suicidal depression and his mother's suicide he had accepted what his doctors had said, that depression was the result of some biochemical change. However, as he examined the events of his own life and that of his mother Jean, he began to see that depression was not a biochemical anomaly. It is, he wrote, 'an attempted defence against the terror of losing your invented sense of self: who you believe yourself to be and the way in which you think the world operates. It is fear of annihilation, of doubt, of insignificance.'[59]

Tim studied how his mother had seen herself, how she related to her husband Jack and to her sons Jeff, Tim and James, and how she saw her place in the world. He wrote,

When my mother decided to kill herself, she was both crazy and entirely sane, both severely ill and well. She hanged herself because her story, her idea of herself as a successful wife and mother – the only real test of worth she knew – was no longer sustainable in her shocked mind. She had no function, now that James had left home. She had not succeeded in protecting me from whatever it was that left me wanting my own death – that was left to medicine. Her oldest son had divorced, then remarried without extending her an invitation to the ceremony. The story of her life no longer stood up, but she was not prepared to let it collapse. She was more frightened of that than the noose.

Larger forces were at play. As Southall rotted, another scrap of identity went, the idea, so large for her generation, of pride in being English. At the same time, the illness that is depression cut her off from her own feelings, separated her from Jack.

Under the terrifying magnifying glass that depression, once set in train, becomes, all these things expanded into catastrophes that were *her fault*, since in her view of the world they had to be *somebody's* fault. It wasn't in her philosophy to blame accident or anyone else. Thus it was that she no longer deserved to live. She knew that to carry on living meant that the person she had always imagined herself to be could no longer be sustained. She killed herself to save herself, to avoid change, to duck meaninglessness. And, since depression feels like a collapse of faith, she could see no hope of things getting better.[60]

Suicide is not about letting go and dying. It is about saving yourself and about punishing yourself and other people. One high-achieving, adorable young woman I once knew punished herself with suicide because she had failed to achieve perfection in a task she had set herself. She had never failed at anything, or even done anything badly, but now she was failing to be a perfect mother. Unfortunately, motherhood is a task which every woman who undertakes it fails. Being a parent is a task marked by failure, and this is one of the burdens that parents have to bear as best they can. But my friend, for whom perfection was the only acceptable standard, could not accept this, and so she punished herself for failing. I do not know how conscious she was of the fact that her death would also punish her family.

Every suicide is a message to the living. The person might leave a note saying, 'You'll be better off without me,' but no loving message can hide the fact that suicide is a rejection of family, friends and the world. The world may be indifferent to being rejected, but to friends and family the message is, 'I didn't care enough about you even to try to go on living.' To the person's children the message is, 'When life is difficult, give up.' It is quite common for the children of suicides to end their own life in this way.

At a conference recently a young man came up to me and said he wanted to thank me for my book *Depression: The Way Out of Your Prison*. He said, 'I'd decided to kill myself and then I read what you'd written about suicide and I didn't. I'm so glad now that I didn't.' He looked very happy.

This young man had discovered that life is worth living. Life *is* worth living, and death, ordinary, unpredictable, uncontrollable death, comes all too soon.

Of course it is easy for me to say that, because I do think that life is worth living. You do not. Whether you see death as the end or as a doorway to another life, whether you believe in God, or the Devil, or the Forces of Good and Evil, or whether you have no religious beliefs at all, your particular beliefs about the nature of death and the purpose of life inspire in you fear rather than hope. They ensure your suffering – and yet they have their advantages.

Every belief, like everything else in this world, has its advantages as well as its disadvantages. The God of vengeance will deal with your enemies just as He deals with you, while the belief in sin certainly adds a piquancy to life. Some activities which might otherwise be quite dull can be found to be exciting because they are sinful and forbidden. There is some satisfaction to be gained in believing in a universal system which is just and perfect, even if the application of that justice means that you are punished and the vision of perfection illuminates your faults. Your beliefs may make you fearful, but because you know them to be Real, Absolute, and Eternal Truths your beliefs give you *certainty*. You prefer to be certain of the future, even if the future is tragic. And a tragic figure has a particular distinction which a contented mediocrity lacks. As much as we fear our death, it is the knowledge of our death that gives the point and purpose to our life, and we want our life to have some significance to ourselves, even if not to other people.

Of course we must be aware of death, in order to survive. We learn to be careful crossing the road, to eat the right foods, not to walk down dark alleyways, to wrap up warmly in cold weather and try not to smoke. A careful respect for death can help ensure a long life not just for yourself but for those around you. Respect rather than fear, for, as Epictetus said,

Why, do you not know then, that the origin of all evils, and of baseness and cowardice, is not death, but rather the fear of death.[61]

Our death lies in the future, so if you fear death it is the future that you fear.

4. Only bad things happened to me in the past and only bad things will happen to me in the future

'I just feel that my past is getting larger, my future's getting smaller and I haven't got time for the present,' said Bob, one of the heroes of the BBC TV series 'Whatever Happened to the Likely Lads?' (Bob and Terry, once likely lads, were then approaching thirty, and were looking back to their child-hood and adolescence as their golden age. The theme song of the series ends with the words 'The only thing to look forward to is the past.') Bob's words, uttered in his usual rueful, anxious way, made us all laugh, the kind of laugh that comes when we are presented with something which we know is, sadly, only too true about ourselves.

If time were a house, then our present should be a large airy, sunlit room where we can move freely in it and from it, whenever we wish, into the past, a small, cosy, cheerful room, or into our future, a wide open doorway on to a welcoming vista. But if *your* time were a house, your past would be a huge, dark, menacing room, containing your present, an insignificant treadmill where you have to run fast to stay in one place and your future a dark tunnel ending in a blank wall. There was a time when you thought that if you turned your back on the past and ran as fast as you could the future would open up, rosy with promise. However, once inside the prison of depression you know that running on a treadmill makes no progress, that there is nowhere to progress to, and all you are left with is a past which is filled with fear, anger, jealousy, shame, guilt, regret, grief and loss.

The famous French psychiatrist, Henri Ey, considered that the most important feature of depression was the way in which the person's perception of time changed, not just the slowing down of time so that twenty-four hours pass like a week, but the relative importance of past and future, so that the past and not the future engages the depressed person's attention. It is not the kind of interest in the past which many people develop as they approach old age, when they spend a lot of time thinking about past events and telling their stories to every willing and unwilling listener available. Usually the story is told in the framework of 'things were better then than they are now', even when the events recalled involved suffering and hardship, since the person is in the business of showing that he had not been conquered and defeated, but that he had mastered life and enjoyed it, and, since the contemporary world is inferior to that of his youth, nothing is to be gained by living forever. In such a way do elderly people become reconciled to their lives and so reconciled to their deaths. They recall their past to redefine it as good.

But your living in the past is quite different. When you do recall something that was good and happy, you do this not with pleasure but with painful regret. Something, or somebody, has been lost, never to return. When you see this loss as having occurred not by chance but by carelessness or malice your memories are filled with bitterness, anger and resentment. You have suffered many losses, rebuffs, unsettling changes, some of which would be categorised by sociologists as the 'life events' which depressed people, so research shows, collect in greater numbers than non-depressed people[62] (you always knew you were unlucky!) and some of which were the small betrayals, deceits, disloyalties, treacheries, cruelties, dishonesties, denunciations, threats, belittlings, rejections, criticisms, reproaches, indignities, jealousies, animosities, ingratitudes, meannesses, enmities and ostracisms that take place in every community which is not guided by love and forgiveness.

None of us grew to adulthood without having suffered some 'life events' and some measure of inhumanity. How do we come to terms with the unhappiness of our past so that it does not dominate our present? What most people do is that they talk things over with someone. A good friend listens, commiserates, and helps us get things in proportion. But what if there is no one in your life who is interested enough in you to listen? Or no one you would dare to talk to, since the people you know would get angry with you, or belittle you, or punish you in some way? Or you believe that family matters must never be discussed outside the family, and there is no one in the family you can discuss such matters with because you do not want to hurt anyone in your family? Many, many times a client has told me a story of what I would call everyday family unhappiness and ended with the words, 'This is the first time I've ever told anybody about this.' No wonder the past remains as the burdensome present.

It is not just that you have never been able to reassess, redefine, master and lay to rest the past events which still trouble you, but you have been unable to redefine yourself in relation to these events. Long ago you decided that you were a bad person, and subsequent painful events served only to confirm this. In fact, you only remember bad things about yourself, and, if by any chance someone reminds you of an occasion when you did very well at something, you can instantly prove your badness by saying, 'I should have done better.' Now it is a curious matter that what we call 'I' or 'myself' is composed almost entirely of memories, so that to have a sense of identity means being constantly aware of the past. If you ask me what sort of person I am, much of what I would answer would refer to the past. If I answered you in terms of the present, that I am in bed on a cold winter morning, writing this, drinking coffee, coughing, and aware of a vague pain rumbling around inside my pelvis, you would feel that I had told you very little about myself, but if I answered you in terms of the past (I was born in Australia in 1930, married in 1956, had a son in 1957, travelled to England in 1968, worked as a psychologist in the National Health Service for eighteen years, enjoyed my work, the company of my friends, reading, writing and travel), you would feel that I had told you a good deal about myself. My past, it seems, tells more about me than my present. This is curious, as Alan Watts, in his excellent book, *The Way of Zen*, explains,

> We learn, very thoroughly . . . to identify ourselves with a
> . . . conventional view of 'myself'. For the conventional
> 'self' or 'person' is composed mainly of a history
> consisting of selected memories, and beginning from the
> moment of parturition. According to convention, I am not
> simply what I am doing now, I am also what I have done,
> and my conventionally edited version of my past is made to
> seem almost the more real 'me' than what I am at this
> moment. For what I am seems so fleeting and intangible,
> but what *I was* is fixed and final. It is the firm basis for
> predictions of what I will be in the future, and so it comes
> about that I am more closely identified with what no
> longer exists than with what actually is![63]

Thus it is that we use our past to predict our future, and if that part of our past which we call 'I' is defined as 'bad' it must follow that the predicted future matches it in badness. Of course, when you were younger you dreamt of a future which would recompense you for the pain of your childhood. All children have such dreams, but soon there crept upon you

> The conviction that life
> Is coming up with some colossal romantic musical
> For which the casting director has, yet again,
> Overlooked you.[64]

You might abandon, but still mourn, your romantic dreams, while you acquired what you call a more realistic appraisal of the workings of the cosmos

> Life, you know, is set up by this great random computer,
> But it has been poorly programmed.
> Someone has fed in more bad news than good,
> And the messages tick out mad irrelevancies and ironies.[65]

But such a cynical attitude cannot keep at bay your deep all-pervading pessimism. You know that Robert Lowell was right when he said that always,

> if we see a light at the end of the tunnel
> it's the light of an oncoming train.[66]

However, although you are convinced that the future holds nothing good for you, until the isolation of your prison brings you to a complete halt, you are forever rushing, rushing, rushing to get things done. You never pay attention to what you are actually doing since you are busy thinking about what you must do next, and after that, what next, and so on and so on. If hell is ceaseless activity, then this is it. Only by running on the spot can you avoid falling into the bottomless abyss under your feet. And some fool tells you to take it easy! How can you stop when you must work so hard to overcome your badness, to placate and please others, to earn the right to exist, to grasp at a life which might at any moment be wrenched away from you, to get hold of something which might fill the horrible void within yourself.

Philip Toynbee who, in the last years of his life, set out to discover the *purposes* rather than the *causes* of his depression wrote,

> I suspect that each of us suffers from some *besetting* sin, which we must diagnose with great care and much hard thought. Often that dominant sin is not what seems the most obvious one; or rather it lies half-concealed behind some of its more ostentatious forms. In my own case it might seem that lust (in the days of lust in action!) and gluttony (drunkenness) have been my major sins; but now I believe that what lies behind these, and most of my other faults, is a sort of wilful metabolic frenzy; the constant urge to hurry as quickly as possible out of the present moment and into the next one. Get this woman *now; at once!* Drink these drinks *immediately* in order to take instant possession of the whole evening ahead.

He described how he rushed at everything, eating, dressing, gardening, repairing his house, just to get the job over and done with.

> How calmly and thoroughly S works at her windows, scraping off every bit of old paint and crumbling putty! How I rush at my walls, wielding the brush like a weapon!

He realised that

> With the old and obvious error about possession goes a

slightly subtler error about accomplishment. 'I want *to have read* this book; and therefore contain it . . .'. 'I want *to have made* this garden; I want *to have written* this book . . .'. In fact it is desire for possession in another form; another notch on the stick for another Indian killed . . . A greedy grabbing for the future.

No matter what you acquire or get done, nothing assuages your sense of guilt. Philip Toynbee wrote, 'The reason why guilt is so useless is that it keeps our heads buried, and suffocating, in our own past.'[67]

So you live in the horrendous past and the hopeless, fearful future and never in the present. And yet the curious thing is that the past and the future have no reality, except as ideas in our mind. All we ever experience is the present. In the present we can remember (think about) the past and imagine (think about) the future, and our thoughts are *in the present*. Of course, we can be so absorbed in our thoughts that we are oblivious to everything else in our present, and our thoughts may make our present quite unbearable, but, as Alan Watts said, 'There is never anything but the present, and if one cannot live there, one cannot live anywhere.'[68]

However, there are advantages in seeing your past and your future in the worst possible light. We can always try to avoid responsibility for our actions in the present by blaming the past – our parents, our schooling, our social conditions, our genetic inheritance. 'I can't help being like this' is a wonderful excuse for behaving badly. How easy it is to change a cause into an excuse, to claim that a disadvantaged past necessarily means a disadvantaged present and future, and that no effort toward change needs to be made. Even if we do not want to excuse our bad behaviour in this way, we can absorb ourselves in our past so as to avoid the challenges of our present and future. We can be so terrified of adulthood that we resolve to remain a child forever, or we can be so absorbed with the mother of our childhood that we ignore the needs of the old woman she has become, or we can be so lost in the nostalgia for our children's early years that we can ignore the problems with which our adult children are trying to deal. It is so much better to concentrate on the problems of the past, because we are always experts on those. It is the problems of the present that keep on being new and different and demanding flexibility and creativity for their solution. Better to stick to what you know.

When it comes to the future, it is always better to predict disaster than success, since you have a better chance of being right, for the simple reason that it is always easier to destroy than to build. You can always make sure of failure, and then you may not be happy but you will be certain.

As a child I was very slow in learning to ride a bike, and I was an adult before I could walk down a flight of stairs without feeling nervous. I had no physical disabilities, but I had a mother who followed my infant steps with cries of, 'You'll fall, you'll fall!' To oblige her I did. Then she would say, 'I told you you would fall.' Fortunately I had a father who was encouraging and optimistic, so my inhibition in learning was not too great, but I was often reminded of my mother when I talked with Carol.

Carol often told me anecdotes of family life in which she had expected the worst and was not disappointed. On a visit to a neighbour, 'I was just waiting for Peter to smash that Chinese lamp. I was thinking all the time, he will do it, he will do it. Anyway, he knocked over some plastic ornaments – but I knew he would.'

When I asked how she knew these things would happen she said, 'Premonitions. More often than not when I've thought of something it's happened.'

'Does that worry you?'

'No. I think it's an advantage in one way. I think there must be something in it. I get a sort of feeling. You can't always say directly what's going to happen. It's an inspiration that suddenly comes over me that there might be some trouble. It doesn't worry me. In fact, I think it's an advantage.'

'It allows you to start worrying sooner.'

'Possibly. When the car didn't pass its test I wasn't a bit surprised. I could not get out of my mind about the accident my cousin had. Whether somebody's given me a bang on the head and giving me all these premonitions! I wish they'd give me nice premonitions – so that things would still be all right – so I didn't have to guard myself.'[69]

Being constantly on guard against the future is exhausting, but it does have the advantage of directing your attention away from the present. Since the past and the future are ideas in our minds we can insist that the past and the future are exactly as we see them. The trouble with the present is that it has the habit of suggesting that my ideas may not be entirely right. How can I maintain my belief that everybody hates me if I recognise here and now the love you have for me? How can I maintain my belief that the Catholics are in league with the Devil if I recognise the concern of the nun who nurses me in hospital? How can I maintain that everything turns out badly for me if I recognise that the trouble I predicted for today has not eventuated? And if I discover that my ideas are not entirely correct, how shall I know how to behave? Instead of following the rules of behaviour which my ideas demand, I would have to behave spontaneously. Now some of us quite like behaving spontaneously. But you do not. For you, spontaneity means not joy but anger, and anger, you know, is dangerous and evil.

5. It is wrong to get angry

In the journal of the last two years of his life Philip Toynbee spoke very briefly but very poignantly of his childhood. He wrote,

> All that period of my youngest childhood is filled and suffused with love of my mother. She seemed a wise, strong and tender giantess, holding my hand on a walk or swinging me high above her head; a tall figure in doorways or towering beside my bed. During those years, and probably for many years afterwards, the thought that she might be wrong in anything she did or said was as far outside the reach of my mind as the idea that she was capable of dying. (It wasn't until I saw her dead body, nearly fifty years later, that I realised what a small woman she had been.)
>
> So my mother was also a storybook queen except that

she was so palpably present to Tony and me, warm-fleshed, always sweet scented and often singing. Although she reproached us when we behaved badly, and sometimes punished us, that mother was never angry. To have lost her temper would have been a breach of the impeccable serenity which belonged to her as closely as her beautiful hair and face. . . . Tony was much more shy and withdrawn than I was. He was terrified of being made to look a fool in public, while I was a natural clown, and always happy to attract attention. I was also the more quick-tempered of the two, and my mother used the same device to tease Tony out of his sullen self consciousness and me from my noisy tantrums. She would raise her first fingers to her temples, point them down at us like horns, purse up her mouth as if in awe of us and waggle her fingers at our angry faces. We understood that this forbade us to sulk or rage any longer: her gesture was almost an order to us to laugh at ourselves.

Although Tony and I often quarrelled I know now, as I have always known, that we were closely bound to each other under all the apparent ferocity of our rows and arguments . . . Yet our quarrelling was the usual cause of my mother's displeasure, and in most cases she was shrewd in deciding who was the more to be blamed. So we were usually in disgrace separately, and in a disgrace which divided us further. This may be why I remember so clearly an afternoon when we had been equal accomplices in some nursery crime. My mother had spoken to us with that air of amazed disgust which was the worst punishment we ever received; and even my father had been called to our bedroom to add his uneasy quota of disapproval. [My father was] a shadowy figure [but sometimes Tony and I] were allowed to come into our parents' bedroom in the morning; and when I saw them sitting side by side in that great bed I was deeply assured of their strong and unbreakable union. Or rather I was never aware of my need for such assurance. We used to climb into the foot of the bed, pulling the eiderdown over our legs; and when the whole family of four were together I imagined the bed to be a boat which would sail down the river and over the sea.

Certainly this concept of the close family was deeply planted in my mind, and my father was just as necessary a part of it as either my mother or my brother. I never admitted to myself that I loved him less than the other two, for I know from as early as I can remember that such inequality in love is a terrible and dangerous thing.

Philip had a recurring nightmare:

of a high wind blowing down the river as we crossed the Albert Bridge for our afternoon walk in Battersea Park. I was clawing at the smooth surface of the bridge as the wind blew me back and back towards an edge which no longer had any protective paling. But my mother always saved me before I fell into the wrinkled water. [Then] a very clear memory of my grandmother skipping across the hall at Yatscombe, holding a piece of paper above her head and singing, 'A new-born baby! A new-born brother for Tony and Philip!' I suppose we must have been warned of this, but all I remember was a feeling of mildly uncomprehending surprise. There was certainly no conscious shock of jealousy and not the least apprehension of what this birth would mean to us . . . What I remember best is coming into a bedroom and seeing the new baby at my mother's breast; but even at this moment of confrontation I can remember no very strong emotion. I said that the baby looked weak, and asked my mother whether it was going to die. Today the 'true' meaning of my question seems too obvious to mention,[70] yet I know that I felt quite a genuine concern for the wrinkled fragility of that tiny, spluttering creature. And I would guess that this concern was at least as real as any fratricidal impulse in my unconscious mind.

But how did it come about that within a year of that birth I was boarding at a private school half a mile from our St John's Wood house? I wasn't even a weekly boarder, although my mother must have paid occasional visits to the school in term-time.

Children usually accept whatever happens to them without question, and I doubt if it even seemed odd to me that I was boarding at a school where Tony was a dayboy,

and where the parents of all the other boarders seemed
to be living in Africa or India. Many years afterwards,
when this state of affairs, and many others that followed
it, had begun to seem strange to me, my mother
explained that I had become so intolerable soon after the
birth of my brother Lawrence that it was impossible to
keep me at home. Indeed she had always dreaded the
holidays, when the exiled monster would again start to
raise hell in a house which had been a bower of peace in
his absence.

What I do remember is that I was often in trouble now,
and that the notion of my exceptional naughtiness was
one which I learned to accept as a fact in life. I told the
dirtiest stories in the dormitory. I was often beaten by the
tough but charming Mr Campbell, whom all wished to
please. I got myself lost whenever we went on school
outings to Hampstead Heath.

Most home memories of those years have been
obliterated; but I remember that my mother, who had never
seemed capable of ill-temper in Chelsea, was often fiercely
angry with me in St John's Wood. And still it never crossed
my mind that she might be wrong, or even mistaken, in
anything she said or did. (How curious it seems to me now
that we were brought up to believe that all the adults we
knew were good, and that both our parents were
impeccable.) Some time in my ninth year, and second year
at Arnold House, the headmistress was taking a group of
parents round the garden when they came upon Toynbee
Minor peeing into a flowerpot. This had been of course,
the culmination of my offences, the last straw on that
broad back which made her decide that her school
could tolerate me no better than my mother could. This
first expulsion from school must have greatly
strengthened my conviction of sin, for my mother's
accusations had now been endorsed by a quite separate
authority.

After this, with a minimum delay, I was sent off to
board at the Dragon School in Oxford, an institution
which prided itself on being able to lick even the most
misshapen boys into place.[71]

But whatever reshaping this school did of Philip, it did not change his belief that he was essentially evil nor did it teach him how to control his quick and violent temper.

What Philip Toynbee described here is the process by which a small child comes to believe that he or she is bad, evil, and unacceptable. His early childhood was presided over by a strong, good and loving mother who protected him from all sorts of unknown terrors. She had already made clear to him her disapproval of anger, but this did not become a major problem for him until the birth of his younger brother. He could remember nothing of the year between the birth and his expulsion from the family home, but a great deal must have happened. He wrote,

> A family friend saw very clearly that my mother
> transferred much of her overt love from Tony and me to the
> third-born son. This same friend also saw that while Tony
> seemed almost unaffected by this – perhaps he had already
> worked off his quota of jealousy on me – I was soon
> disturbed by obvious though confused resentments. And
> so, the much-told story continues, I was made captive to
> these emotions, and remained their captive for forty
> years.[72]

Philip Toynbee began his story of his childhood with an account of how he, as a small boy, saw himself and his world. This perception was a set of judgements, that is, a set of ideas. However, small children – and most adults – take their perception of themselves and their world, not as a set of ideas, but an accurate representation of reality. Thus, when their situation changes, they cannot simply say to themselves, 'I'll have to change my ideas.' Instead, they feel immensely insecure and utterly frightened.

Philip saw his world as being secure, but this security was built on the strong figure of his mother. When she had a baby she withdrew from her sons. Philip's world fell apart.

'The world fell apart' is not an empty cliché. Neither is 'the bottom fell out of my world'. They are exact descriptions of what happens when we discover that there is a serious discrepancy between what we thought our world was and what it actually is. The world, as we experience it, does fall apart, and, worse, we feel ourselves falling apart. Philip had seen himself as being loved and wanted by his mother, and that he was an integral part of the family. Then he discovered that he was neither loved nor wanted. When our ideas about ourselves fall apart we experience ourselves as falling apart, shattering, crumbling, disappearing. We face being annihilated as a person, and it is utterly, utterly terrifying.

To defend ourselves against annihilation we try desperately to find an explanation. If we tell ourselves that the disaster happened by chance we increase our fear for we are helpless to prevent further disasters. If we tell ourselves that the disaster was brought about by someone else's carelessness or enmity towards us, such an explanation increases our fear because there may be worse to come. So we make the most popular choice, that of blaming ourselves for the disaster. We feel, wrongly, that by taking responsibility for the disaster we in some way take control of it. Moreover, we believe that taking the blame is a virtuous act. So we say to ourselves, 'If I had been really good this disaster would not have happened.'

This is what young Philip did. He decided that if he had been really good his mother would have continued to love him. Because he was bad she had ceased to love him.

Thus Philip created the ideas necessary to build the prison of depression, a prison which enclosed him, or threatened to enclose him, for the rest of his life. *To get depressed all you have to do is to blame yourself for the disaster which has befallen you.*

When young children become depressed they tend not to behave in the way depressed adults do. They tend not to become lethargic and miserable. Children usually become what adults call naughty. If these children are punished for their naughtiness rather than understood and helped, their sense of being inherently wicked is strengthened. This is what happened to Philip.

Well before his younger brother was born Philip had been taught that anger was wicked. After his brother was born Philip learned that the ultimate punishment for anger was complete rejection by the people he loved and needed.

Unfortunately his parents had never taught him any skills in handling his anger, and so he was quite unable to cope with frustration. For the rest of his life he was beset by angry impatience, bad temper and bitter remorse.

Philip Toynbee was certainly not the only child whose life was deeply marred by the birth of younger siblings. Jackie who, when she first met me, would not utter one word of criticism about her mother and who lived in fear of her mother's disapproval was explaining to me that she was the third child in a family of eight and mentioned, in passing, how when she was small she would go to bed at night and then begin to worry whether her tiny brothers and sisters were still breathing. She would get out of bed and go and investigate. As soon as her parents heard her moving about they would come upstairs and slap her hard and order her back to bed. Jackie had not connected this with the terrible terrors that had come upon her after the birth of her own babies. What mother has not crept to the side of her sleeping baby to check that the baby was still breathing? But what if she has already had it beaten into her that this is a wicked thing to do?

For many children it is not the birth of siblings that convinces the child that he is evil. It can be any situation where the child's desires come into conflict with those of the adults around him. Often the clash comes over toilet-training, where the adult's disgust with the natural products of the child's body is taken by the child as disgust with the child himself. Parents who themselves have been taught, and never questioned, that anger is wrong, find any sign of temper in their child quite intolerable. Rather than teaching the child how to cope with frustration and how to use his anger constructively, they demand that the child inhibit a response which for human beings is as natural as breathing. Sometimes the child decides that anger is wrong, not because he is forbidden to express his own anger, but because the anger of the adults around him, amongst themselves, is so violent and uncontrolled that he lives in terror. Children who grow up in households where everybody is angry all the time, or in households where nobody gets angry with anybody ever, grow up believing that anger is wrong. Consequently they cannot manage to live with anger, their own or anyone else's.

So, for whatever the reason, you have grown up believing that it is wrong to get angry. How do you manage to live with this belief?

What a great many people do is to deny that they ever get angry. No matter how difficult or provoking other people may be, no matter how much your desires are thwarted, you never get angry. You are always calm and smiling. Except, of course, when you have those dreadful migraines that usually come on after you have visited your mother, or when your ulcer plays up, usually on the morning of the monthly conference at work, or when you are stuck in a traffic jam and you start trembling so much you can hardly drive once the traffic starts moving. But you do not like to complain about these things at home or at work, because you do not want to upset your family and you would not want anyone at work to suspect that you do not do your job perfectly all the time. You know how quick some people are to criticise, and if there is one thing that really upsets you, it is criticism.

When Chalky Giles came to see me to find out why he could no longer cope with his job of deputy-headmaster of a local school, I told him about the six beliefs one must have if one wants to be depressed. He laughed ruefully and agreed that he had them all. (His image of his prison was being trapped in a dyke, the deep ditch which lines most of the roads and lanes in Lincolnshire.) At the end of our first talk I set him some homework, to write a character sketch of himself as it would be written by a sympathetic friend. This, he protested, was a very difficult task, for, while he would have no difficulty in listing his faults and in berating himself, to say anything good about himself and to talk about himself with sympathy was quite impossible. I insisted. So the next week he presented me with the following account.

I have known Chalky for the last ten years when he married Rachel and came to live in Huxby. To me he seemed perfectly happy and quite a witty and effervescent person. He could always be relied on to make some cheerful, humorous comment. He appeared confident when he was chairman of the tennis club and could organise his committee and he was liked and respected by all who met him. However, over the last few years I have seen him in a depressed state when he is like another person, as if he has a split personality. Gone is his humour and ability to joke, to be replaced by moaning about the mess he is in and the gloomy outlook that lies ahead. On the surface of it all I can't see what he has to get depressed about for he appears to have all the material needs for a comfortable life, and has a good wife and a beautiful daughter. He is fit and healthy physically when not depressed and always seems to be bursting with energy. I know now that 'he sails close to the wind' most of the time. If only he would believe in himself and realize that he can do his job well. He tries to please everybody all the time and sets himself too high standards. He is not content with what he has achieved and worries far too much about the future and what people might say or do to upset him. He never really enthuses about anything but tries to appear happy, contented and on top of things. He never tries to offend people or show annoyance but always wants to be the peacemaker.

He is very concerned and helpful when anyone else needs a helping hand, but he doesn't seem to like to help himself when he is depressed. He is quite capable at his work and is well liked and successful with nearly all the pupils, both past and present, from the village.

He is a fool to himself because he could so easily destroy his job security and family by letting himself get so low and depressed. It always seems to happen in the early part of the year when the weather is bad and he tends to stagnate when coming home from work.

Chalky had run into difficulties when he had been promoted from class teacher to deputy head. Like many people, what Chalky wanted above all else was to be liked. He had not realised that if you take as your rules for living trying 'to please everybody all the time' and trying never 'to offend people or show annoyance' but always wanting 'to be the peacemaker', then you must never take a position of authority and decision making. In a position of authority, whatever it is, you cannot avoid offending some people and you cannot avoid being criticised. Rather than offend others and be criticised by others some people refuse to accept any role which might confer some authority ('I always go along with what my husband wants', 'Do what you think best, dear. Don't ask me to decide'), but this solution will run counter to the need to justify one's existence by achieving or by doing everything perfectly. You can then find yourself in the difficult position of trying to win by letting all the other contestants come first.

One of the problems of never wanting to offend people is that you find yourself doing things which you do not want to do. Mary said, 'It's just that I get put upon. People will say, "Oh, Mary will do it." In the bank I keep changing my job to get the hang of the work, and it's surprising how many things follow me around from job to job . . . I don't like to say no . . . I get given a lot of things other people don't want. People give me clothes that's too small for them. I don't want them but I can't say no. I feel awful if they find out I don't wear them.'[73] Being put upon in this way makes you feel resentful, but, if you dare not speak out and protect yourself against the encroachments of others or even complain to someone else, then the resentment destroys whatever enjoyment or satisfaction that might have accrued from doing something for somebody else.

One of the ways through which people manage to deal with the frustrations and irritations of living or working together is through humour. They use humour to defuse anger. Every group of people that get along well together has its own special jokes and teases, most of which are developed as commentaries on the curious and often irritating characteristics of the individuals in the group. The ability to joke and be joked about, to tease and be teased, is something we usually learn as small children in our families. The person who grows up in a family where there are no jokes, where everything is taken absolutely seriously, usually has great difficulty in being able to tell whether another person is being serious or joking. Since the most outrageous and aggressive things are said in joke and since all jokes carry a kernel of truth, if you cannot tell whether another person is joking or not you will often be hurt, confused and offended by the people around you. Of course, if you can recognise a joke but believe that to joke about a person means that you do not like or admire that person, then all jokes about you will be taken as insults.

Mary had married a very witty and humorous young man who used his humour to cope with all sorts of difficult situations. However, Mary took everything he said very seriously and so was often confused about whether or not she had angered him. One day I asked her what she thought would happen if she upset people. She said, 'They won't love me. They'll get cross with me. I'm terrified people will get angry with me. Sometimes I worry about things I've said that don't upset people but I think they might do. They don't appear to be upset, but I wonder when I've said something I don't really mean, and I think I've upset them even if they don't appear to be upset, and I'm always worried in case they are – and I get upset so easily. I think everybody's like me. Nobody has to shout at me to make me really upset. I take things the wrong way. I suppose everybody is just like me.'[74]

Everybody is not like Mary. There are some people who cannot possibly deny that they get angry, since their anger is a violent, raging torrent that rises in them and bursts forth, crashing against and damaging everything and everybody that gets in the way. And even when the raging torrent is still, the person lives in fear that it will burst forth again, a force which cannot be subdued or controlled. Some people in the grip of such anger inflict real damage and injury on their possessions, their loved ones, or even a passing stranger. Others use only the weapon of their tongue, but their murderous fantasies show them what they are capable of, given the opportunity, and they see the opportunity all around them. Sometimes the murderous fantasy becomes so powerful and engrossing that the person finds it hard to distinguish thought from action and comes to believe (as young children do) that wishing someone dead actually causes the death of that person. Some people believe that their guilt should be as great for the thought as for the action (as if thinking about scrubbing the kitchen floor is the same as doing it, or thinking about sending money to Oxfam is as virtuous as actually giving money to Oxfam.)

Jean was a very timid person but on occasions she would fly into the most terrible rage. She wrote to me and said, 'Sometimes I see violence in almost everything I look at. I fear that poker, the axe, the kitchen knife – I fear their potential – as I realise I fear my own potential. Facing my own potential violence I find very hard. We visited the Art Gallery in Aberdeen on Monday and I could marvel at the violent emotions at work in a lot of the works there. The stairs were made of marble and so cruelly cold and hard. As I carried little Emily down them I could feel their threat. I know in myself that what it says on your wall poster is true – that the world is not how it seems but how you are – though I can't remember the precise words. ['We do not see things as they are. We see them as we are.'] I suppose that in my "perfect" world there is no cruelty or violence. Or harsh words or guilt or whatever.'

Some people feel very guilty about their bad temper but use their temper as a defence against a cruel world. Carol said, 'I have to hurt or be hurt. The minute I put my defences down nearly always something happens and I get hurt. I might be looking for it – I don't know. I don't know how to cope with being hurt.'[75]

Peter's rages were extreme but they gave a subtle reward. As he told me, 'The person who suffers after a row – I know other people do, don't misunderstand me – the person who suffers extremely is myself. I get shattered. I think about it for months afterwards. I suppose in a sense I punish myself for it. I'm not sure that there aren't times when I promote anger in order to lay the stick on myself. In a sense, one sort of feels that for some reason or other it's appropriate that I should punish myself. I deny myself things on occasion. Self-denial. I think it does me good – it's like "If I don't do this God won't punish me".'[76]

There is one great advantage in regarding anger as wicked and evil. If you see anger as simply part of the drive to survive and to create, the drive which has enabled puny humans to overcome enormous obstacles, then as you develop ways of mastering and using your anger (e.g. don't thump the mechanic whose ineptitude has damaged your car; write a stern letter to the Managing Director, demanding recompense and suggesting ways in which the work of the garage could be improved), all you can claim is the gaining of wisdom. But if you regard anger as a vice, evidence of your essential badness, then all your attempts to control your anger you can regard as evidence of virtue. How delightful is the vanity of practising our virtues! In fact, you can devote so much time to being angry and being guilty about being angry, and feeling virtuous because you are feeling guilty about being angry that there is no time left over to do or even to *be* anything else. 'It's exhausting being angry,' said Julie, 'but if you subtract the anger there's nothing there.'[77]

For some people, in the last analysis, not being angry is more dangerous than being angry. Peter deplored his bad temper, but, as we explored the ways in which he might come to curb or dissolve it, he said, 'I can identify with anger. I can say, "Yes, I'm angry about this", and the reason I am angry about it is so and so – I can and I will on occasions say to myself, "Well, it's not something to be angry about", and it may make me angry, but it's an unrealistic action on my part because it isn't important enough. I tell myself that I can translate virtually any situation into this sort of equation and whatever it is, life is short, it's only me getting angry over something I feel and it doesn't justify anger. And then I get frightened because I think, okay, if that's the way it is, then I'm in danger on a long-term basis, and if I spread it over the whole of my outlook, my attitudes, my behaviour, maybe I shall stop feeling. I don't want to stop feeling. I want to feel pleased about things and cross about things because I feel that, without feeling, motivation goes and I don't think I'll become a vegetable, but I'd become so bland that I'm no longer a person, and I know that's not a good argument but it's where I come to war with myself about feelings. I would like to be serene and wise and able to take everything in my stride and that would be a lovely ego thing, I tell myself, I think with my head. But I don't feel that with my gut. My gut says that I've got to care because if I don't care about this or I don't care about that, then I cease being *me*.'[78]

And so it is better to be *me*, even if me is a wicked me, than not to be me at all.

I am often asked if being with depressed people makes me depressed. I always answer no, but in truth there is one thing about being with a depressed person which I always find very worrying and wearying. This problem did not arise with my clients since, when we talked together, it was in a time and place which have been set aside, free from interruptions and harassments, and where I could relax and give my full attention to the other person. I no longer work as a therapist but the problem still can still arise when I visit a self-help group run by depressed people. I might make this visit when I have finished a day's work or I have travelled some considerable distance. On these occasions I am not always full of sweetness and light. Sometimes I feel tired, distracted, harassed, ill or crabby – sometimes all five together, and consequently in danger of not being on my best behaviour. A trivial matter, such as a taxi not arriving or a train being cancelled when I am making my way home, can irritate me, but woe betide me if I reveal any of this irritation to a member of the group because that member is likely to immediately assume that I think it is all her fault, that it is all her fault, that I do not like her, I have never liked her, I shall never like her. What follows is an ominous silence (she will not speak to me because she knows I do not like her, but when I finally realise that I am not being spoken to, I think I must have done something to offend her, but do not know what), or else protracted apologies with each of us trying to take the blame for the incident. To avoid all this I have to remember never to show any anger or irritation when in the company of anyone who is depressed. Thus I have to dissemble, something I dislike doing, first because I am too lazy a person to be an effective liar, and, second, if I am found out it will only reinforce the person's belief that other people are not to be trusted. I think to myself, 'If only she would realise that just because a person gets angry in your presence, or even gets angry with you, it doesn't mean that that person does not like you.' Then I realise that this is simply my way of seeing things. It is not hers. She knows quite well that if someone gets angry with her that person does not like her and will not forgive her for what she has done. Why?

Because this is the sixth rule that builds those prison walls so firm and high. You know that when someone gets angry with you that person dislikes you and will never forgive you. You know this is so, because, when someone hurts and angers you, you never forgive.

6. I must never forgive anyone, least of all myself

When we were children we each spent a lot of time working out what we hoped and believed would be the story of our life. We dreamed of growing up to be like the adults we admired and we feared turning into the kind of people we despised. Sometimes we despaired of being able to live up to certain standards, and sometimes we became angry and frightened as we found ourselves being pushed by our families and teachers into something which did not fit our dream (I dreamed of escaping school and family to lead an exciting life of travel and writing. My heroine was Dorothy Thompson, an American journalist whose wartime travels were recorded in the newspapers I read. But I was told, 'Girls don't do things like that. It would be different if you were a boy. You should become a teacher. That's a good, safe job.') The fate of our childhood dreams always bears out what George Bernard Shaw said, that there are only two tragedies in life. One is not getting what you want, and the other is getting it. If our childhood dream does not eventuate, we mourn it; and if it does eventuate, we discover that it does not bring the complete happiness that we expected. Prince Charmings can make dreadful husbands, and what do you do after you become rich and famous? Life is always different from our dreams.

However, that does not stop us trying to make life conform to our dreams, especially when our dreams are our only defence against a harsh and cruel world. When we were little and made up the story of what we wanted our life to be, only part of that story followed from our belief that life was wonderful and that good things were in store for us. Part of our story sprang from our joy, but only a part. The other part, and for some of us, the major part, sprang from our fear, our experience of being cruelly and unfairly treated. When we were small children we were weak, fully in the power of other people, and, when these people used their power to punish, shame and ridicule us, we did what all impotent human beings do when they are threatened with complete destruction and annihilation by their enemies. We vow revenge. We vow never to forgive.

Sometimes the dream we create is based on the theme of 'I'll show them'. We dream of becoming so brilliant and famous that our family and teachers will be able to do nothing but stand amazed and abashed, overawed by the magnificent figure that we have become. Some people do achieve great success in the pursuit of this dream, but rarely do they find that the returning hero gets the welcome home of which he dreamed. Teachers have the habit of dying or forgetting who you were, and relatives are either singularly unimpressed with anything you do or else they appropriate to themselves all the credit. Thus success can seem very flat, stale and unprofitable. If, on the other hand, you have vowed to heap scorn on your enemies by becoming a world-famous figure and you fail to do this, then you find it very difficult to accept what most of us who dream of fame have to accept, that world fame, or universal, total acclaim is a fate reserved for very few people. You can make yourself very miserable by rejecting all your successes on the grounds that they are not good enough. They do not confound your enemies.[79]

Sometimes the dream we create is based on the theme 'They'll be sorry'. Tom Sawyer enjoyed the perfect working out of this dream when he and his friends hid in the church to listen to their own funeral service. How lovely it would be to hear our relatives saying how sorry they are that they hurt us and treated us unjustly, and what good and wonderful people we were! The trouble with relatives is that they never seem to do this, and some of the relatives I have met in the course of my work could not do this, even to save their own lives. But that will not stop you trying. There are many depressed people who are prepared to starve themselves in the hope that their family will kneel round their deathbed and beg forgiveness. There are others who are prepared to let the locked doors of the lunatic asylum clang behind them, just so they can say to their grieving, repentant relatives, 'See what you made me do!' However, relatives who drive you to these extremes are usually the sort of people who never beg forgiveness nor ever admit any responsibility for your distress. Your dream fails, and the reality is that you have entered upon the career of a psychiatric patient, a career which, once begun, is difficult to leave.

Fortunately, not all the people who get depressed carry revenge to such extremes. Instead, behind the façade of pleasantness, compliance, graciously agreeing with everybody, never (or rarely) saying anything nasty about anyone, you remember all the injuries done to you and you still feel angry and unforgiving. Some of you find it impossible to voice these feelings because you dare not criticise the people on whom you depend. Some of my clients have given me the impression that they still more or less have the childhood belief that their mother knows everything they think and do. Other clients I have found feel obliged to report to their mothers and partners what is discussed in the therapy session. One woman I knew went straight from my office to her mother's home, while another woman knew that the minute she arrived home her mother would phone her from the other side of England to check on what I had said and especially to see if I was blaming her for her daughter's predicament. Another woman found it very hard to talk to me about the things her husband did which upset her (not very terrible things really – just the acts of a typical loving, obtuse, unthinking man) because he would question her about our therapy session. I suggested to her that she simply say that she had forgotten. This was not a complete lie, since she was in that stage of depression where it is very difficult to think straight. (A bad memory is a wonderful alibi and should never be relinquished.) The problem about not being able to talk about your resentments is that you are then prevented from going through the stages necessary to achieve forgiveness and reconciliation. By giving expression to our anger in some direct and truthful form (that is, saying how you feel instead of saying nothing and being upset), by talking the matter over with a sympathetic friend, by thinking about our feelings and our relationships freely, not inhibited by rules of 'I mustn't criticise my mother/father/husband/wife', we can come to terms with the painful experiences we have suffered. We master them, learn from them and, by letting them go instead of holding them close, we cease to be oppressed by events in our past and are better able to cope with events in our present.

But to do all this we have to believe that it is right to forgive. Not everyone sees forgiveness as a virtue.

Some people see not forgiving as a virtue, and so they refuse to forgive themselves. For them part of trying to be good is to confess their sins, not to a priest who can give absolution, but to themselves. They see their sins as being so great, so horrendous, that absolution is impossible. Many people believe that they must keep secret from everyone the unforgivable wickedness that is inside them, and that consequently they must never let anyone get really close to them and thus discover how wicked they actually are. Many of those labelled as being unable to make a long-term commitment would actually like to make a commitment but they feel they cannot run the risk of being found out. They might tell themselves that having a long-term partner would not add anything to their life and that they are perfectly happy as they are, but, in telling themselves this, they dare not admit to themselves that they are lonely. They are, in effect, not forgiving themselves.

When we do not forgive ourselves we are making no attempt to see our supposedly great acts of wickedness in the context of when and where they happened. Often we act badly, not because we intend to be bad, but because our knowledge at that time is very limited. Children's knowledge of life is necessarily limited, and so is the knowledge of people who refuse to look at their parents with an adult, critical eye. Often we act badly because, at the time, so much was going on in our life that we were confused and under great pressure. Later, when we know more or our life is calmer, we can remember what we did. We can feel ashamed of what we did, wish we had acted differently, and thus learn from our experience. However, if we decide that what we did was unforgivable not only do we fail to learn from these experiences but we become the tortured and the torturer, locked together in lifelong pain. Even more, we do to others what we do to ourselves. We refuse to understand why they behaved as they did. We refuse to forgive them.

As a consequence of this way of thinking some people who get depressed do not always present themselves as pleasant and compliant, not speaking evil of anyone. They may do this outside the home, but inside the home, whenever anyone offends they sulk – not quietly and unobtrusively but in as dominant and noticeable manner as possible. (Actually, there is no point in sulking if nobody takes any notice.) Some of you have perfected the art of Not Speaking. This is where you go about your usual domestic chores but without saying one word to anybody, no matter what anybody says to you. (Heavy sighs which mean 'Here I am yet again sacrificing myself to an ungrateful family' are allowed, as are cries of distress in the kitchen, following some small accident, while the family are settled watching television in the living room. The cries of distress are particularly effective if the accident has been caused by the laziness or negligence of your family.) Some of you prefer Retiring to Your Bedroom in a High Dudgeon. It is necessary to have a well trained family for this. You have to be sure that they will hover around your door, anxious to cater to your every whim. It is no good if they laugh at you, or scamper off to attend to their own affairs and leave you to starve or to perish for want of a cup of tea. The games of Not Speaking and Retiring to Your Bedroom in a High Dudgeon can give a great deal of satisfaction (if revenge was not sweet we would not bother with it), but they do have the problem of how do you start speaking again or leave your bedroom without feeling foolish. If you have succeeded in getting your family to apologise to you in the way you feel is appropriate then you can graciously agree to overlook their errors and to rejoin family life, but so often families not only fail to understand how they have offended you but they also fail to understand how they should mend their ways.

I can laugh at such ways of behaving now, but I grew up with a mother who, when her family offended her, would retire to her bedroom and not speak. On two occasions when

I was a schoolgirl her sulk lasted for six months. However long her sulk lasted, when she did emerge from her bedroom she would indicate that she was prepared to talk to us by making some banal domestic remark. My father and I dared not make any comment, and certainly dared not make a joke, lest she disappear back into her bedroom and re-impose the pall of misery that encompassed the house when she was in one of these moods. Try as we might to please her, we could not because each of us persisted in our unforgivable error. Mother could not forgive my father for being her husband, and she could not forgive me for being her daughter. After my father died my mother forgave him. I think that by the time she was old she had forgiven me because by then she had stopped criticising me, but, if she had, she never mentioned it. The word 'sorry' was not in her vocabulary, and, because it was not, she threw away so much possible happiness.

As a child my mother had had a religious education, so she must have often heard the words of Jesus

> Judge not, that ye be not judged. For with what judgment ye judge, ye shall be judged: and with what measure ye mete, it shall be measured to you again.[80]

These words certainly applied to my mother. Jesus pointed out that the rules or judgements that we apply to other people we expect other people will apply to us. So, if you believe that it is wrong to forgive, you must expect that other people will not forgive you when you harm or upset them in any way. This is one of the reasons why you find other people so frightening. Even when they are nice to you, you cannot be sure that they are not harbouring grudges against you, and when you feel certain you have offended someone you are often too scared to meet that person again. You try to avoid all the places where you might encounter the people you might have offended and so the number of places where you dare to go become smaller and smaller. It never occurs to you that that person might have dismissed the offence entirely or, if forgiveness was required, to have forgiven you. You expect to be judged as you have judged.

This, of course, is the rule you apply to yourself. The one

person you must never forgive is yourself. You never let any of your mistakes go by saying to yourself, 'That was bad luck,' or, 'No point in worrying over it,' and forgetting what you did. You go on and on at yourself, never forgiving yourself, no matter how many punishments you inflict on yourself. In your eyes your crime is that you exist, and you will never forgive yourself for that.

If you believe in a God who judges us then you know that God will not forgive you. Jesus had a great deal to say about forgiveness. He told Peter that he should forgive his brother not seven times, but 'seventy times seven'.[81] He preached,

> But I say unto you, Love your enemies, bless them that curse you, do good to them that hate you, and pray for them which despitefully use you, and persecute you.[82]

He told the parable of the servant who was forgiven by his master for not repaying a debt of ten thousand talents but who would not forgive another servant a debt of a hundred pence.[83] On learning of this the master withdrew his forgiveness. When Jesus taught the prayer

> And forgive us our debts as we forgive our debtors

He explained,

> For if you forgive men their trespasses, your heavenly Father will also forgive you. But if you forgive not men their trespasses, neither will your Father forgive your trespasses.[84]

So, if you cannot forgive yourself or other people you know that you are damned.

Jesus had a lot to say about forgiveness but it is one aspect of His teaching which has been largely ignored by most of His followers. Had it been accepted and acted upon world history would be quite different – no pogroms, no religious persecutions between different Christian sects, no wars or acts of vengeance. Northern Ireland would have always been a haven of sweetness and light, and nuclear weapons would never have needed to be invented. All too fantastical. Much better to justify our aggression by remembering Jesus saying, 'I came not to send peace but a sword.'[85]

While Jesus was quite clear that we should forgive one another and so obtain God's forgiveness, He did make some rather obscure remarks about the unforgivable sin of speaking against the Holy Ghost.[86] Just what this sin is and why it is unforgivable has caused much debate, and many believers have worried terribly that they have unwittingly committed it and so are irretrievably damned. The Catholic Church lists the sins against the Holy Ghost as presumption, despair, resisting the known truth, envy of another's spiritual good, obstinacy in sin and final impenitence. These categories could be narrowly interpreted to fit every crime and peccadillo, but they can also be interpreted to encompass what Simon Phipps, the Anglican Bishop of Lincoln, explained to me was the interpretation he gave to the unforgivable sin against the Holy Ghost. He said,

> I suppose it would mean absolutely basically turning your back consciously, deliberately on what you saw as what God stood for. There are lots of sins, lots of things which you might do which might be called sins, categories of ways in which we do damaging things, but this sin against the Holy Ghost means not so much that you do something as you actually decide to *be* something which is totally over and against what you see God to be. I think the Holy Ghost, the Holy Spirit, is an attempt to put a name to the actual impinging upon our experience of God.[87]

What Simon was saying and what religious thinkers of all faiths have said in their own particular ways is that if, when we glimpse some profound and awesome aspect of our existence as an individual and as part of the cosmos, an aspect which we know without the necessity of proof is true, and then we deny that truth, we do ourselves great damage. Such a discovery was not confined to religious thinkers. Freud rejected the religious account of how we damage ourselves by rejecting what we know is true, but devoted his life's work to showing how similar denials created what he called the splitting of the psyche. This he regarded as the essence of neurosis. Such denial is simply lying to ourselves. We know something but we tell ourselves that we do not know it. Some people who fear anger tell themselves that they never get angry. They call their anger fear, and then become exceedingly anxious. They might be angry with their parents, but they tell themselves that they have the best parents in the world, sheer angels in fact. Having told themselves one lie they have to go on telling themselves more and more lies in order to keep the first lie in place. When we lie to ourselves we split ourselves into the person who knows the truth but is shut out and the person who lies. Thus we prevent ourselves from experiencing ourselves as one whole person.

Freud said that psychoanalysis was concerned with healing the divided psyche and rendering it whole. Sartre considered the problem from the existentialist point of view and spoke of 'bad faith' when we pretend we are something we are not. The trouble with pretending is that if you start it early enough in life, you end up forgetting who you were before you started to pretend, and so you fear that if you stop pretending you will disappear. The 'holistic' therapies which have developed over the past forty years aim at finding ways of discovering who you are and of making yourself whole. If, as a small child, you decided to see yourself as bad so as to preserve the adults you depended on as totally good (which they were not, and you knew they were not, since they were fallible human beings and not angels) and to put from your consciousness the realisation which came to you when you were under threat, that we are part of a formless, ever-changing, moving, shapeless nothingness and everything-ness, and, if in adult life you have not reviewed all this by accepting the awesome uncertainty of which you are a part and by reapportioning responsibility and then generally forgiving and forgetting all round, you have, in fact, decided to *be* something which goes against what you know – and deny – to be the truth, and so you have wilfully done great damage to yourself, something which we all know is unforgivable, if not in God's eyes, then in our own. We are each responsible for ourselves and we should cherish ourselves.

The various religions of the world all have ceremonies of healing, cleansing, forgiveness and rebirth. The various psychotherapies use non-religious rituals and words, but they, like the religions, help the person become whole again by creating a sense of being forgiven, if not by God, then by one's own conscience. (Some people would argue that the words 'God' and 'conscience' refer to the same thing, that being at peace with yourself means being at peace with God, and vice versa. But this is not important. What is important is for you to know the right words for you for your experience.)

So these are the reasons for forgiving. You have lots of reasons why you should not. It can be that you just hate saying sorry and admitting that you have made a mistake. Many of us say sorry when we do not actually mean it. We are sure that we are right and the other person wrong, but we use 'sorry' as a kind of social grease that helps us get along with one another without too much friction. We can do this when our 'sorry' relates to something we regard as relatively unimportant. However, if the matter is important we can find it impossible to say sorry because to do so would be to admit that our ideas were wrong, that that part of the world was not what we took it to be. There was a discrepancy between what we thought the world was and what it actually is, and such a discrepancy threatens us with annihilation. We cannot risk that, and so we refuse to say sorry.

It can be easy to say sorry and tell yourself that you have forgiven the person who hurt you, but you still feel the hurt and, indeed, hang on to it. Forgiving means letting go of the hurt as well as the cause of the hurt, and, like Carol, you may not be prepared to do this. As she said, 'I think I can forgive but I don't think I could forget. This is my trouble. I never forget. With us when the air gets heated between us we tend to bring all these things back. I've got to have something to fire at Bob when he starts on me. I'm grateful that Bob has put up with me. But gratitude can only go so far. You get to the point where you're just taken for granted. I've realised after thirteen years of marriage I was never a person that could say I was sorry. That was a lot of our trouble. I keep things inside and build up a resentment.'[88]

Of course, if someone hurts you and you forgive that person you just put yourself in a position to be hurt again. When I asked Joan what she did when a shop assistant got angry with her she said, 'I should be hurt and I wouldn't go into that shop again . . . If I know somebody who's nice and then they're angry, I don't want to know them any more.'[89]

There is another danger which Kay described. She and her husband often argued, and when he said and did wounding things she 'would just stop speaking. Because I detested him at the time. It would go on for a day or two and after that I would wish I were speaking. He would say, "You silly thing. Why aren't you speaking? You know you've got to speak in the end." I enjoyed it. But I didn't enjoy it for long. I've gone on for over a week, but after two days I wished we were speaking. It's a wanting to go back to normal, really. After a couple of days I wouldn't feel the same and I wouldn't eat either . . . Since I have been like this he has said, "If only you knew how much you have hurt me." But he'd never shown me. If only he had shown me that I had hurt him in a way I should have been pleased to think that in some way I had hurt him, but I think we would have had a better relationship. But I just wanted to see that I had hurt him. I wanted him to feel like I did. Sometimes I would break down and cry when he had upset me, but I didn't want him to go that far. I just wanted to know that I had hurt him. But he never did . . . Sometimes I wanted to say I was sorry but I just couldn't.'

Kay described how they had quarrelled and to hurt him she had refused to go to his firm's dinner dance, a function she very much wanted to attend.

'I just lay on the settee and I was miserable with myself. I wanted to go, but I couldn't tell him.'

'What did you want him to do when you said you weren't going?'

'I was laid on the settee and I wanted him to come and say, "Please come, please come, darling." And he didn't you see, and it shook me. That was three years ago and, looking back, that, I think, was the start of this depression. I should have said nothing and should have gone with him. We should have been all right then.'

I asked her, 'What do you think would have happened to you if you had never stood up to Jack?'

'Well, I might have done better. It might have made him feel small. Or I might have just become a servant to him.'[90] If you experience yourself as weak, or so bad a person that you have no right to stand up for yourself, then you do see yourself as being in danger of being wiped out by those people who hurt you, and whom you see as much stronger than yourself. So you build a fence around the emptiness, the void you feel inside, by vowing never to forgive. Indeed, you can come to define yourself almost totally in terms of your vows never to forgive but to seek revenge. Over the past decades, generations of children in Northern Ireland, the Middle East, the Balkans, India and Pakistan, have been told by their elders that their very reason for existence is to avenge the crimes committed by their enemies. Unfortunately, many of these children have grown up believing what they have been taught and so resist every attempt to resolve the conflicts between Protestants and Catholics, Arabs and Jews, Serbs, Croats and Muslims, and Hindus and Muslims, because such a resolution would take away their purpose in living, the very means by which they define themselves.

Sometimes we call not forgiving 'intolerance' or 'righteous anger' and define it as a virtue because we are intolerant of the evils we see in the world. Tony scorned 'tolerance' because he saw tolerant attitudes as no more than a cover for cant and hypocrisy. His ferocious intolerance caused him and the people around him a great deal of pain. The pain did not end until he 'had what he described as a profound and revelatory experience when he discovered that he could contrast his intolerance not just with pusillanimous tolerance but with the assured detachment which is the essence of Zen Buddhism.'[91]

It is this detachment, and not forgiveness, which we should create, especially when we have suffered a massive, irreparable injury, or are still struggling with the effects of an injury inflicted long ago. If, say, we have a child whom we love and that child is killed through the stupidity or malice of someone, we can find it impossible to forgive that person. Or, as in my case, every day is a struggle against the effects of a chronic illness which was a result of childhood neglect. In either case, we have a choice of dwelling on our loss and injury and feeling bitter and sad, or we can detach ourselves by turning our thoughts to other matters. We can remember our child as he was when he was alive but we turn our thoughts away from the circumstances of his death, and away from our anger and despair. If, as I go through my daily health routines, I find myself on the edge of thinking about how my family could have saved me from this, I say to myself, 'Now, what am I doing today?' I have identified what events set me to thinking about my childhood in a miserable way (for instance, a letter, email or phone call from my sister) and I try to keep such events to a minimum. I cannot pretend this is easy to do, as those of you in a similar position will know, but because I value myself I do what I can to look after myself. I do not tell myself I have forgiven when I have not, and I certainly do not berate myself for not forgiving. I simply practise detaching myself from that aspect of my childhood by not dwelling on it.

Forgiveness as detachment is a strength and not a weakness. This is part of the Buddha's teaching in the terms that *dukkha*, suffering, is the result of our trying to impose our desires on the world and to insist that what happened in the past is still with us. Wanting revenge is a way of avoiding the guilt we feel when we believe we have acted wrongly, and the helplessness we feel when we know that there was nothing else we could have done to prevent the disaster. To desire revenge is to suffer. If you do not wish to suffer, give up the desire for revenge. We may try to hang on to the past by not forgiving. We can try to keep our dead alive and with us by not forgiving, with reproaches to ourselves ('I should have looked after my mother better'), or to the dead ('Why didn't you say you loved me?') but all we achieve out of trying to make reality repeatable is *dukkha*, suffering.[92]

And you have indeed made one part of your reality repeatable. You try to protect other people by blaming yourself, you feel guilty about your shortcomings and misdemeanours and fear that you will be punished, you get more frightened, and then angry with the people who make you feel guilty and frightened, then you feel guilty about being angry with the people you should protect, so you blame yourself and feel more guilty, more frightened, more angry and so on forever and ever. There seems to be no way out. There is no way out, since you forbid yourself the key that will unlock the door. You will know no peace until you discover how to forgive yourself, to forgive other people and to let others forgive you. Only then will you be free of the past, be able to live in the present and to look to the future with hope. But how can you do that when you believe that it is wrong to forgive?

These six opinions, held as Real, Absolute and Immutable Truths, can be expressed, interpreted and acted upon in many different ways, and each person who gets depressed has his or her own individual way of doing this. Of course, opinions are not just ideas in our heads. They are feelings, emotions and actions. They determine the decisions we make, but they do not have to become conscious in order to do so. You can decide not to buy yourself some desirable shoes without consciously thinking, 'I don't deserve them.'

To understand how these six opinions can combine together to form the peculiar sense of isolation which is the essence of being depressed, we need to look at these opinions in terms of one basic essential feeling, a feeling that is so intrinsic to our existence that we do not have a single word for it but a number of words which have all sorts of meanings and connotations. Some of the words which refer to this feeling are –

Spirit, soul, heart, psyche, quintessence, vital principle, energy, vigour, vim, force, intensity, potency, dynamic energy, verve, fire, drive, vivacity, liveliness, outgoing, radiance, vitality, life force, élan vital, vital spark, joie de vivre, passion.

When we think to ourselves, 'What a lovely day it is. I'm really looking forward to what I'm going to do today. Life's turning out really well. What nice friends and colleagues I have. How I love my family! I did that really well. I do enjoy meeting people. We had a good laugh together over old times', and such like, that feeling of life within us goes out towards everybody and everything. 'We experience a sense of the outgoing of the spirit, a sense of the force of life, a sense of freedom and movement which may range from mild placidity through vigour and vitality to immense and marvellous joy, relish and delight. Such an experience is accompanied by some degree of confidence, creativity, optimism, courage, and benevolence.'[93]

But when we think to ourselves, 'What a horrible day it is. I dread what the day will bring. Life is terrible. I haven't a friend in the world. My family are a great disappointment to me. I make a mess of everything. I'm terrified of other people. I can never forget the dreadful things that have happened to me', and such like, that feeling of life within us does not go out to anybody or anything, but rather it shrivels within us. Then we feel that 'we merely exist, that we are diminished, constricted, isolated, inhibited, helpless, despondent, anguished, barren, desolate, fearful, pessimistic and bitter.'[94] We are enclosed and isolated within ourselves, and we learn the truth that torturers down the ages have always known. Many people can manage to survive the greatest pain, injury and privation, but the one torture that affects even the strongest and bravest of us is solitary confinement. We need, just as we need air, food and water, to be part of the woven pattern that is human life. If we are isolated from it, if we isolate ourselves from it, then we suffer the torture of the damned, and the longer we stay in solitary confinement, the greater the torture becomes.

So it is that if we hold these six opinions and make them the basis of our every action and decision then we impose on ourselves a sentence of solitary confinement.

Many people go through life believing that they are not so much evil as simply not good enough. They struggle hard to make up their deficiencies, but since they see themselves as unacceptable to other people, other people make them nervous. They find anger hard to deal with, but they value forgiveness so they do not brood too much on their past. They have some hope for the future since they have based their life on a philosophy which allows some optimism. Such people would not call themselves depressed but they may, at times, be aware of a sense of being burdened in a world of muted colours. A stone lies on their heart. This might be the pattern for their entire life, or, if they are lucky, great happiness, a success which they are able to accept, removes the stone forever and they feel light and free in a colourful world. But if disaster comes upon disaster and they can no longer believe that if they are good they are safe, or if one day they realise that they are no longer young, that the opportunities for the life they dreamed of are lost forever, if the love they need has vanished, then they despair and mourn and do not forgive. The burden on their heart becomes the prison walls of depression. However, for many such people their depression is no more than a walk through a dark valley while they come to terms with their life. Because they have always allowed the possibility of forgiveness they have the capacity to accept change. Because they have always allowed the possibility of love they do not turn totally against themselves but give themselves a measure of kindness and allow others to be kind to them too. Love and forgiveness (aided perhaps by the cheering effect of antidepressant drugs) leads them out of the dark valley.

Susan described her experience of depression as being in rough and dangerous waters, and trying to gain a foothold on a rocky incline. The first time she was depressed she could, in her image, see figures on the top of the incline, reaching their hands down to help her. She was able to find the strength within her to scramble to safety. In the words of her psychiatrist, she responded to antidepressant drugs. But in each succeeding period of depression the water got deeper and rougher, the helping figures fewer and further away, and the less strength she had to secure a firm footing. Even when she felt herself to be on dry land she was not secure. She was only one step away from a precipice. On her next admission to hospital she 'did not respond to medication or ECT'. She saw no figures offering to help her and she was not able to help herself. And neither should there be any help for her. She believed in a forgiving God but a just God. She was wicked and lazy, and had not helped her family in the way that she should. So she was being justly punished for her wickedness. Her depression was her punishment and it was right that she should accept her punishment and not try to escape it.

So, if you have not taken love and forgiveness into the dark valley with you, you will not discover the path out of the valley. Those people who get depressed and stay depressed, or who go from one period of depression to another, with the time in between each period filled with the sense of the depression lurking in the background are those people who see as Immutable Truths that they are essentially evil and must work hard to be good, that other people are dangerous and must be feared, that the only religious and philosophical ideas which reveal the Truth are those which lead to fear and despair, that the past is irreconcilable and the future hopeless, that anger is to be feared and that it is wrong to forgive. If you are one of those people then you know how for some of your life, before you became depressed, you were strong and active enough to work hard at being good. You had found some limited ways of coping with other people and there were one or two people in your life you could risk loving and trusting. You put from you all awareness of death and when you thought of the disasters that would certainly befall you, you thought, 'Not yet.' You avoided anger as much as you could, and, while you cherished your injuries like a miser cherishes his gold, you did not spend too much time counting these, for you still had some hope for the future. But then something happened. Perhaps it was the last of a line of disasters which destroyed your hopes, perhaps it was the death or defection of a loved one, or perhaps it was the gradual realisation that you could not keep up the pretence of being good any longer. You are a wicked person and this disaster, whatever it is, is your punishment. The bottomless abyss yawns beneath your feet. The black cloud descends, the door clangs shut. You are in the prison of depression.

Chapter 4

THE DEPRESSION STORY

We all love stories – telling stories and listening to stories. When we watch a film, or go to a play, or read a novel we might not already know the actual story told in that film, play or novel, but we already know the plot or theme of the story. There are a great many different stories but very few plots. The two most common plots are the love story plot and the good triumphing over evil plot. The love story plot is that of two people meeting, falling in love, and having some misunderstanding or encountering some adversity. The ending may be that of living happily ever after or that of a tragic separation. The love story plot can be part of the most popular of all plots, that of good triumphing over evil. In real life evil quite often triumphs over good, but stories with such a plot rarely get told in films, plays and novels. We all like happy endings, and, if the ending cannot be happy, we need an ending which assures us that, one way or another, good will at last triumph.

Not all stories get turned into a film, play or novel. We each have our own story, our life story, and all these life stories have a simple plot – we are born, we live, we die. However, within this main plot there are many sub-plots, and here I want to tell you about a plot which I call The Depression Story.

Everyone who gets depressed has his or her own individual story about becoming and being depressed, yet all of these stories have the same basic plot. I have mentioned all the elements of this plot in the preceding chapter, but now I shall put them together in the order they occur.

First, I have to set out what you need to know in order to understand The Depression Story. To understand the love story plot we have to know about falling in love, and to understand the good triumphing over evil plot we have to know about good and evil. To understand the depression story we have to understand how human beings function in every moment of their lives.

How we function as human beings

When you look around you it seems to you that what you are seeing is part of the world, perhaps it is a room, a garden or a street. Yet, what you are seeing is not a particular part of the world as it actually is. What you are seeing is a picture of that part of the world. This picture has been constructed by your brain, and the picture is inside your head. Your brain then plays a trick on you. It persuades you that, instead of the picture being inside your head, the picture is all around you.

Your brain constructs all your pictures out of the memories which are stored in your brain. These memories come from your past experience. You see what surrounds you as a room because your brain has constructed this picture of a room out of all your past experiences of a room, and you call this picture 'a room' because that is what you have learned to call such a picture. Another person in that room with you will not construct a picture of that room which is exactly the same as your picture because that person's experiences of rooms are different from yours, even though both of you have learned the same language and thus call the picture 'a room'.

No two people ever have exactly the same experiences so no two people ever see anything in exactly the same way.

Some of the differences in the way people see things come from differences in the physical equipment each person has for seeing. Suppose you and a friend are standing side by side at the edge of a pavement, waiting to cross a busy street. You both look to the right and you both see a car approaching. In the retinas at the back of your eyes you have a full complement of the cones which turn all your pictures into colour. This means that you live in a colourful world, and so you see a red car approaching, but your friend does not because he lacks the requisite cones in his retinas to make his world colourful. He sees a grey car approaching.

Moreover, you and your friend differ in how you see cars generally. Perhaps you have always been passionately interested in cars and so you know a lot about cars, while to your friend a car is nothing more than an object which gets him from A to B. Thus, when you both look to the right your friend sees a grey car which he has to let pass before he crosses the road, while you see a brand new Golf GTI which makes your heart leap for joy while you envy its driver.

A very ordinary scene, two people waiting to cross a street, but you and your friend each interpret it in a different way.

What determines our behaviour is not what happens to us but how we interpret what happens to us.

The interpretations we create are meanings. Creating meanings is our basic, constant function. We start creating meanings when we are babies in the womb and our brain gets to a certain stage of development, and we go on creating meaning every moment of our lives until our brain ceases to function. Only a small proportion of the meanings we create we put into words. Emotions are meanings, as are the pictures we see in our mind's eye, and the feelings of some sort of discomfort in our body. We can be in bed and busily creating those meanings which we call a dream and at the same time we create a meaning, though not a conscious meaning, which tells us that our leg is cramped and we need to turn over.

We do not just create one meaning and then discard it, create another and then discard it. All the meanings we create our brain stores in the pattern of connections between the multitude of neurones in our brain. The pattern of connections in our brain and the pattern of meanings we create change with every new experience, but this pattern or *structure of meanings* remains as a whole, and from it as a whole comes our sense of being a person.

You are your structure of meanings: your structure of meanings is you.

All the meanings you create are guesses or theories about what is going on. As you and your friend are waiting to cross the road each of you forms a theory about the speed of the approaching car. Neither of you can tell the exact speed of the car, but you might guess that it is travelling at 60 miles per hour and that, once it has passed you, you will have enough time to cross the road before the next car comes along. Your guess needs to be a good one because if it is wrong you could be in trouble.

The structure of meanings which you experience as your sense of being a person is actually a set of guesses about what you, your life and your world are actually like. When your guesses approximate quite closely what is actually going on everything seems to be real and predictable, and you feel secure because your guesses are being confirmed as correct. But, whenever you discover that you have got some of your guesses badly wrong, you feel shaky and frightened – shaky because your meaning structure has been disconfirmed, and frightened because your sense of being a person is being threatened with annihilation.

Thus, if you and your friend are standing there and you say to your friend, 'That's a new Golf GTI coming towards us', and then, as the car goes by, you see that it is an Audi, you feel that you have received a blow. Your friend might be indifferent to what sort of car it is, but you discover that you are not the authority on cars that you thought you were, and this discovery comes like a blow which leaves you shaky and frightened.

Whenever you discover that there is a serious discrepancy between what you thought you, your life and your world were and what they actually are your structure of meanings receives a blow which threatens to shatter it. You feel that as a person you are falling apart, shattering, crumbling, disappearing, being annihilated. You feel a nameless dread which can rise and rise until you are consumed by terror. You have to do something to hold yourself together. You have to find some way of defending yourself.

There are many kinds of defences, and one of these is the prison of depression.[1]

Laying the foundations of the prison of depression

When you were born you came into the world full of unself-conscious self-confidence. You did not lie in your cot worrying about whether people would like you and whether you were pretty enough or clever enough to satisfy your parents. You were you, and you were not surprised when there was a smiling face looking at you. You became very attached to one of these smiling faces, but one day this face was not smiling at you at all. It had become an angry, cold, ugly face, and you were very frightened.

This experience was followed by other experiences from which you learned that, as you were, you were not acceptable. With this discovery you lost your unselfconscious self-confidence. With this discovery you laid the cornerstone of the prison of depression by coming to believe that

As I am, I am not acceptable. I have to work hard to be good.

Believing this, you became a good person. Good people always believe that, as they are, they are not good enough, and that they have to work hard to be good. Different people define 'good' in different ways, but, however they define it, good people are always striving to be better. Only good people can use the defence of depression.

The belief that you are, in essence, not good enough leads on to the other five beliefs, that other people are such that you fear, hate and envy them, that life is terrible and death is worse, that only bad things happened to you in the past and only bad things will happen to you in the future, that it is wrong to get angry, and that you must never forgive anyone, least of all yourself. When life goes along reasonably well for you, you think of yourself as being only mildly unacceptable and the other five beliefs do no more than lurk in the back of your mind, but, when life goes badly for you, you become more and more critical of yourself and the other five beliefs come to the fore.

Believing that you are unacceptable and always trying to be good is a miserable, fraught way to live, so children who live like this have to believe that one day they will be rewarded for their goodness. In your day-dreams about what you would do when you grew up you told yourself stories of how your goodness would be recognised and rewarded, how you would be loved and admired, and how those who have hurt you will admit their wrong and beg your forgiveness. You wanted to believe that your rewards would follow as night the day, and so you came to believe that you lived in a Just World where goodness was always rewarded and badness always punished. You might have made your belief in the Just World quite explicit as a central part of your religious beliefs, or you might have held it implicitly, believing that goodness ought to be rewarded and badness ought to be punished. In every film you watched and every novel you read you expected goodness to triumph. If it did not, you found that film or novel deeply unsatisfactory.

Thus you had become a good person living in a Just World.

And thus you laid the foundations for the prison of depression. All you needed to complete the prison was for a disaster to happen to you.

Encountering a disaster

There are three kinds of disaster which you could suffer.

First, something happens to you which everyone would agree was a disaster. Perhaps someone close to you dies, or you have a terrible accident or contract a serious disease, or your home and all your possessions are destroyed by fire, or your business goes bust, or you lose your job.

Second, you witness a disaster the like of which you have never seen before, perhaps a terrible train crash, a suicide bomb, a football stadium disaster, or perhaps you see a stranger who is very similar to you in many ways die a very tragic death.

Third, you suffer a disaster which is known only to you. It might be that you discover that your partner is faithless but you say nothing for the sake of your children, or that you have waited all your life for your father to say that he loved you but he dies without any acknowledgement of you, or your secret love dies or leaves you, or you have always promised yourself that when the children were grown up you would return to study, but when the time comes your family prevent you from doing this, or perhaps one day you look in the mirror, are shocked at how old you have become, and realise that your dreams can never come true. Perhaps you do not recognise that you have suffered a disaster because you do not know what you truly thought and felt.

The third kind of disaster is perhaps the hardest to bear because, if you have not confided in anyone, there is no one to help you bear your sorrow. Something happens, something which to an outside observer is minor, even trivial. However, this event brings together a number of threads in your life, and so an apparently trivial event becomes loaded with meaning. It is a meaning which shatters you. This is what happened to Gwyneth Lewis. She had gone to visit friends who lived on a farm in west Wales, and she had offered to help them with the sheep wintering in a shed.

> The shed was divided so that the sheep expecting triplets were in one pen, those carrying twins in another and so forth. Our job was to separate the ewes that weren't pregnant from the rest, which we did, using a system of railings and gates. Rhian explained that this had to be done so that they knew which of the sheep needed extra rations. The 'empty' ewes wouldn't be fed.
>
> When I heard this I felt I had been hit in the stomach. Rationally, I knew that what Rhian meant was that only the pregnant sheep would be given extra food, but that's not what I heard emotionally. In my stomach, what I understood was that childless women are useless and don't deserve to be nourished. I began to starve.[2]

For excellent practical reasons Gwyneth Lewis and her husband Leighton had decided not to have children. She had felt that this decision was right for each of them and for their marriage, but she had not taken account of how she still embraced society's belief that 'equates motherhood with virtue' and sees 'childless women as calculating, selfish harridans'. As a result, 'I ending up feeling like an immoral, hurtful and unacceptable human being.'[3] Gwyneth Lewis had spent her life striving to be good, and now she discovered just how wicked she was. Thus there was a serious discrepancy between what she thought she was and what she actually was. Later she could write,

> The day before I finally stopped I woke up knowing I was in big trouble. It wasn't that I was just tired – although I was – my blood felt all wrong. I knew I'd no more energy to run away from what was bothering me. Depression was about to take the whole matter out of my hands and to show me another, better way of coming to terms with myself. I had to grieve for the life I was never going to have without children. The adjustment required in your expectations and view of yourself, particularly in relation to time, is huge. Part of my work of my depression was, I'm sure, to allow me to get used to this new reality.[4]

Both the first and second kind of disasters have the effect of showing the person involved that there is a serious discrepancy between what he thought his life was and what it actually is. If he blames himself for the disaster then the depression which follows has the task, as Gwyneth Lewis describes it, of teaching him that he has to adjust his expectations and view of himself.

The second kind of disaster can be very hard if you are surrounded by people who tell you that you're stupid, you're hysterical, you ought to pull yourself together. It is even harder if you are told that, following the disaster you witnessed, you have become ill with post-traumatic stress disorder. People then talk to you about the tragedy you witnessed but not about what that tragedy meant to you. They do not give you a chance to talk about what it meant to you to discover that death is real and will come to you, and that no amount of goodness prevents disaster.

The first kind of disaster can be made even harder to bear because the people around you offer comfort but it is not the kind of comfort you need. Perhaps your elderly and ill mother has died and friends offer the comfort of, 'It's a blessed release for her,' while you are silently screaming, 'I need my mother. I can't manage without her! I've let her down. I've failed her.'

Whatever the kind of disaster, it shows you that there is a serious discrepancy between what you thought you, your life and your world were and what they actually are. This serious discrepancy is a major threat to your meaning structure. You feel that as a person you are falling apart, shattering, crumbling, disappearing, that is, being annihilated. William Styron called this 'anxiety, agitation, unfocussed dread.'[5] Andrew Solomon gave a longer description. 'There is a moment, when you trip or slip, before your hand shoots out to break your fall, a passing, fraction-of-a-second terror. I felt that way that every hour after hour after hour.'[6]

In this perilous situation you ask yourself, 'Why has this disaster happened to me?' Because you believe in the Just World where nothing happens by chance, you cannot decide that the disaster was simply bad luck. You are left with 'It was someone else's fault,' and 'It was my fault.'

You are a good person. Good people blame themselves. So you decide, 'It was my fault.'

Now everything falls into place because everything is explained. If you had been a really good person this disaster would not have happened. Now you know that you are worse than being simply unacceptable. You are wicked, and your wickedness caused this disaster because this disaster is your punishment for your wickedness.

Everything is now explained, and you have made sense of it all. Now you are safe – safe in the prison of depression. Its walls are around you and they keep you safe from the chaos which was threatening to overwhelm you.

But you are completely alone. You can see and hear other people, but they are on the other side of the walls of the prison and you cannot reach them, indeed, you do not want to reach them.

How did this aloneness and the walls of the prison come into being?

Building the prison

To understand how the walls of the prison are constructed we need to understand how we operate in relation to other people, and why connectedness to other people is so essential to us.

We are our meaning structure, and our meaning

structure – how we see ourselves, our life, our world – means that we each live in our own individual world.

However, if we each saw our own individual world as being like a balloon, and we all floated around like a host of balloons quite unconnected one from the other, we would not survive for very long. We would not survive physically because it is extremely difficult to maintain our body solely by our own efforts. We would not survive as a person because individuals who try to live completely on their own lose touch with what is going on around them, and they lose the ability to distinguish what goes on around them from what goes on inside them, that is, to distinguish their perceptions from their thoughts and feelings. As torturers and jailers have always known, the quickest way to destroy a person is to put that person in completely solitary confinement for an indefinite period. This is why the defence of depression is perhaps the most painful defence we can ever choose.

So it is that we have to connect ourselves to other people, and these connections, though invisible, are more real to us and far stronger than any road or bridge could ever be.

When we are with someone we trust and feel affection for, a connection goes out from us to that other person. That person does not have to be beside us for us to feel that connection. We can feel connected to people far away, or people whom we once knew but who are now dead, to people we know only by reading about or seeing them on television. We can feel connected to people not yet born – our children, our grandchildren. We can feel connected to people we have never met but who are related to us, or who share our outlook on life. We can feel connected to fictional characters in books or films. We can see our pets or certain of our possessions as people and feel connected to them.

In the same way we can feel connected to ourselves – the 'I' that acts and the 'I' that watches 'I' acting. Both operate together as one. We can feel connected to our past that defines our identity and can comfort and warn us. We can feel connected to our future which we view with hope and joyful expectations.

We can feel connected to everything around us. As we

walk down a busy street we can feel ourselves to be part of the crowd, part of society. As we walk in the countryside we can feel connected to the fields, the trees, the wind, the sky.

Thus we are connected to everything. We might have to live in our own world of meaning but we are connected to everything that exists.

But only if we value and accept ourselves.

Turn against ourselves and hate ourselves, and every one of these connections fails.

When you blame yourself for the disaster that has befallen you, you turn against yourself and hate yourself.

Thus you divide yourself in two – the 'I' that acts and the 'I' that constantly criticises and denigrates the 'I' that acts. The 'I' that criticises is always punitive, cruel and rejecting, while the 'I' that acts feels punished, worthless, vulnerable and frightened.

Hating yourself, you cut yourself off from other people because you are frightened of them. If they can see how wicked you are they will punish and reject you. They may even try to destroy you. Moreover, you have to protect other people from the foul malignancy inside you which could contaminate, even kill them. So you cannot bear them to touch you or even come close to you.

You cut yourself off from your past because there is no comfort or protection there, but endless evidence of how wicked, useless and totally unacceptable you are.

You cut yourself off from your future because you cannot hope for anything better. You know that all that lies ahead is nothing but the punishment you deserve for your wickedness.

You cut yourself off from everything around you. You are an outcast from society and from nature, and rightly so. You are too wicked to belong.

By believing yourself to be totally wicked you have cut yourself off from every aspect of your life. Every aspect of your life frightens you, and you put up a barrier to protect yourself. The broken connections and these barriers form the walls of the prison of depression.

The whole process between asking, 'Why has this disaster happened to me?' and finding yourself in the prison of depression is quite unconscious because every meaning, every thought involved in the process is a much-practised habit. Thus the process is completed extremely quickly, in the blink of an eye. We can all move at remarkable speed when we are in danger. If you were crossing a street in the belief that you could do so safely, and a speeding motorbike came from nowhere and bore down on you, you would move at Olympic speed to the safety of the pavement. Similarly, when your sense of being a person is threatened with annihilation you can construct a defence in the blink of an eye.

If you have already laid the foundations of the prison of depression then you can put it all in place in a second.

But, do you have to stay there? Or can you find a way out of the prison of depression.

The key to the prison of depression

The key to the prison of depression is within your grasp. All you have to do is to change how you see yourself and how you see the world.

Instead of seeing yourself as being bad and unaccept-able and having to work hard to be good in order to keep yourself safe and earn the right to exist, you see yourself as valuable and acceptable and, if you choose to do good, it is simply because it pleases you to do so. You do not expect the world or anyone else to reward you for being good.

What follows from this belief is that you are no longer frightened of other people, and so you no longer hate and envy them. You remember pleasant things about your past and become reconciled to the bad, hurtful things. You no longer fear your anger, and so you can deal sensibly with your own anger and other people's anger. You are able to forgive yourself and so able to forgive others, or at least detach yourself from them when the feeling of forgiveness does not arise.

To see yourself as valuable and acceptable you have to cease to be so judgemental of yourself. You have to abandon all the ridiculous demands you made upon yourself and the equally ridiculous standards you set yourself, and put in their place a few reasonable demands and set yourself some reasonable, achievable targets.

Valuing and accepting yourself does not merely free you from the prison of depression. You find yourself emerging into the world with a most glorious sense of freedom. No longer is your cruel taskmaster, the 'I' that watches, burdening you and frightening you. You are simply yourself, and you are whole and free.

Discovering this freedom you no longer need to see the world as a Just World, dominated by an implacable Power who deals out rewards and punishments in ways impossible for mere mortals to understand. You can see that some things happen by chance, some things are the result of actions by others, and some things are the result of your actions, and that most events are a result of a mixture of all three. You accept that you control very little of what goes on in the world, but you know that you do control how you interpret events. You know that you can choose to create interpretations which cramp and confine you, or you can choose interpretations which lead you to feel free and happy.

Making such changes in how you see yourself and your world can be difficult, but it is possible to do so. I know a great many people who have done this, and an even greater number of people have written or spoken to me and told me that they have made these changes and their life is now something infinitely better than what it was.

This is the end of the story of depression and it has a happy ending. However, just as the love story plot and the good triumphing over evil plot always have a villain who strives to separate the lovers and prevent good from triumphing, so the depression story has a villain. It is pride.

Chapter 5

WHY NOT LEAVE THE PRISON?

The short answer to this question is 'I'd rather be good than happy.'

However, preferring to be good rather than happy is not something that only people who get depressed do. To some extent we all do it. I remember saying this in a lecture on depression to a group of psychology students and teachers. They all looked surprised since, like most psychologists, they regarded themselves as hedonists, preferring pleasure to pain. To explain I simply said, 'It's Saturday afternoon.' They all laughed and acknowledged I was right. There we were, crammed into a dreary lecture room, applying ourselves to serious matters instead of taking part in all the delightful things that we could do on a Saturday afternoon. We certainly were preferring to be good rather than happy.

There were some people in that room who knew how serious a point I was making. Others, the ones devoted to joyous and successful living, would have argued that they followed the principle of enlightened self-interest, that they were prepared to endure some discomfort in order to gain future pleasure. But those who knew what it was to be depressed knew that they were involved in a continuous battle to be good, and in this the sacrifice of a Saturday afternoon was a small matter.

I first realised the significance of wanting to be good rather than happy back in 1968 when I was learning about a form of psychological testing called the repertory grid and when I was spending much time talking to patients who were quite severely depressed. One of these patients was a woman,

Mrs A, who had had all the usual treatments of drugs and ECT, all without any sign of permanent improvement. I asked her to do a grid where, first of all, she drew up a list of twenty people, including herself, who were in some way important to her. Next she drew up a list of the terms she used in assessing these people. Then she grouped the people she had listed according to each of her assessments. This gave a grid of numbers which was then analysed on a computer to see how her ideas or opinions clustered together. What this showed was that she divided the people in her world into good and bad. Her good people were 'not critical of other people, are affectionate, easygoing, soft, generous, are used by other people but do not complain. The bad people are mean, hard and cruel, aggressive, nasty and hurtful, have no feelings, are fault-finding and self-opinionated and use other people.' Mrs A put herself among the good people. A sensible way of judging people, you might say – except for one thing. All the good people, she said, were poorly; all the bad people were well. 'Poorly' in Yorkshire covers every physical and mental state where one is not well. It certainly covers being depressed. In Mrs A's way of viewing her world, every time the doctors tried to move her from being 'poorly' to being 'well' they were trying to move her from being a good person to being a bad person. No wonder all their treatments failed![1]

None of us wants to be changed from being a good person to being a bad person, and most people accept a degree of unhappiness so as to meet what they see as their responsibilities. Looking after husband, children and a house, or doing a dull job, day after day, year after year, in order to support a family certainly does involve a degree of unhappiness in order to be good. But this is different from seeing your unhappiness – depression – as evidence that you are good, or, at least, that you are trying to be good.

'Oh, no,' you cry, 'I don't want to be unhappy. I don't want to be depressed. I'm not like your Mrs A. I'm not making myself into a good person by being depressed.' Are you sure?

In the effort to be good we all do peculiar things. When we start in life believing that we are not good enough we have to do all sorts of things to improve ourselves. The more bad and unacceptable you see yourself as being the more drastic the things you must do to be good. Being depressed is one of these drastic things.

There are many ways in which a person can work out the equation

being depressed = being good.

If you regard yourself as essentially bad, then you can think that you do not deserve to be happy. Being depressed is what you deserve to be. Not just not deserving happiness, you can see depression as your punishment for not being good enough. You should have tried harder, done better. At the same time you can see your depression as the punishment for your badness and the evidence of your badness, because no matter how much you strive to overcome your depression you fail. You try to pull yourself together, to make an effort, to do the things your doctor and your family tell you you should do. But all this effort does not work. You are still depressed. So you must accept your depression as punishment (good people always accept their just punishments – good little children hold out their hands to be smacked and do not run away or hit Mummy back, and good adults always pay their fines) and you must work harder to overcome your depression (good people always try again and do not give up).

It is no wonder that you get confused, trying to do these two opposing things at the same time.

Probably all of us, when we were little, were told by some adult that if we were good we would be looked after but if we were bad we would be abandoned. A common sight in any shopping centre is of a child dawdling behind his mother who, exasperated, turns to him and yells, 'If you don't hurry up I'm going to leave you behind.' The child who knows she does not mean it continues to dawdle, but the child who fears she might obeys and hurries to his mother. Sometimes, when a child loses his mother in the crowd and in fear begins to cry, the mother, returning, instead of comforting him, says, 'You're a naughty boy. If you did as you're told, this wouldn't have happened.' Some children in these situations are wise enough to know that his mother would never leave him and that it was her fault that he lost sight of her (that is, on occasions his mother lies and is careless) but the child who would not dare think such dreadful things about his perfect mother grows up believing that if you are good, really good, there will always be someone there to take care of you. You might devote your life to trying to get your parents to care for you totally, or, if it is borne in upon you that parents cannot protect their adult child totally and make your life smooth and secure, you expect *them*, the government or society or the medical profession or God, to protect you and make your life smooth and secure. You want to live in a world organised by immutable laws derived from an infallible source. (A colleague once told me how an adolescent client was in difficulties over her Social Security benefits but she assured my colleague that she would be all right because, she said, 'They aren't allowed to let you starve.' Really?) However, when you do discover that *they* are incompetent at protecting you, you get very angry. How dare the government be so stupid! How can the medical profession be so ignorant when they ought to know how to cure every illness! How dare God go back on His promises!

What promises? The promise that if you are good you will be safe. Don't ask where the government, society, the medical profession, or even God made this explicit promise. You know for certain that the way the world operates means that goodness and rewards balance. The better you are, the more rewards you get. You might not become rich and famous, but at least you know that you will be safe. Whenever you see good people suffering or when things do not turn out the way you want you get angry, even resentful. This is not the way the world *ought* to be. The idea that we have to be responsible for ourselves and that the ways of the world are neither good nor just is too terrifying for you to contemplate. You cannot tolerate such uncertainty. You do not trust yourself, so how can you take responsibility for yourself? You would rather stick to the belief that if you are good someone, somewhere, somehow will look after you.[2]

But right now it seems that you are not being looked after. Perhaps it is not because of the incompetence of the powers that be. Perhaps it is because you are not good enough. You must try harder.

If being good means being depressed, then you cannot *afford* to leave your prison.

Chapter 6

WHY I WON'T LEAVE THE PRISON

1. I have high standards

We all want to be good, and most of us are prepared to put up with some unhappiness in order to be good, but there are many different ways of defining 'good', in setting goals and standards for ourselves and in dealing with ourselves when we fail to reach these standards.

People who do not get depressed see themselves, although with some faults, as essentially good. Since they do not have to battle to overcome great wickedness they regard themselves as good if they are 'good enough', that is, they do not expect perfection but just a reasonable attempt to do as well as can be managed in the circumstances, and when they fail to achieve this modest goal they chide themselves in the mildest of terms and feel reasonably sure that next time they will do much better.

You who get depressed despise such mediocrity. Since you regard yourself as essentially bad with insufficient virtues to redeem yourself you expect – nay, demand – perfection, and when you fail to reach it (as you must, since you regard yourself as inherently flawed) you berate and chastise yourself harshly as you believe you deserve. Even as you suffer you despise those who lack your high standards. You have before you the image of perfection. You know what Melvyn Bragg meant when he wrote, 'Most of us have known a time – however long ago, when the notion of perfection seemed worth the sacrifice of everything else.'[1] But you still feel that perfection is worth the sacrifice of everything else – or at least your happiness – while Melvyn Bragg was saying that this is a youthful belief that most of us outgrow. Most of us come to realise that the world is imperfect and that we need to accept these imperfections as best we can. But not you. You will not forgive the world for not living up to your expectations, for not being perfect the way you want it to be. You have suffered, and in striving to be good you have sacrificed much. In a just world goodness is rewarded, and your reward must be a perfect world. You will not settle for less.

Because you are frightened of other people, and because you are not sure just how to make the world perfect (that is, to get everyone to do what you want, and to abolish death, old age, suffering and natural disasters like earthquakes and blizzards) you can, perhaps, concentrate on making your family perfect. You can reject the world for failing to live up to your standards but, unfortunately, the world is unimpressed with your rejection. You can, though, make your family very aware that you will reject them if they do not live up to your standards. You can make your love conditional on their good behaviour, and if they accept this, you have them in your power. So you demand that they be perfect parents and children and partners, that they keep their bedroom perfectly tidy, be in at your stated hour, get their hair cut a decent length, cook food as it should be cooked, never have friends of whom you do not approve, keep to your routine and so on. They do try – at least, sometimes – but they fail, because children cannot help but be their age, and parents get tired of adolescent demands, and wives get tired of mothering their husbands, and husbands get confused by conflicting demands. Sometimes you feel confused yourself about the demands you hear yourself making. You find yourself wanting to do something in an easy fashion, or to stop, or to rest, or not to be so demanding of others, but there is a voice within you that drives you on. You obey because if you do not you will be overwhelmed by guilt. Jackie described to me how she and her husband Ron decided that on Saturday mornings she would lie in while he minded the children, but every Saturday morning she would get out of bed soon after him and follow him around, telling him where he was not doing things properly. 'I can't stay in bed' said Jackie, 'When

I was a child it was a rule that the girls had to get up and do the housework. I feel guilty if I stay in bed. I know Ron knows how to look after the children but I can't let things be.'

Not letting things be, constantly carping over faults, impatiently wanting things to be done, being resentful and unforgiving when your standards are not maintained, all adds up to what Jung called 'the well-known bad moods and irritability of the over-virtuous'.[2] Since your family soon come to fear your bad moods, irritability and constant criticism, it is no wonder that you sometimes feel that they do not love you.

As much as you rail at your family, you criticise yourself even more. It is as if you are two people, your wicked self and a harsh, punitive critic whose standards can never be met.

What is this self inside us, this silent observer,
Severe and speechless critic, who can terrorise us
And urge us on to futile activity,
And in the end, judge us still more severely
For the errors into which his own reproaches drove us.[3]

Carol's mother had taught her that 'The easy way is never the best way'[4] and now the severe and speechless critic in her head was scornful if she looked for ways of making her housework easier. Chalky said, 'If I don't feel tired at the end of the day I don't feel I've worked hard enough.'

Who sets these crazy standards? Is a floor more virtuously clean because it was scrubbed by hand, not a machine? Does a child's knowledge increase proportionately to his teacher's increasing exhaustion? But there is no arguing with these kinds of rules. I might joke about them and you might smile in sheepish acceptance of my jokes, but, if underneath you still hope that there is a book of immutable laws from an infallible source, and that this source or power will protect you if you keep these laws, then there is nothing I can say or do that will help you take life easier. Your mother or father might be many years dead, but if you still scurry to obey the parental voice when it speaks in your head, giving orders applicable in another time and place but not here and now, and if you still hope that your obedience will secure your parents' protection and love, then you have sentenced yourself to a lifetime's hard labour, and much good will it do you.

In a study of women's experience of neglect and abuse in childhood and adult depression one woman told the researchers that 'as a child she had sobbed her heart out in the school toilets because she was afraid to go home and tell her father, a school teacher, that she had scored ninety-nine out of a hundred in her maths exam. Despite being top of the class, she knew she would be severely reprimanded for failing to achieve one hundred per cent. Her father's disparaging remarks guaranteed that she would never feel pride in her accomplishments. This sense of failure haunted her into her adult life: despite dazzling career achievements she was continually plagued by self-criticism and doubt.'[5]

Sometimes the parents you obey are not your earthly parents but the ideal parents in your head. When Tracy was nine years old her mother left the family. Tracy was very upset by her mother's desertion, even though she had not been, in Tracy's eyes, much of a mother. 'I'd go into her bedroom when Dad was at work,' Tracy told me, 'and she'd be in bed and I'd see a man's head coming up from under the covers. And I never had any clean knickers.' Tracy vowed that she should never forgive her mother, and she constructed a picture of an ideal mother, someone who never deserted her family, who looked after her children and her home perfectly. By the time she was nineteen Tracy had a house, a husband and a baby. She rarely left the house because she had to keep it perfectly clean all the time; she had to keep the baby clean, dry, neat and tidy in good clothes and healthy and properly fed. Her husband would have to ask permission before he touched anything in the kitchen, and usually he complied, but sometimes he would grow so exasperated with her he would hit her. 'I ask for it,' she told me, 'I say dreadful things to him. I get so panicky. I get this tight feeling in my chest and I think I'm going to explode. I can't stand going to my friend's house – she lets it get so mucky. I don't think she's a fit mother. I'm worrying now what my house is like while I'm here talking to you. I don't want people to think that I'm like my mother.'

However, no matter how much we try to be good and to obey our parents, or our ideal parents, and our conscience, no amount of good behaviour will make our life secure and save us from our death. We are all fallible mortals. We all die. But for you death is the Great Imperfection.

You come to believe that you can attain perfect security if you can have complete control over yourself and your relationships with other people. You set high standards in your relationships. You want your loved ones to be completely truthful and open with you and always loyal and trustworthy. You want to be sure that the love and care you bestow on them is not wasted but responded to in what you consider the proper manner. (i.e. 'If you really loved me you wouldn't upset me by coming home late/expecting me to entertain your friends/watch football with you. If you really loved me you'd know what I was feeling without me having to tell you.') You expect your loved ones to be perfectly self-controlled, but this is no more than what you expect of yourself. You set yourself the standard of perfect, composed self-control, and when rage or misery or even joy pours through some small chink in your armour you berate yourself and fear that you are going to pieces, going out of your mind. Even when the self-control appears, at least outwardly, to be perfect, inside you are angry and frightened, since, as Alan Watts said, 'Any system approaching perfect self-control is also approaching perfect self-frustration ... I cannot throw a ball as long as I am holding on to it so as to maintain perfect control of its movement.... This desire for perfect control, of the environment and of oneself, is based on a profound mistrust of the controller.'[6] Because you see yourself as bad, you cannot trust yourself to *be*. Because you cannot trust yourself to be, you cannot trust yourself to *become*, to allow yourself to grow as a plant grows. Rather you have to *make* yourself, like you make a box. A box can be made just as you want it, perfectly symmetrical, whereas a plant grows by unfolding itself in its own asymmetries. In regarding yourself as a manufactured box rather than a growing plant you see yourself as an object, not as a living being.

In making yourself do all the things that your high standards demand, you turn everything you do into joyless work rather than pleasurable activities. You expect that other people have the same high standards as you (or even higher) and so you can be constantly trying to reach these standards and constantly feeling exhausted, and frustrated and angry at your failure. You encourage others to depend on you (after all, you know better than they do how to be the perfect mother, father, son, daughter, student, boss, counsellor and comforter), and when the burden of these dependencies begins to weigh you down you start to be angry and resentful, and then guilty, because being angry and resentful does not meet your high standard of being the Perfect Comforter and Friend, the one who is responsible for the wellbeing and happiness of all those around you. Not for one minute will you allow yourself justified anger with the people who lean on you rather than be responsible for themselves. After all, they do not have to be responsible for themselves while you are there looking after them and knowing what is best for them. Left to themselves they could make mistakes and that would never do.

Some people who get depressed have set themselves the rule Never Complain. No matter what happens they Say Nothing. Not for them the pleasure and relief of complaining. Some people who never complain do so because they have learnt that it is futile to complain to their nearest and dearest who, if complained to, will either not listen or tell them that what has gone wrong is their fault. Some people never complain because they feel that if they complain they weaken themselves and allow other people to feel superior to them. They want to do good to other people: they do not want other people to do good to them. They may have the generosity to give but they lack the generosity to receive.

Those people who get depressed and who do complain do not find that complaining produces any pleasure and relief. It can never be a relief, since no matter how much you complain the feeling of anger and frustration never goes away. You cannot find complaining in any way pleasurable, since you are trying to keep your anger in check. Moreover, when you do complain, the people you complain to either take no notice or else they give you stupid advice like, 'You work too hard. You ought to take things easier,' or 'You do too much for your family. You ought to go out more. When did you last have a holiday?', or 'You worry over things that are never going to happen. What's the point? Take each day as it comes, I always say.' How could you possibly take such advice? You must keep up the high standard of your work. Who will look after your family if you don't? And you know quite well that the only way to stop terrible disasters from overwhelming you suddenly is to identify all the possibilities and to worry about them. Worrying about a future disaster, you believe, can stop the disaster from happening. Not being able to maintain your high standards is something that you can always worry about.

You have to maintain your high standards because you cannot bear the thought of being mediocre and ordinary. You want to be the Most Perfect, Wonderful, Intelligent, Beautiful, Successful, Admired and Loved Person the World Has Ever Seen (don't we all!) and if that does not work out you are not going to be mediocre and ordinary like the rest of us. You would rather be the Worst, Most Despised, Confused, Evil, Failure and Outcast the World Has Ever Seen. You hate yourself, but like those people who discover that notoriety can bring the same rewards as fame, you come to take a secret pride in your very badness. There is, you are sure, nobody in the world like you. You might find your essential badness, as you see it, quite unacceptable, but there are aspects of yourself which you deplore but which, viewed from another angle, fill you with pride.

Some of you suffer painful loneliness but take a pride in keeping yourself to yourself. At school you may have felt yourself to be an outcast, but secretly you despised the other children who were rough, common, or snooty, or stupid. You grew up regarding everyone outside the family as foreigners. Now neighbours rarely cross your threshold and you rarely cross theirs, and you can be certain that this is the correct way to behave. People should know their place. You are as formal in your dealings with a bus conductor as you would be with the Queen. You do not join sporting and social clubs because you have better things to do with your time. You cannot spend time just chatting to people when there are all those important things that you have to do. (Concentrating on the virtue of not wasting time banishes the recollection of the breathtaking, paralysing fear you feel when you have to join a group of people.)

Your fear of other people and your pride in being independent may be so strong that you want to remain alone all your life. If this is unbearable you may risk a close relationship with one other person, but you can come to see this relationship threatened by your inability to share a joyous sexual union. To deal with this you may pretend to enjoy sex, and you achieve a good performance, but the pretence is wearying and makes you feel that what should be the most important relationship is nothing but a hollow sham.

Since sex can be a metaphor for all kinds of power struggles among men and women there is no single explanation why things go wrong in bed, but there is one idea still around, despite Freud and the sexual revolution, that lays its chill hand on a loving couple. It is the belief that sex is disgusting. A virtuous woman does not like sex but endures it for the sake of the family. A virtuous man worships his wife, a virtuous woman. He has sex with bad women. There are still many men who can see women only as sex objects or as sexless good women. One young man of my acquaintance would often declare that he saw women as his equal in every way. Without exception, every one of his girlfriends was from Southern Europe, dark-haired and passionate. But when he married it was to a prim virgin of Anglo-Saxon stock, blue-eyed and fair-haired, the attributes of an angel. A man who sees women as either a sex object (that is, stupid, of little value, discardable without guilt) or wholly good (that is, submissive, unaggressive, non-competitive) has found an excellent way of dealing with his fear that women are more powerful than him. But the poor wife, knowing that her husband has never actually met her, much less accepted her, feels very lonely.

Because you believe that you know best, at least in all matters concerning yourself, and because you want to do everything perfectly, you find it very difficult to admit that you have made a mistake. In the face of all evidence to the contrary you go on and on, making the same mistake, keeping yourself in an unfulfilling job or a barren relationship, rather than let the world see that you are capable of failure like everyone else. Sometimes you will not even admit to yourself that you have made a mistake. You berate yourself for not doing things well enough, but you never question your basic assumptions about how you should live your life. However, while it is possible to lie successfully to other people, provided you have a good memory, lying to yourself is never a good idea. To lie to ourselves we have to split ourselves in two, the person who knows the truth and the person who lies. The person who lies tries to ignore the person who knows the truth, but this person refuses to be silenced completely. The truth will come out, not directly, but in all kinds of confusing and painful ways, sometimes in dreams and slips of the tongue, or in actions which the person finds alien to himself, but, whatever way, this undermines his self-confidence. Lie to yourself and you become less of the person that you might have been.

It is easy for me to say that. You know that if you look too closely at yourself and your life, if you discard your childhood dreams of perfection, then the despair you feel now will be as nothing compared to the despair that would overwhelm you. I make it sound all too easy. Buck up your ideas and everything will be all right. I know it is not like that, as Jean reminded me when she wrote to me. She said,

I have managed to re-acquire all my depression and bitterness . . . and am having an indulgent time . . . My overriding feeling is that it isn't really fair to write to you like this. I want to write letters of blue skies and birdsong. I think I get close to the pain sometimes. I can remember it as a child, the tightness in my chest when I was alone and I didn't know what to do with myself. Always waiting for stage directions. I wonder if living in an isolated situation intensifies the feeling, as I can always remember taking long, solitary, painful walks. I wonder what mother was doing at the time – probably wondering what her mother had been doing when she was spending solitary hours. Anyway, I know the pain is there, and that I want someone to make it better and tell me what to do to stop it coming back again – and guess what – I'm going to have to start all over again. I know vaguely where the path is. Is it common to step back onto the shore having once plunged into the raging torrent? Actually, I suspect I only dipped my toe in to test the water, knowing my inability to commit myself to anything beyond self torture. I have had glimpses of the raft that carries one in the choppy water though – there always is that confounded chink of light that in the end has to make you laugh uproariously at the whole farce.

I apologise for this letter, as I don't suppose it does anything for you to read it – but it has made me feel better to write it. Harry Williams wrote something rather good about feeling even more angry than ever after receiving Holy Communion – I can't remember the exact context, as I have lent the book to my sister, but I know the anger well. There is a perfection – of thought and emotion that the human mind is capable of, and the human heart of accepting – I wonder if some of the rage has to do with getting small glimpses of such from a million miles away.

And indeed it has – to glimpse perfection, to reach out for it and to be frustrated, again and again. You reject the imperfect and reach out for the perfect. Yet as Father Harry Williams[7] knew well, we cannot reach the perfect until we accept the imperfect and see them fuse together in a perfection more wonderful than we could ever construct in our narrow imaginations.

That, of course, sounds like mystical nonsense. You know quite well that you must reject the bad and concentrate on the good. You want to be entirely good, entirely right. The trouble is it is so hard to get hold of what is good and right, and if you relax your grip for just a moment what you have grasped will be swept away. If only you could get hold of the good and right in all their entirety.

> If we could get the hang of it entirely
>   It would take too long;
> All we know is the splash of words in passing
>   And falling twigs of song,
> And when we try to eavesdrop on the great
>   Presences it is rarely

That by a stroke of luck we can appropriate
 Even a phrase entirely.

If we could find our happiness entirely
 In somebody else's arms
We should not fear the spears of the spring nor the city's
 Yammering fire alarms
But, as it is, the spears each year go through
 Our flesh and almost hourly
Bell or siren banishes the blue
 Eyes of Love entirely.

And if the world were black or white entirely
 And all the charts were plain
Instead of a mad weir of tigerish waters,
 A prism of delight and pain,
We might be surer where we wished to go
 Or again we might be merely
Bored but in brute reality there is no
 Road that is right entirely.[8]

You are prepared to be bored, in fact you usually are, rather than see the brute reality that no road, no course of action is entirely right. You want to see the laws of right and wrong, prescriptions of how people ought to live their lives, as immutable laws of the universe, and not as conventions which people create to guide them through their lives. You prefer to see them as immutable laws, fixtures of the universe, since that way you gain certainty. You prefer to know where you are, even if it is in a prison. Even if you see our rules about right and wrong behaviour as something that people create, then you cannot rejoice that you are free to change the rules. You do not consider the pleasure of creating something better; you fear the uncertainty that any change brings, and you are quite sure that any change can only be for the worse. You cannot accept with your heart, though you may know with your head, that good and bad, right and wrong, are inextricably intertwined. You reject the wise words of Lao Tsu,

 Under heaven all can see beauty as beauty only
  because there is ugliness.

All can know good as good only because there is evil.
Therefore having and not having arise together.
Difficult and easy complement each other.
Long and short contrast each other;
High and low rest upon each other;
Front and back follow each other.[9]

Without dark we would not know the light. Without death we would not know we were alive. Without imperfection we would not know perfection.

Imperfection is all around you and inside you. Perfection is somewhere else. This is so clear to you that if I say to you, 'I'd like you to consider how you see your self and your ideal self', you know exactly what I mean. 'Self' is that bad, useless thing you see yourself as being. 'Ideal self' is the person you aspire to be. If I asked you to tell me about the values you use to judge yourself and other people, and then I asked you to rate your 'self' and 'ideal self' on these values you would put a very great distance between 'self' and 'ideal self'. If I computed the relationships among your ratings and set the results out in a graph, it would look something like this.

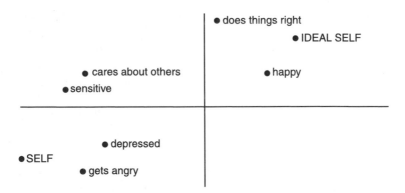

Not everyone produces a graph like this. Some people, I have found, look at me strangely when I talk about 'ideal self'. It has never occurred to them that they could be, much less *should be* different from what they are. Some people can see the point of considering an ideal self, but when asked to describe their ideal self, give no more than a slight gloss to their present self. They would like, perhaps, to be a bit more confident, achieve a modest success, in short, to gain the goals which they have set themselves and which they see themselves as eventually achieving.

Only the people who get depressed put between self and ideal self an unbridgeable chasm. And in the chasm is great despair – and pride.

2. I am a sensitive person

Many of the people who get depressed describe themselves as being sensitive. I often hear this word being used when my client is telling me how much she or he cares for other people. As I listen to accounts of how much my client does for other people, how much other people's problems become my client's concerns I am impressed, yet again, with how good my depressed clients are. They would reject the idea that they are good, but they would agree that being sensitive to others is a virtue. Being sensitive means caring about others, and this is what we all should do.

You would agree that we all should be sensitive. So many people are not. They are completely hard and uncaring. Not you. You feel sometimes that your awareness of another person's suffering is especially keen. You do not just know how the other person feels, you feel it yourself, right inside you. It is not just the suffering of the people around you that distresses you, but the suffering of every person in the world. You feel other people's suffering so much that you get to the point where you cannot bear to read the newspapers or to watch television. The sight of such suffering can make you feel very depressed.

Being a sensitive person also makes you very vulnerable to the rudeness and bad temper of other people. Some people, hard, uncaring people, are never upset if someone is rude or angry with them. They can just shrug it off. But you cannot. You get hurt, and the hurt stays, and as often as not this makes you feel very depressed.

In short, being a sensitive person means that you are a caring, loving person, which means that you are being good.

Also, being a sensitive person means that you get upset and hurt, which means that you get depressed. Therefore, to be good you must get depressed. Being depressed is evidence that you are being good.

Some people who get depressed have linked their notion of themselves as a sensitive person with their notion of themselves as a creative person. They value their artistic ability and see it as coming from the same source as their sensitivity to everything around them. Beauty excites them joyously; the suffering of others pierces them like a sword; while criticism and anger all but destroy them. Their depressions may be terrible, but they resist any therapy which might abolish the depression since any method which could eradicate their depression would threaten to destroy their creativity, the source of their being, their reason for existing. This kind of reasoning can be seen in the writings of Virginia Woolf and Sylvia Plath, both of whom preferred to die rather than to put their creativity at risk.

Still, both these women did achieve a great deal, and, as much as criticism hurt them, they were prepared to risk it and to present their work to the world. Unfortunately, some people who get depressed argue to themselves that, 'My sensitivity shows that I could be a great artist but my sensitivity makes me too depressed to create.' Thus one can have a sense of being special without having to prove it. It is much better to think of oneself as someone who would have been a great artist if only I was not such a caring person/I had had a chance/the world had not been against me, etc., etc., than to have tried and – worse than to have failed – to discover that one was merely ordinary.

Whether or not you regard yourself as a creative person, you do regard yourself as a sensitive person, easily upset by other people, even though you do not always show it. One of the things that does upset you is the way other people do not understand you. All of us like to be understood, at least by one or two people in our lives, and the people who get depressed do seem to have inherited and collected relatives who show a remarkable inability to understand other people. You have no one you can really talk to.

As long ago as 1970, two sociologists, George Brown and

Tirril Harris, showed that a common feature of women who get depressed was that they had no one they could confide in.[10] Since 1970 all the studies which examined the differences between women who got depressed and women who did not showed that two women could be living in equally difficult circumstances but the woman who had a relative or a friend in whom she could confide was much less likely to get depressed than the woman who lacked friends and had relatives who ignored or criticised and rejected her. Women are much more likely than men to value having a confidante and to complain when they lack someone to talk to. Many men lack the skill of confiding in another person, and they often fail to understand how important such conversations are. When offered the chance of talking to a counsellor, women who are suffering mental distress usually seize such an opportunity, and they are grateful but not surprised when talking to a counsellor proves to be far more beneficial than taking pills. Men in mental distress will often refuse to see a counsellor, or they agree to do so but see no point in the exercise. When they discover the benefits of such conversations they are amazed.

We all need to understand that having someone to talk to is essential for our well-being. Not having someone to talk to leaves us feeling desperately lonely. However, for some of us, just talking to someone who is sympathetic to us and is on our side is enough, but for others, especially you who get depressed, the longing to be *understood* outweighs the simple need to talk to some sympathetic, uncritical friend. If you experience this huge need to be understood, you get impatient with relatives and friends who offer you sympathy and a willing ear but who clearly do not understand you. They say they love you, but you know quite well that if they truly loved you they would understand you, and so their incomprehension upsets you even more.

If this is how you see not being understood then you have never considered the possibility that we can love someone without understanding that person. Not only is it possible, it is extremely common. Children cannot understand their parents fully, yet they love them. Parents do not always understand their children, yet they love them. Romantic love can only flourish in an atmosphere of mutual incomprehension. (In the middle years of our marriage, my husband would say, jokingly, that as a wife I had only two faults – namely, I could not iron his shirts as well as his mother did, and I understood him. His joke reflected a mutual disenchantment.)

However, wanting to be understood can mean wanting to possess that person. We can want the other person to be so absorbed in the business of understanding us that he or she has no time for other people. A child deprived of his mother's loving attention (he might have got plenty of her angry attention) can grow up desperately wanting this lack to be made up, and so comes to express this need as a longing that his mother understand him. Since his mother is now an ordinary, middle-aged or elderly woman who could become a nuclear physicist more easily than she could develop this superhuman understanding, he is bound to suffer terrible disappointment.

We can also desperately want people to understand us because we see that as a way of avoiding being hurt. Cruelty is always a failure of the imagination: if someone really understands how we feel, if they feel our hurts as their own, then they will do all in their power not to hurt us. You do not like upsetting other people. You wish other people would not upset you.

But understanding other people is quite a complicated business. Sometimes we feel that we understand another person because we see that person as being very like us in character or in what has happened to that person. We identify with that person and feel sympathy for him. Sometimes we are correct in seeing a similarity. The person sees it too and is pleased to accept our sympathy. But sometimes we are wrong. There is no similarity, and so the way we express our sympathy is not appreciated by the recipient. Haven't we all, at some difficult time in our lives, squirmed with embarrassment when someone has gushed, 'I know exactly how you feel!'

For, in truth, no one can ever know exactly how we feel. Each person's experience is different from everyone else's, since each person is different from everyone else. Each person sees his own world in his own terms, his own values, attitudes and opinions. If we want to understand another person we have to set about the task of discovering what these values, attitudes and opinions are, and in doing so we ignore our own needs and feelings. The other person occupies the stage while we are the audience, involved in the action of the play, as an audience is, but not taking part in it or influencing the action. We can seek this kind of understanding with equanimity when we have no personal connection with the person we are trying to understand. Therapists can do this with their clients who come to them as strangers, provided, of course, that the therapist does not have a theory to prove or a passionate desire to prove himself to be the world's greatest therapist who cures all his clients. (Avoid all therapists who need, for their own sake, to make you better; but be warned, they come in many guises.)

However, if we set out to understand, really understand, someone who matters to us, then we are in danger of being hurt. We may discover that the person is really very different from what we thought he was. Or, worse, we may discover that the person does not value us in the terms in which we wish to be valued. Discovering this, we may feel rejected. And being rejected is something some of us are not prepared to risk.

3. I will not risk being rejected

Anyone who is rejected by someone he loves and needs discovers why our language contains metaphors like 'heartbroken', 'sick at heart', 'heavy hearted'. Rejection pierces the heart like an arrow. You actually feel a sharp, violent pain in your chest, just where your heart is. Your breath does not reach your lungs, but stays caught in your throat. You sweat and feel faint. If only someone would come and pull the arrow from your heart and make you whole again. Sometimes this does happen, and you feel your heart mend. But when this does not happen and time goes by, the sharp pain of a broken heart turns into a dull, heavy ache. The sharp pain can return at any time – when you awaken from a sleep or see something that reminds you – so sharp that tears come to your eyes, and with it the terror of a world from which all security has fled. (When we lose someone we love we often say, 'The bottom has fallen out of my world.') The months go by, and the dull ache in your chest becomes a heavy weight pressing on your heart. The years go by, and you become so used to this weight that you forget what it is to be free and light-hearted.

People who get depressed have suffered a great deal of rejection in their lives. Some of this rejection has been the kind a child experiences when he is brought up by parents who, though meaning well, are so wrapped up in their own concerns that they do not take the time to understand how the child feels. If these rejection experiences start early enough and are frequent enough, the child can be so sick at heart that he does not know what it is to be light-hearted. To know that we are sad we must at one time have been happy, and so, if a child feels from birth unloved and rejected, he grows up sad but not knowing he is sad. He cannot name his wretchedness but acts upon it, usually in ways which conflict with the demands of society. People like this cannot name their state as being sad, rejected and depressed (until they come in contact with psychiatrists and learn to mimic their language) since they do not know what it is to be happy, accepted and free.

People who get depressed and who know that they are depressed know what it is to be happy and accepted, even though they may never have allowed themselves to be free. As a child you experienced your parents' love and so were aware when it was withdrawn. So painful were these experiences that you had to do something to reduce the pain quickly – to remove the arrow yourself. You exchanged the sharp pain of rejection for the slow misery of guilt. Perhaps you did what many children do, that is, blame yourself when your mother dies or your father deserts the family, or when you were beaten by your parent you told yourself that you were bad and deserved this cruel punishment. Like every therapist I have often had the experience of being shocked and horrified by a story told by a client where the client as a child was the victim of a brutal assault by a parent, and for the client to conclude the story with, 'I was a bad child and deserved the punishment.' Perhaps your parent when punishing you, whether by a beating, or by expelling you from the family group, or by telling you what a disgusting child you were, would conclude by saying to you, 'I'm doing this for your own good.' Your good parent punishes you in order to make you a better person.

Thus you can tell yourself that your good parents had not rejected you. You were a bad child who deserved punishment. Your badness meriting punishment was a continuing state, so you went on feeling guilty. Expecting more pain, you did what you could to prevent it by trying to be the good child your parents wanted and by resolving never to risk being rejected. You desperately wanted people to love you, but you became very wary of giving your love to others. You reasoned that the less you loved another person the less it would hurt when the inevitable rejection came. You loved, but never completely, never enough to forgive the person for being what he or she was or to let that person go. You might come to hate your parents or your partner, but you hang on to them in the desperate hope that one day they will say the right word, make the right gesture, and your bleeding, broken heart will be healed and you will be a loved and happy child again. You have not realised that to heal the wounds of rejection there must be mutual love and forgiveness.

The problem with growing up fearing and expecting rejection is that you cannot enter into any adult relationship in the expectation of happiness. With friends and acquaintances you cannot help but be reserved, suspicious and easily offended. You may decide never to marry, or, if you do, you choose someone you see as being safe, and you place very great restrictions on your love. You hope you have guarded against rejection, but in this world people rarely value us to the degree and in the terms which we desire, so in every relationship something is sure to happen which we can interpret as rejection. As a result of this way of thinking you are always lonely.

When I first came to England I went to work in a clinic where there was a good deal of research going on into the physiological changes that occur in depression, and in particular in the changes in people who become depressed at regular intervals. The doctors were sure that the regularity of mood change must be caused by some metabolic change, but in case some 'psychological factors' played some part in these changes I was asked to do some testing of these patients. In fact few, if any, patients get depressed at regular intervals, so there were not many patients for me to see. However, when I started work there was one such patient. The case notes showed that she became depressed every August. Unfortunately, over the years, the periods of her depression had became longer and longer and her response to pills and ECT slower and slower, so she no longer came to the clinic but was on a ward in the large psychiatric hospital. I went to see her. The ward was bleak and dingy, affording little privacy to the women there. Maud was a quiet, gentle woman in her late fifties. My tests showed nothing extraordinary about her. She was very intelligent, very depressed, and, so I gathered from what she said about herself, very lonely.

I was a complete novice in the business of therapy. All I could do was to give her some companionship and to listen. After she had known me for quite some while she told me something which she had never told any of the doctors because, she said, she did not wish to be disloyal to her husband. One evening years ago, she had been putting her daughter, her only child, to bed when the little girl, prattling on, told her mother something which made her realise that her husband was unfaithful to her. This all but wrecked her marriage. They stayed together, but the estrangement from her husband and later her daughter whom she saw as siding with her husband continued. It was in August that she discovered that her husband had rejected her. It was in August, another August, that her beloved grandfather died, and in another August that her mother died. (Deaths, we know, can be felt as rejections.) August was the cruellest month of her year. It seemed to me that it was unnecessary to look for physiological reasons for her annual depression. I shall always be grateful to Maud, because she removed the pain I was experiencing (I was helpless in my sorrow for her) since she eventually ceased to be depressed, left hospital and re-established a loving relationship with her husband and daughter. Moreover, she did raise many questions in my mind about why people get depressed and what should be done about it, and so she launched me on what seems to have turned into a lifetime's work. In the course of this I have learnt a great deal.

One of the things I have learnt is to have a greater appreciation of how much people need people. It is not just that no man is an island. No man or woman can *be* an island. We do not exist just within the boundary of our skin. Our body may have the skin as its terminus, but we, ourselves, exist as part of an indivisible network of human relationships. We may set up boundaries and barriers – black and white, men and women, Jew and Arab, Catholic and Protestant, rich and poor – and we may insist that those outside our barriers have nothing to do with us, but our very act of exclusion simply serves to underline the fact that one group only exists in relation to the other. I define myself by the existence of the Other, the Foreigner. I know I am a woman only because there are men; I know I am old only because there are young; I know I am I because you are you.

We try to make the divisions between ourselves and other people real, and we may act as if these barriers are real (and so we do not speak to our neighbours because they are Pakistani, or we send our children to private schools so they will not mix with rough working-class children, or we would not contemplate worshipping God in any church other than our own denomination), but we must be careful not to exclude everybody. We must include some people in a group with us for, as each of us knows quite well, if we stay on our own for long enough we become odd. I like my own company, but if I spend a few days without meeting friends or talking on the phone I find that I am holding imaginary conversations out loud. I begin to wonder whether this will become a permanent habit and I shall be like those solitary people I have seen (and heard) on the streets of London and New York who speak aloud only to themselves and never to others. My solitary conversations cease once I am in company again, but in awareness of our need for others I always respond when some person, usually elderly, in a shop or on a bus, starts a conversation with me about the weather or the cost of food. We can starve for lack of conversation just as we can starve for the lack of food.

We need other people in order to maintain our sense of existence as a person. It is always difficult to talk about our sense of existence because it is hard to find the right words for something which is rarely discussed. Your sense of existence is the arena in which you experience everything that happens in your life and, as it is always there, you can take it for granted and not be aware of its peculiar qualities. Whenever in a lecture or workshop I talk about how we can experience our sense of existence I find that some people there are very clear in their own minds about how they experience their sense of existence but others are not. Among those who are not clear about their sense of existence are those who are such good people that they have concentrated so much on what they *ought* to feel they have lost touch with what they *do* feel. There are those people who are so drawn to what goes on around them in their external reality that they have spent little time observing what goes on inside them in their internal reality of thoughts and feelings. There are others too who have spent so much time acting out different roles that they find it hard to be just themselves. Indeed, they may have little idea just who they are.

In a workshop I try to help people discover how they experience their sense of existence. We examine not just the sense of existence but what goes with it, the threat of annihilation. Because we know that we are physically alive we are always aware of threats to our physical survival. Because we know that we exist as a person we are always aware when something threatens to annihilate us as a person. Remember how you feel when someone completely ignores you when they should be paying you attention, or someone makes you feel helpless, or treats you, not as a person but as an object to be used and abused. You feel diminished, demeaned and humiliated, so you have to do something to establish that you are rightfully a person of value and importance. If you cannot do this, you feel hurt and frustrated, and, worse, if this situation continues, you begin to feel that you actually are an insignificant person of no value, deserving no better treatment than what you are given. If then you make the dread discovery that there is a serious discrepancy between what you thought your life was and what it actually is, the experience of falling apart is even more terrible, and you readily seize upon the explanation that you are to blame for the disaster that has befallen you.

We are always trying to maintain our sense of existence and to ward off threats of annihilation. In fact, every decision we make has in part the aim of maintaining ourselves as a person. Hence your way of experiencing yourself is absolutely central to every decision you make and everything you do.

Each of us experiences our sense of existence and sees the threat of annihilation in our own individual way. However, I have found that in whatever way each person describes these experiences each description has within it one of two general meanings.

It seems that each of us experiences our sense of existence in one of two ways.

For some people existence is experienced only in relation to other people, and the threat of annihilation is seen as complete rejection and abandonment. Such people find that they exist in the relationship they have with others, perhaps as part of a family or part of a group, being observed and observing, being loved and loving, needed and needing. They need to be liked. Louis Theroux, television interviewer and son of the novelist Paul Theroux, said, 'I am someone who likes to please people. I like to be liked and I like to be obliging.'[11] Because such people are so engaged by their relationship to others they may not have a strong sense of being an individual, and instead have a sense of existing in terms of playing a role. Louis Theroux said, 'I think it can be a terribly damaging thing to be on television. For one thing I think it's addictive if you're on a lot – the recognition, being a big shot. The other thing is that you come to impersonate yourself, and you forget what it is about you that is real, and what performance.'[12] Louis is one of the people I call a People Person or an extravert.

Such people comprise half the world's population. The

other half are those people who experience their sense of existence very differently. What they need to survive as a person is a sense of individual development and achievement, the gaining of clarity, organisation and control, and what they fear most is losing control and falling into chaos. These people are pleased if people like them but this is not their top priority. Their top priority is to fulfil their sense of achievement. This achievement need not be fame and fortune. For many introverts achievement is a matter of doing a task to the best of their ability and achieving a result which reaches the standard they have set themselves. Praise from others is pleasant but not essential. Living up to one's own standards in order to achieve that which they regard as important, and warding off chaos form the essence of an introvert's life. Some introverts would sum up the principle of their life as simply doing one's duty to the best of one's ability, and what better example of this could there be than that of Queen Elizabeth II. From the moment when, as a small girl, she was told that she would one day be Queen she set about preparing herself to fulfil that role to the best of her ability. She has never sought popularity. Those who know her do not describe her as warm and friendly, but everyone, including republicans, praise her for the exemplary manner in which she has always carried out her royal duties. She is one of those people I call What Have I Achieved Today Persons or introverts.

Introverts need people, though in a different way from the way extraverts need people. Introverts need people to keep them focused on what is going on around them. Introverts are always busy thinking. Without other people being around an introvert can become totally absorbed in what is going on in his head. Moreover, since they need to know that they have achieved something, all introverts have a small group of people against whom they measure their achievements. They feel they have achieved if they have the approval of this group of people, or would have the approval of this group were they still alive. Introvert physicists might measure themselves against Einstein, and an introvert Queen might measure herself against a royal ancestor.

Thus none of us can escape from needing other people

so that we can exist and not fear annihilation. But you who get depressed have decided to express your need for other people in ways which make it very hard for you to live.

Take the first form of existence – wanting to be part of a group and fearing isolation. If you see yourself as basically acceptable and valuable and therefore with something to offer other people, you have no fear of joining groups, of being part of a family, having friends, being accepted. If disaster wrenches you away from your family, as much as you suffer loss, you know that you are able to find new friends and to help other people. But if you see yourself as basically bad and unacceptable, then the threat of expulsion from your group is expected and feared. Since you do not value yourself, you cannot see people as wanting you to join them, either as a friend or a helper. If disaster wrenched you away from your family you could not see yourself surviving, and so no matter how much you come to hate your family you cannot let them go. They are your reference points of existence, and you fear that if you lose them you will disappear.

When I was with my dear friend Martin not long after his wife Bridget had died unexpectedly, Martin tried to explain to me what Bridget had meant to him. He said, 'Bridget validated me.' He and Bridget had a large group of friends, but he told me that he had always seen them as Bridget's friends, and that, as Bridget was no longer there, he was sure that these friends would desert him. He recognised how much he needed people around him. He said, 'I need other people to validate me. When I'm with other people I'm all right, but when they leave and I'm on my own, I feel I'm a bubble that's about to burst.' Martin greatly underestimated how much everybody liked him. He soon found that he had many friends.

Andrew Solomon, another extravert, described how, as a child, he was always 'fearful of rejection'. When he went away to college he was 'blissfully happy', but 'sometimes, when I was alone, I would suddenly feel isolated, and the feeling was not simply sorrow at being alone, but fear. I had many friends, and I'd go and visit one of them, and I could usually be distracted out of my distress.'[13]

In the second form of existence – individual development

and achievement as against chaos – the person who sees himself as basically acceptable and valuable can pursue the goals of achievement and individual development without fearing that he is basically flawed. When you value and accept yourself you choose reasonable qualities on which to judge yourself, and you judge yourself in reasonable terms. You want to do things well, but you do not demand that you do everything perfectly. When you do not value and accept yourself you make utterly unreasonable demands upon yourself. You must achieve every aspect of your life, and achievement can be nothing less than perfection. Failure means being overwhelmed by the chaos that lurks menacingly close by.

Introverts need approval, but only from a group which they themselves have selected, whereas extraverts want to be liked and accepted by as many people as possible. Thus, one way or another we all need acceptance and approval. Rejection is always a threat, but if we allow this threat to dominate our lives we can never be free to be ourselves. We can become so submerged in a group we lose all sense of individuality, or, in seeking the approval of all others, we become afraid to act. And this is what you have done. Having decided never to risk rejection, you hesitate to make any move which might upset other people. It might be so long since you expressed any personal preference that you have forgotten what your personal preferences are. (I could ask you, 'What do you do when you give yourself a treat?' and you would look at me uncomprehendingly. In any case, you know you do not deserve a treat.) Or in your endeavours to win universal approval you have discovered to your cost the truth of that old saying, 'Try to please all and you shall please none.' Of course, all this desire to please and to avoid rejection does not mean that you always behave peaceably and meekly with your nearest and dearest. Sometimes you behave very badly, so as to test the limits of your family's acceptance of you and to show by hurting and being hurt that you matter to them. I speak as a daughter of a mother prone to depression. She rejected others in order to forestall them from rejecting her. She treated her family outrageously, confident that our guilt would prevent us from ever rejecting her.

However, even Mother was careful not to overstep certain limits. Thus as much as you provoke your family with temper tantrums or by saying bitter and cruel things, you keep to your family's rules about what are the limits of what is allowed to be said or done. No one leaves home. All families have rules, usually unspoken, about how arguments are to be conducted. In some families shouting and abuse, verbal and physical, are allowed, while in others fights are conducted silently with tight lips and closing doors. (My mother did both.) In some families one person may be the overt target for attack while it is forbidden to attack openly another person who, yet, is the focus of all family fights. In some families it is forbidden to let the neighbours know that there is a row going on, while in others certain family members are allowed to slam out of the house and go to the pub or put on a token show of leaving home and never coming back. But playing out the pattern of the family row serves only to reaffirm the unity of the family.

You often wonder why your family puts up with you, and you feel guilty and try to repress your anger and resentment. But at the same time you are striving to be so very good since you are trying to make people love you because you are so good. You think that surely, if I am very, very good, my family will love me. After all I do for them, they must love me.

But do they? Does anyone love us just because we are good? Can we make anyone love us? Will being the perfect daughter stop your mother preferring your brother to you? Will being the perfect wife stop your husband from noticing other women? Will being the perfect husband stop your wife preferring the children to you? Alas, the answer to all these questions is no. The curious thing about love is that it can only be freely given. We can force people to obey our orders. We can coerce them into behaving respectfully towards us. We can even coerce them into behaving as if they love us by making them feel guilty (the greetings card industry flourishes on this), but that warmth of the heart which we call love does not spring into being at command, either the command of those who wish to be loved or those who feel they ought to love. No amount of good behaviour or feeling that one ought to love will create love or bring it back when it has fled. As Nina Simone sang, 'You've got to learn to leave the table when love's no longer being served.'[14]

But that is a very difficult thing to do when you see yourself as needing the love and approval of others in order to survive, and as fearing rejection as you fear death. You cannot separate yourself from someone who hurts and belittles you. You dare not upset other people, since by their possible criticism and rejection of you they have the power of life and death over you. You are helpless.

But are you? Are you really helpless? Or do other people have only the power that we give them? Any form of government will collapse if the majority of the people cease to acquiesce to it. The pomp and ceremony of government are no more than the Emperor's new clothes which exist only in the eyes of the beholder. It is just the same in individual relations. We can see other people as being powerful and important, and feel frightened of them, or we can dismiss them like Alice in the Court of the King and Queen of Hearts with, 'You're nothing but a pack of cards!' We can invest other people with the power to harm us by their criticism and rejection, or we can say, like streetwise children, 'Sticks and stones'll break my bones but names'll never hurt me.' We make ourselves sensitive to the words and actions of others. We can choose whether we shall be hurt, or whether we shall ignore them, or whether we shall see them as ridiculous and so be amused.

However, there is one great advantage about seeing yourself as helpless and in the power of others. You do not have to be responsible for yourself. Other people make all the decisions, and when things turn out badly you can blame other people. And things always turn out badly. You know this. That's why you always expect the worst.

4. I prefer to expect the worst rather than to risk disappointment

One of the first words I learned when I was a small child was 'pessimist'. At home something would happen or be about to happen and I would hear my father make a favourable or joking comment, and then my mother would say, no, it wasn't anything to be pleased about, I always knew it would turn out badly, you're too soft, you ought to know better than to trust these people, remember when so-and-so happened, that was bad enough but this is going to be worse, you shouldn't be so stupid as to think that this was going to turn out all right because it won't ever be better. My mother was fond of that saying, 'It's an ill wind that blows nobody any good', but as far as she was concerned the only winds that blew were ill winds. My father would counter her arguments with, 'Why do you always look on the black side? Why are you such a pessimist?'

My mother never deigned to answer this question. I did not know why, but I did know what a deadening effect her relentless pessimism had on my small world. So I tried to counter it by holding steadily to the hope that things would turn out well and that I would have a happy life, just as my father promised that I would. Thus I acquired what my clients call my foolish optimism.

Now I know why my mother was always pessimistic. If you are an optimist you live a life full of uncertainty, always at risk of being struck down by the pain of disappointment. As a pessimist you may not ever feel cheerful, but life is certain. Everything, you know, will turn out badly. There is the bonus that occasionally you might be surprised by something actually turning out well, but this is rare and something to be suspicious about since, as you well know,

> The Victorian moralists understood these things.
> If you were greedy, they said,
> And wished it to rain chocolates,
> It would rain hard centres, and knock you down.[15]

Bearing this in mind you try never to fall into the crime of hubris, of getting above yourself, proclaiming your virtues and thus incurring the wrath of the gods. You might not fear being struck down by one of Zeus's thunderbolts, but you do fear that if you come top of your class, win the race, collect the prize, you will be dangerously exposed to malicious criticism and rejection by others. You fear success for you know that if something good happens then something worse must follow. You may see the hand of God in the inevitable disaster, but in case God is slow in evening up the score or simply because you cannot stand the tension of waiting for the inevitable disaster, you rush in and create your own disaster. The ideal disaster combines a confirmation of your pessimism with self-punishment. Thus the tension of waiting for a disaster and the tension of guilt may in one action be relieved by being turned into the pain of a broken leg or the inconvenience of being without the car for a month. You may not be happy but you do feel more in control of your life.

Even when you do not do anything as drastic as crashing your car or falling down a flight of stairs, you can render the outcome of most events certain by your pessimism for the simple reason that it is easier to destroy than to build. It is easier to lose the race than to win, to refuse to enter rather than compete, to undermine confidence rather than to encourage it, to stress the dangers without seeking the courage to face them, to carp, criticise and reject rather than to risk building something positive yourself.

This way of thinking is not confined to those who get depressed. I have two friends, both kind, good people, who always have some small problem to tell me about whenever I go to see them. These are never major, intractable problems, but everyday, annoying matters that take time to put right. They can be put right by being assertive, usually by contacting the appropriate authorities, perhaps the manager of a firm or the appropriate member of parliament. Wanting to help, I advise them about what course to take, and, as I do, I see a little smile creep over their face. They know for certain that what I suggest will not work so they are not going to try. I used to wonder how it was that people like my friends manage to encounter so many problems and small disasters, but now I know why. If you concentrate on small, manageable disasters you can avoid the fearful chaos which you see as threatening to overwhelm your world. As a client said to me once in a burst of candour, 'There is a great, heart-thumping fear out there, but I can deal with that by creating my phobias.' Phobias are manageable, domesticated fears, defences against worse terrors and therefore not easily relinquished. By concentrating on what you know would happen if you ignored your phobia – say you actually left the house to go shopping, you know that you would faint and everyone would stare at you and that would be *terrible* – you can avoid bigger problems and even bigger calamities over which you would have no control.

Optimists are so often proved wrong. No matter what success, there is always a fly in the ointment. Something always goes wrong. What satisfaction you can feel when you have your convictions confirmed! And what security there is in suffering!

5. My problems are greater than anyone else's

or

Anyone who hasn't got my problems has no problems at all

People who get depressed are often amazed to discover that there are other people in the world who feel as they do. Sometimes it is a relief to find that you are not alone in experiencing what you suspect may be a peculiar madness. But even after you are told just how common depression is in the entire human race, you still have a sneaking suspicion that no one has ever felt as bad as you do. You look at the people around you who show no sign of depression and you feel that, although these people have the occasional practical problem, they do not suffer as you do. In feeling this way you are, in fact, operating under that universal law that 'Anyone who hasn't got my problems has no problems at all'. People in rich nations look at those of the Third World and say how lucky Third World people are, not having to endure the tensions of the modern world. Men look at women and say what an easy life women have, just caring for a home and children or doing women's work which is always easier than men's. Women look at men and say aren't they just like kids, playing games and avoiding all the real responsibilities that women have. I have met homosexuals who have told me that heterosexuals never experience uncertainty, jealousy and rejection. There are stammerers who believe that fluent people never have problems in communication. Then there were all those clients who sat opposite me when, I was sure, I was showing signs of illness (sometimes I cough a lot) and tiredness (it shows when I do not get my eight hours' sleep) and who told me how they know that a wise and competent person like me could not possibly have any problems. They also told me that the opposite of being depressed was being perfectly happy. Anyone who is not depressed is perfectly happy all the time. If only!

Usually my depressed client does not say this to me directly but by implication during a discussion, say, about his brothers and sisters. He asks me why it is that he is the only one in his family to suffer like this. Everyone else is perfectly happy. He goes on talking and mentions, in passing, his oldest sister who gave up a good job to stay at home to look after their ageing parents and who now rarely leaves the house, and a younger brother who ran away from home and has never been heard of since. Matters like these my client does not see as reflecting a degree of unhappiness. He is sure that he alone suffers, since he alone in his family is the bad one, born bad, and his evidence for this is the fact that his brothers and sisters are happy, as they must be since they were born good and were brought up by such excellent parents. So we go on talking over the weeks, and then one day he tells me, in great amazement, how his favourite sister, who he *knew* was happily married, had phoned him, greatly distressed, to say that her husband had left her, how she had wasted the best years of her life, how she had never wanted to marry, how she had wanted to go to university but their parents had prevented her, saying that education was wasted on a girl. He is appalled by these revelations, not just in his concern for his sister but by the realisation of how little he knew of his closest and dearest sister. Sometimes this is the point where he suddenly sees that the role he has written for himself in the drama of his life as the patiently suffering scapegoat, noble in his tragedy, his self-sacrifice allowing his family to live their lives in peace, does not fit reality. Sometimes this is the point where my client stops and considers. Sometimes it is not.

I could tell this story over and over, in many different versions, and show how, when we are entranced by our own suffering, we become oblivious to the suffering around us.

This happens to all of us when the pain of toothache or cancer dominates our thinking. All of us, too, missed a great deal of what was going on in our families, especially when we were in our teens, since we were so wrapped up in our own concerns, and thus in adult life we can come to discover all sorts of things about our parents and siblings that we never knew. Of course, my burdens are heavier than anyone else's, since mine are the only burdens I have to bear. However, if we want to convince ourselves that nobody suffers the way we do, if we want to measure our significance in the world by the degree of our suffering, then we have to ignore the suffering of others. We dismiss suffering humanity by saying it is not our concern – by switching off the television and by refusing to read the newspapers – and we dismiss the suffering of those close to us by denying that they are suffering, by saying that they are perfectly happy, have nothing to complain of, don't realise just how lucky they are and so on. Of course there are many people, not just those who get depressed, who adopt such attitudes to other people's suffering. They wish to be simply totally selfish and so they make themselves quite unaware of other people's suffering, while you who get depressed would say that you cannot bear to read the newspapers or to watch television because they upset you too much, while you care deeply about your relatives. And so you do. But caring does not always include knowing about and understanding. Caring about can become a way of increasing your own suffering rather than a way of opening out your understanding of another person. Of course, if you are one of those people who believe that 'worrying about' is the same as 'loving', then even as you show concern for others you increase your burden of suffering. It may not have occurred to you that if you habitually say to your family 'I worry about you' instead of saying 'I love you', your family will stop telling you things so as not to worry you and thus you go on, unaware of the kind and the full extent of the burdens each member of your family carries.

Even as your family tries to relieve you of burdens by trying not to worry you, you hang on to them and grow very skilful in turning every new event into another burden.

('Tom got me a new vacuum cleaner. I'd hate to tell him it's too heavy and makes my back ache', 'Joan's baby's lovely but it upsets me to see how tired she looks', 'Dad wants to buy me a new car but I said no. I'd feel terrible if anything happened to it.')

You can collect burdens too because you do not like to upset people by saying no. You collect burdens because you are the only one that does things properly. Once the burdens are collected you do not relinquish them. There is a certain nobility in having more burdens than other people. You can take pride in your burdens and reassurance in the suffering they bring.

6. I would think there was something wrong if I wasn't suffering[16]

Suppose you were alone on a spaceship which was fast running out of fuel and you had to decide on which of the two available planets you would land. Both planets had adequate food and shelter which you would need since you were likely to be there a long time, but the inhabitants of each were very different. On Planet Alpha the inhabitants would simply not notice you. They would go about their business and ignore you. They would never speak to you or acknowledge your presence. On Planet Beta the inhabitants would certainly notice you, but only with hostility. They might not kill you outright, but they would harass you, plot against you, and appear friendly only to do you harm. Your life would be one long engagement with an enemy.

Which planet would you choose?

If I put this choice to Captain Kirk or Dr Who the answer would have to be Planet Beta. Planet Alpha would yield no stories, no adventures. Without opposition, nothing happens in our lives. Some of the people I have put this problem to have said that after a lifetime of harassment and opposition they would quite enjoy some peace and quiet, and so would choose Planet Alpha, but even they admit that such a life could be very lonely. One would need to have considerable inner strengths to survive such isolation. So, many people choose Planet Beta, even though it means being the object of other people's malice. At least you are noticed. Your life has some significance for yourself and other people.

Not many of us, as yet, have found ourselves on spaceships, but many of us do find ourselves in environments where we are ignored. Think of all those elderly people without families, living in a busy city where no one stops to pass the time of day, much less to care whether they live or die. Some resilient old people make strenuous efforts to establish and maintain contacts with the postman or the woman next door and to create relationships with a budgie or a radio, but some old people take the option of believing, not that no one notices them, but that everyone does. They see themselves as the object of a vast conspiracy. They are being watched by their neighbours, or by bugging devices in the television. The governments of Russia and the USA are trying to poison them. In secret headquarters all over the world plans are being drawn up for their destruction. Doctors call such people paranoid and deluded, but the good thing about this kind of delusion is that they make the person who has them seem more important, at least in his own eyes. And the good thing about paranoia is that you are never alone. Someone, somewhere, is thinking of you.

Many of us, too, were faced with the choice of Planet Alpha and Planet Beta when we were children. Many children grow up in homes where they are more or less adequately sheltered, fed and clothed, but otherwise they are largely ignored by their parents. So each child has to find some way of gaining the parents' attention. Some children discover that if they fall ill or have an accident their mother is suddenly at their side, giving love and comfort. Thus the child is soon set fair for a lifetime of illnesses and accidents. (If you are like this and have defined your depression as an illness then you will have to find other ways of seeking love and comfort rather than through illness before you will be able to give up your depression.) Some children discover that if they are naughty their mother takes notice of them. True, being noticed means being punished, but at least it does mean that you are important to your mother. Many children soon learn that the only way for them to be noticed in school and in society is for them to break the rules. Then, at least, the headmaster, the police, the judge, and, if you are lucky, the newspapers and television, take notice of you. Your life has some significance. (The moral of this for parents who want their children to turn out well, is to reward good behaviour much more than you punish bad behaviour.)

Most of us grow up in homes where sometimes we were ignored, sometimes we were noticed and loved, and sometimes noticed and punished. For some children the belief 'I suffer; therefore my life is significant' is established in complex ways. The child who decided to see himself as bad in order to see his parents as good has to follow the first act of self-sacrifice by many, many more, and such sacrifice is always accompanied by suffering. Thus suffering becomes a way of life. You may not consciously think 'I suffer; therefore I am', but you do get very nervous every time you are threatened with happiness. (One woman told me, 'I don't think I ought to be comfortable.' She did not risk saying 'happy'. Another woman, when I asked her how she had enjoyed a particularly nice party, replied, 'I didn't enjoy it as much as I ought to have enjoyed it.' See the devotion to suffering revealed in those answers.) You may not feel that if you stop suffering you will disappear, but you do feel that you can only justify your existence by your suffering, and so, after a lifetime's practice, you become an expert in suffering.

When the light-bulb jokes were doing the rounds, one went, 'How many Jewish mothers does it take to change a light-bulb?' and the answer was 'None. I'll just sit here in the dark.' I am sure there are plenty of Jewish mothers who change their own light-bulbs. It is all those depressed people who sit there in the dark. I have been so impressed with the way depressed people can turn any event into an opportunity for self-sacrifice, self-blame and suffering that I once considered writing a book called '1001 Ways to Be a Martyr', but gave up the idea when I realised that a thousand and one was too small a number to cover the inventiveness of the committed martyr. Another project much discussed in our psychology department was the Suffering Olympics, to find who was the Greatest Sufferer in the World. (There were some expert sufferers among the psychologists as well as among the clients.) We had to abandon this idea because we could not work out a way of giving a prize to the Greatest Sufferer since one of the necessary attributes of the Committed Sufferer is that you Always Lose.

It is all very well to joke about these matters, but we live in a culture which has suffering and sacrifice as the central theme of its main religion. The symbol of Christianity is the Cross and Christ's bleeding, broken figure. He sacrificed Himself so that we can have eternal life. Not just by baptism but also by martyrdom can we wash away our sins and enter into the Kingdom of Heaven. The Church does not encourage martyrs the way it once did, but the idea that we should consider others before ourselves is central to the teaching of the different Christian churches. Judaism makes much of atonement through suffering, especially the suffering of the innocent. Islam teaches that the martyr in the Jihad or Holy War has secured his entry to Paradise. Believing this, many young men and some young women sacrifice themselves for their compatriots and their religion. Through suffering and self-sacrifice we reach salvation.

Since the human baby takes so long to grow to self-sufficient maturity, it is necessary for the survival of our species that we have some rules about caring for other people and putting their needs before our own. If we are to live in any kind of harmony we need to have rules about sharing and considering other people's needs. However, when it comes to putting our rules into practice we run into all sorts of difficulties. When I have the flu, should I stay home and expect other people to do my work, or go to work and spread my germs around? Should I put my parents' needs before those of my children? Is it permissible to lie or to kill in order to save the lives of other people? Is my first duty to society or to my family? And so on. Endless moral dilemmas.

These moral dilemmas have been argued by theologians and philosophers for hundreds of years without any satisfactory resolution being reached. The sad thing about our lives is that such dilemmas do not wait until we are grown up and educated to present themselves. We meet them when we are children, in situations fraught with fear, anger and uncertainty, and from which there is no escape. Jackie wrote the following story from her childhood which she called *The Noddy Clock*.

It was a sunny day. My brothers, sisters and I had been playing out, so it was decided that an early bath was in order. Normally we didn't run for a bath but today was different. The box of paints and left-over wallpaper was too tempting for us to mess about. We were told to hurry up and get bathed. My mum and dad were in the garden with the younger ones chatting to the neighbours. I remember it was two in and two out in double quick time today. Downstairs I ran in my towel to get my pyjamas and there I saw it – the worst thing that could have ever happened. Our special Noddy Clock was lying on the floor smashed to pieces.

Panic overtook me. 'No painting today, that's for sure.' Who did it? How did it happen? Well, for me the sunny day soon became a dull one. We were all rounded up together on the settee. 'Who did it?' We all in turn answered, 'Not me,' and the response was a smack for each of us, and so on until there were four or five tearful faces all with the same thing on their minds. Nobody owned up. I had the feeling, small as I was, that everyone was telling the truth. But the truth of the matter was the clock was broken and somehow something had caused Noddy and Bigears to be on the floor instead of in the clock face.

After seeing all the kids like this I had a thought. If I admitted breaking the clock perhaps the punishment would cease and we'd be able to paint, so I said to mum and dad, 'I did it'. The other kids were sent into the dining room and the paper and paints were put on the table for them. I was taken upstairs and taught that day that I wasn't being punished for breaking the clock but for lying. I understood all this, but I felt awful because I had not lied. I'd lied in the fact that I had owned up to something I had not done. My punishment was to go to bed without any tea.

My feelings.
I learned so much by this day:
(a)   Being the eldest girl feeling the pain of the younger children and not wanting them to suffer.

(b)   Wanting the peace of the family and the sunny day to carry on.

(c)   The feeling of guilt for lying in the end.

All of you who experience yourself as essentially bad, evil, unacceptable to yourself and others have, as children, been put in situations like the one Jackie describes, a situation from which there is no escape (young children cannot leave home) and out of which there is no peaceful and happy solution. You dealt with these situations as best you could, but you were left with a feeling of guilt and a sense that you could alone and somehow put matters to rights by sacrificing yourself and taking on the burden of suffering. You may not even remember the original situation, but so strong were the emotions that you felt and so impressive the conclusions you drew from it that they became part of the foundation of the structure you call your life. You might have decided that you would devote your life to helping others, and so strictly do you apply this rule by trying to ignore your own interests and well-being and to meet the needs of others, that you create for yourself a great deal of suffering. You have set yourself the task of making the world perfect, to abolish all suffering and injustices, and, when you fail, you despair. Even when you do achieve something you find that people do not always show the proper appreciation and gratitude for your sacrifices, and you cannot help feeling sad and resentful. When people do try to help you or to give you things – love and sympathy as well as presents – you find that other people's generosity makes you frightened. You can give, but you cannot receive, and so you find the thought of illness and old age, when you would have to depend on other people, very frightening.

Another set of conclusions you might have drawn from the profound moral dilemmas of your childhood is that life, your life, is a tragedy. Not for you the humdrum mediocrity of happiness. You are a lone figure, singled out by Fate, or God, to play a significant but tragic part on life's stage. The heroes and heroines in the theatre of your imagination did not always end their adventures hand in hand with their lover to live happily ever after. You had alternative plots where you saw yourself as the heroic figure, after curing the sick and freeing the oppressed, riding off alone into the sunset, or in a defiant stance before a firing squad, or mourned over by chastened fellow countrymen who, at last, have recognised your true worth. With this tragic role in mind you grow up always expecting the worst, and find that your life is full of disasters, so much so that you may come to feel that you are damned. But, at least, if God has gone to the trouble of damning you, it does mean that He has noticed you.

Seeing your life as a tragedy does have its advantages, just as self-sacrifice has the advantage of making you feel virtuous. But in your determination to see your life as a tragedy you may do the things which actually make it a tragedy (not pursue a career commensurate with your talents, marry the wrong person, take to drink to drown your sorrows, etc., etc.); and in seeing your role in life as sacrificing yourself for others, you may go beyond the practical things that you can do for others and instead see your altruistic acts as some form of ritualistic self-sacrifice by which you inflict pain on yourself in order to secure the safety of others. You might use self-sacrifice as the only way to solve all family problems or as the way to resolve all family crises. Many of the obsessional rituals which some depressed people feel compelled to carry out have this as one of their meanings.[17]

So, in your guilt at your failure to be perfect, in your need to sacrifice yourself to atone and to protect others, in your identification of yourself with unhappiness rather than happiness you create for yourself a great deal of suffering. You feel that such suffering gives your life a significance which a happy, contented life would certainly lack. You do not consider that life, ordinary life, contains enough natural disasters, mishaps and losses without you creating more.

But it is those natural, chancy, spontaneous mishaps, disasters and losses which you fear. You prefer to create your own disasters in the attempt to control them, while you avoid the random disasters of the wide world by staying safe inside your prison of depression.

7. Besides, it's safe inside the prison

Once, when I was talking to a group of psychologists about depression and I had asked them to give their images of depression, one psychologist said,

> The worst part is when I'm coming out of the depression. When I'm depressed I feel I'm in a bathysphere deep under the water. There I'm in complete darkness except for a small circle of light which must be coming from the surface. The bathysphere is floating in the deep water, so I have to be careful not to move about too much. If I did the bathysphere might plunge to the bottom and I would be done for. When the depression ends I suddenly go up to the surface, and that is terrible, because floating on the surface is the wreckage of my ship – all the things that have gone wrong while I've been depressed and now I have to put them right. I always think of it as a Spanish galleon that's blown up, and now I have to gather up the pieces and build it again. I hate that.

This is a powerful image of the dangers and the safety of depression. Terrible though the prison of depression is, it seems to be a refuge from still greater horrors. You are afraid that you could plunge further into bottomless depths of complete destruction, madness and death.

> Which way I fly is Hell; myself am Hell;
> And in the lowest deep a lower deep
> Still threat'ning to devour me opens wide,
> To which the Hell I suffer seems a Heaven.[18]

Dangers, perhaps even greater dangers, threaten you if you leave your prison of depression for the ordinary world. There you might have to change, and change always involves uncertainty. The good thing about being depressed is that you can make every day be the same. You can be sure of what is going to happen. You can ward off all those people and events that expect a response from you. Your prison life has a regular routine, and like any long-term prisoner, you grow accustomed to the jail's security and predictability. The prison of depression may not be comfortable, but at least it is safe.

8. The deadliest sin

All of us, when we were children, created our personal myth, the story which we believed would be our life, not just so as to have a map to guide us through life, but to bolster up our pride in response to the insults the world had inflicted on our small person and to give us courage enough to attempt the journey. Unfortunately, we all grow up thinking that the map, our myth, is the reality, and so when our map proves to be inaccurate, as it must, since reality rarely conforms to myth, we all have to face the fearful task of recognising that our map is nothing but a map and that we need to change it, to bring it more in line with reality. To do this we have to admit that we are wrong, and for some of us, particularly you who get depressed, admitting that you are wrong is something that you find very hard to do. Given the choice, you would prefer to be *right and suffer* than *wrong and happy*.

As you well know, when we say we are wrong we create an area of uncertainty. If what you thought proves to be wrong, then you could be wrong about other things, and that could lead to discovering that nothing in your life was what you thought it was. This is too terrifying. If you cannot tolerate uncertainty then you cannot afford to admit that you are wrong.

Absolute certainty may appear to you to be a wonderful thing, giving complete security, but have you ever considered that if you want absolute certainty you must give up freedom, love and hope?

Freedom means making choices and allowing other people to make choices.

Love arises spontaneously and is freely given. It cannot be coerced into being and produced on demand.

Hope can only exist where there is uncertainty. Absolute certainty means complete hopelessness.

If we want to live life fully we must have freedom, love and hope. So life must be an uncertain business. That is what makes it worthwhile.

But you want absolute certainty and you have too much pride to admit that you could be wrong. You take pride in seeing yourself as essentially bad; you take pride in not loving and accepting other people; pride in the starkness and harshness of your philosophy of life; pride in the sorrows of your past and the blackness of your future; pride in recognising the evil of anger; pride in not forgiving; pride in your sensitivity; pride in your refusal to lose face by being rejected; pride in your pessimism; pride in your martyrdom; pride in your suffering.

Pride, so Christian theology teaches, is the deadliest of the seven sins since it prevents the person from recognising his sins and repenting and reforming. Sin or not, it is pride that keeps you locked in the prison of depression. It is pride that prevents you from changing and finding your way out of the prison.

Chapter 7

OUTSIDE THE WALL: LIVING WITH A DEPRESSED PERSON

Living with someone who is depressed is extremely difficult. It involves much, much more than living with someone who is physically ill.

Whenever I have a teaching session about depression with a group of health professionals I often begin by asking how they feel when they are with a depressed person and what images they have of this experience. One day I met a group of nursing auxiliaries whose job it was to visit old people in their own homes and to help them bathe regularly. As a consequence these women had to deal with a great deal of unhappiness and depression in their patients. As we talked of the feelings that looking after these old folk aroused, one of the women mentioned that her husband had been depressed since he had retired. As she spoke it sounded very much like what many women say after their husband retires – how she cannot get her work done because he is around the house, how grumpy and difficult he is, wanting meals at particular times and expecting things to be done when he wants them, and so on. The group continued talking, and later we came to the question of what images we had of being with a depressed person. Then this woman spoke again. She said, 'I feel that I'm in a boat in a heavy sea. Sometimes I feel I'm at the top of a wave, and then I go down into a trough again.'

'What sort of boat is it?' I asked.

'An open boat – a rowing boat – but there's no oars or sails or rudder.'

'Are you alone in the boat?'

'Yes!'

'When you're at the top of the wave, can you see land or another ship?'

'No. There's nothing in sight. Just rough ocean.'

As she described her image we each became aware of how terrible her plight was. Her husband, in his depressed state, made her feel helpless and alone. The doctors, she said, gave confusing advice and no help. She could only react to things as they happened and could not change or control them. She was trapped in an isolation as terrible as that of her husband. She was sorry for her husband, but she also felt angry and frustrated – and then guilty because she knew it was not right to be angry with someone the doctors said was ill.

This is the curious thing about depression. People call it an illness, but if you live with it you know it is not like any other illness. If someone you care about has a physical illness or an injury – bronchitis or cancer or a broken leg – you feel simple concern and sympathy for that person. You might feel anger at the injustices of life or at the carelessness of other people who have inflicted this suffering, or at the limitations of the medical profession, and you might occasionally feel impatient with your loved one who fails to rest properly or to take his medicine regularly, but you do not find yourself possessed by a terrible rage with your loved one. Sick people can be querulous and difficult, but they usually do not turn on you and say hurtful, cruel things just as you are giving them extra love and comfort. Sick people are not usually impervious to reason. They do not demand that you never leave the house while most of the time refusing to speak to you when you are there. Sick people do not rush upstairs and lock themselves in their bedroom when a neighbour drops in, nor do they sit in silence all day, brighten up and chat happily when visitors call, only to relapse into a hostile silence when the visitors leave. Having someone sick in the house can disrupt family routine, but sickness does not usually create a continual atmosphere of anger, mistrust and uncertainty. No matter how serious an illness is, you can come to understand it, and even if you can do nothing but let the illness run its course, you can see the pattern and not feel as if you are the helpless victim of uncontrollable and dangerous forces. You might say to someone in the family, 'Don't come too close. I don't want to catch your cold', and if someone has a dangerous infection medical science will protect you, but how can you be protected from the danger you feel of having a great well of despair open up in you? Being with a depressed person can be a very difficult and dangerous business.

William Styron dedicated his account of his severe depression to his wife Rose who had devoted herself to his care. As he recorded, when he was depressed he could be extremely rude to people, even to the people who gave him a most prestigious prize, the Prix Mondial Cino del Duca given annually in France to a scientist or writer whose work contains humanistic themes. Even worse, he had become completely dependent on his wife. He wrote,

> My own sense of self had all but disappeared, along with any self-reliance. This loss can quickly degenerate into dependence, and from dependence into an infantile dread. One dreads the loss of all things, all people close and dear. There is an acute fear of abandonment. Being alone in the house, even for a moment, caused me exquisite panic and trepidation.[1]

It is not just relatives who report a confusion of feelings, many of them bad, which arise when they are with a depressed person. I have talked with psychologists, nurses, doctors and social workers, and they all say how they begin by feeling great sympathy and concern for their depressed client, but soon they begin to feel frustrated because somehow nothing they do for the depressed person seems to work. Frustration leads to anger, but they know that they should not get angry with the people they are supposed to be helping. Worse, they then find themselves feeling confused and helpless. If you are in the business of helping people and you see yourself as being very competent and helpful, then being made to feel incompetent and helpless is a threat to your sense of being a person. You are not the person you thought yourself to be. Some professional people, too, report the sense of danger, that being with a depressed person will awaken their own latent depression. It is no wonder that some professionals refuse to treat depressed people while some bring consultations to a quick end by reaching for the prescription pad.

The images of being with a depressed person that professional people give are of two kinds. There are the images of wandering in a fog, not knowing where they are going, or being involved in some strange geometric pattern that cannot be completed in any satisfactory way. The other kind of image is that of being on the outside of a prison wall, knowing that the depressed person is inside the prison, wanting to help the depressed person but being unable to reach him. One image given by a psychologist was of being outside a circular brick prison. There were no windows, but the depressed person inside would remove one brick. The psychologist told me, 'When I see a brick being removed I try to put my hand through the hole to touch my client, but as I do he slams the brick back into place. Then he removes a brick on the other side of the prison, and I dash round there to try to get my hand through the hole, but as I reach there, he slams the brick back into place and I'm left on the other side of an impenetrable wall.' This image shows very clearly how the message that the depressed person gives is, 'Help me, help me – stay away.' It shows too how painful, confusing and guilt arousing this is to the person outside the prison.

What can you do?

Ways of thinking about the problem

When something goes wrong in our relationships with other people there are three kinds of questions we can ask in order to discover what happened and what should be done to put it right.

1. Who is to blame for this?
2. Who is responsible for this?
3. What does this mean?

Each of these questions represents a different way of conceptualising the problem. Often in discussions about relationships we use all three kinds of concepts and so we get very muddled. If you are worried that I am going to blame you for your relative's depression then you must read this section very closely and make sure you understand it.

1. Laying blame

Something goes wrong and we look for the culprit. 'You dropped my best teapot', 'He backed the car into the gate-post', 'He took the car without permission', 'She spent the housekeeping money at bingo'. When we find the culprit we can say, 'It's your fault. What are you going to do about it?' We expect the person at fault to be contrite and to make reparation. If he or she does accept the blame and does make some reparation then all (or most) is forgiven and life pro-ceeds smoothly again. However, sometimes the person does not accept the blame and instead puts up arguments like, 'It's your fault I dropped the teapot. You gave me a fright when you shouted', 'If you had cut the hedge back I'd have been able to see where I was going', 'You said I could take the car – don't you remember?', 'If you took me out more I wouldn't need to go to bingo to give me a break from all this cooking and cleaning and looking after you and the chil-dren'. Then the argument starts and goes on for hours, weeks, and, in some families, for years.

Matters are not made any simpler by saying that the offence is a crime and calling in the police. The culprit may be found and brought to court, and, if found guilty, fined or sent to jail. Just why people get fined or sent to jail is not quite clear – is it to punish them or to teach them better ways of behaving? This whole question of crime and punishment is very complex, and I raise it here only to say that if we think in terms of blaming, feeling guilty and never forgiving, all we do is make our relationships worse and make even greater problems for ourselves. So, please, leave blame and guilt aside and think about these issues in terms of *responsibilities* and *connections*.

2. Being responsible

In the course of my work as head of a department of clinical psychology I often had to draw up a job description for one of the posts in the department. The job description had to show very clearly what the holder of the job was responsible for and whom the holder was responsible to. All this could be clearly defined and followed. If a problem arose about who was responsible for what, we could resolve it through discussion and reference back to our job descriptions.

From this orderly way of defining and limiting responsibility I would go and talk to my depressed clients and what did I find? They were responsible for everything! There wasn't anything which could happen in the entire universe that they could not see themselves as responsible for and feel guilty about. Usually they confined their responsibility to their family and their job. They were entirely responsible for the happiness of their partner, children, parents, brothers and sisters, grandparents and, if they were so minded, to the entire range of their cousins and in-laws. None of these relatives was capable of being responsible for themselves. If my client was working, then no matter what his job was, he was responsible for the welfare of the entire organisation, no matter if it was an international business or vast government department. My client saw himself as responsible for everything, and when he saw himself as failing in his responsibility he would say, 'I feel so guilty. I should take mum and dad out more often/I should have made sure my son worked harder for his university exams/I should have set an example to the others in the office/If I had given my sister more help her husband wouldn't have left her/It's my fault if any of my pupils fail their exams', and so on.

The essence of a job description was the understanding that the holder of the post agreed to carry out certain tasks and to be responsible for himself in doing these tasks. He had to report to or be accountable to a senior colleague, but in his work he was responsible for *himself*. When I talked to my depressed clients I found that while they were prepared to be responsible for everything and everybody in the universe there was one exception. They were not prepared to be responsible for themselves. They saw themselves as passive and helpless. Things happened to them. They did not choose to do anything. They were compelled to do things by forces out of their control. They saw themselves as unable to avert disasters or to take positive steps to achieve success. The black cloud of depression descended without reason, without any choice or design on their part. They were compelled to meet other people's demands and they could not choose to refuse. The world was the way it was and they had no choice but to live in it at its behest. They were the people that they were and they had no choice but to suffer themselves, to be the cross which they had to bear.

When I sent the first draft of this book to Jean for her comments she wrote back,

> One thing I have chewed over and over is the first part where you set out the six opinions. In nos 2 and 6 you use the word 'must'. I have never felt the compulsion of must in holding these opinions, though they are two of my 'favourites'. I don't feel that I must fear people. I just do. I don't see anything about them that must be feared – they just are terrifying, and the same with forgiveness. I don't feel that I mustn't forgive myself – I just don't. I rather feel that the element of compulsion that 'must' gives these makes them seem more of a positive decision than I think they are. In adopting such hopeless attitudes I don't think there is a positive decision. It's really a small point, but I immediately thought, 'I don't feel that "must"'.

It is not a small point. It is the essence of living your life in a prison, and of finding your way out of that prison.

If we consciously tell ourselves that we must do something we are allowing an alternative where we do not do that thing. If we say to ourselves, 'I must write to Auntie Millie' it is because for the last few days or weeks we have not written to Auntie Millie. In contrast, there are things we do which we never tell ourselves we must do because we see these things as being part of the conditions of our being alive. We rarely have occasion to tell ourselves that we must breathe, and most of us rarely have to remind ourselves to eat. These are very basic matters, but to them we can add other activities which for us do not have the feeling of 'must' but rather that of being as natural and compulsive as breathing. Those of us who feel most comfortable when we are not surrounded by chaos clean, tidy and organise, and those of us who hate being alone seek the company of other people. All these are unspoken 'musts', as are the moral or religious rules we follow. Some of us feel compelled to devote ourselves to the care of others, while some of us would not fail to attend church, mosque or synagogue daily.

All of these unconscious 'musts' do have alternatives. It is possible to live in clutter, or to live alone, or be selfish, or never enter a place of worship. However, it is also possible to behave as though these alternatives do not exist, and to tell ourselves that the unconscious 'musts' we follow are Absolute Truths, existing outside space and time, incontrovertible and unchangeable, allowing no choice or modification.

Most people grow up not understanding that all we can ever know are the meanings which we each create. Thus most people grow up believing that the world *is* the way they see it, and they *are* the way they see themselves. To them, they and their world are fixed and unchangeable. However, each of us is in a constant process of change because every new experience changes us. Similarly the world changes all the time whether we acknowledge the changes or not. For such people change is frightening, not liberating, and so they reject new inventions and new ideas. Many of my contemporaries reject video machines, emails, faxes and mobile phones, and so do not recognise that video machines allow us to choose when we watch the television programmes we want to see, while emails, faxes and mobile phones enable us to keep in close touch with friends and family. It is possible to live comfortably without these inventions, but, if we assume that we cannot change, that we have 'a personality' and it cannot change, we stay trapped in a prison which our beliefs have created.

There are many more prisons than the prison of depression. Each of us builds our own prison when we decide upon the ideas which we want to regard as the solid, enduring truths of our world. Some of us build large, spacious prisons where we can roam with ease and where we feel free enough to change some of the boundaries of the prison when we wish. But some of us build narrow, dark prisons where we feel cramped and pressed upon. We believe that we cannot change any aspect of our prison. Our prison simply is. We do not even feel that we must behave in a certain way, because, as Jean said, 'must' contains a positive decision. If, when we build our prison, we deny that we have made any decisions and claim that all the decisions have been made by other people or powers beyond our control, then we can feel that we are not responsible for ourselves. If our prison is cramped and miserable, it is not our fault, and so we can come back to the sorry round of blame, guilt and not forgiving.

Freedom consists of recognising that we choose our own prison and of deciding to create a spacious, light, airy prison filled with delightful things, a place where change is created and welcomed. Freedom means recognising that everything we do is the outcome of a choice (bearing in mind that not all choices are made consciously, and that 'not deciding' means 'choosing not to decide'). Freedom means being responsible for yourself, and it also means looking very closely at your relationships and deciding to what degree and in what way you are responsible for the welfare of other people.

Within organisations it is fairly easy to decide what responsibility we have for other people. For instance, as head of a department of psychology, I accepted that it was my responsibility to provide the appropriate experience and opportunity for study for the psychologists who come there for training, but it was not my responsibility to make sure that they worked hard enough to pass their examinations. That was their responsibility. However, where loved ones are concerned it is much harder to set limits to our sense of responsibility. I want my son to have a happy life, so I find it hard sometimes to say nothing if I think he is making a decision which could have unhappy consequences. It is not just a matter of wanting our loved ones to be happy. It is the pain we feel when we know they are not happy, or are weak or in danger. I remember, as quite a small child, feeling an overwhelming and exceedingly painful pity for my mother. To end this pain I had, in some way, to help her, but it was help she neither understood nor wanted. What she did want from me was something I could not give, that I should give up my life and instead do and be exactly what she wanted. When my depressed clients talk to me of their sensitivity in their relationships and when they say things like, 'As much as my mother annoys me, I couldn't ever say anything to upset her', or 'Dad can manage to look after himself, but I go round to see him every morning, just in case there's anything he needs', I know they are talking, at least in part, of their painful, loving pity and of how they try to deal with it. We try to protect our loved ones in order that we should not pity them.

However, there are limits to what protection we can and should give. When our children are babies we need to protect them, but once they start to move around and explore we have gradually to decrease our protection, for if we try to go on protecting them we prevent our children from growing up to be ordinary, confident adults, capable of looking after themselves. Many of the depressed people I have met have told me of loving parents who protected them and of how they find the world such a terrifying place (it must be – why else would their parents need to protect them?) and of how they lack the confidence to live their lives. As parents we must define the limits of our responsibility to our children, limits which change as the child grows older, until the child is an adult and our responsibility is that of a good friend. For the child, growing up means seeing our parents become older and in need, sometimes, of our help. But the relationship and responsibility should still be that of good friends – loving concern and interest, with minimal criticism and advice, help when asked, and allowing one another to make our own decisions since we are all grown up.

What we should always remember is:

It's not what happens to us which matters but how we interpret what happens to us.

This is what makes being a parent so difficult. You can feel that the rules you expect your children to follow are fair and not at all burdensome, but if your children see you as an unjust tyrant that is what they will respond to, not to your interpretation but their own. You try to put some ideas into their heads – right and wrong, keep safe, be clean, be well-mannered – but they do not take in these ideas in the way they take in a sandwich you give them. They interpret what you say and create ideas about such matters which are their own, and which may not bear much resemblance to your ideas. My son accepted my general idea that a home should be efficiently organised, but his idea of good organisation and mine are very different. Moreover, you are not the only person presenting ideas to your children. There are the rest of the family, teachers, friends and acquaintances, and the ubiquitous media. Each child has different experiences, each child interprets everything in his or her own way, and so each child sees everything differently from you.

Always remember that you cannot control your children's interpretations or anyone else's. We all interpret everything in our own individual way. We choose our interpretations from an infinite range of possible interpretations and because we always have a choice we are always responsible for our interpretations. You have a choice of how to interpret your responsibility for others and, while you might decide that you have no responsibility for anyone or that you are responsible for everybody, you are responsible for that interpretation.

Without losing any of the virtuous aspects of pity and concern for our loved ones, it is both possible and necessary for us to define the degree of responsibility we have for each of our loved ones and so be able to say, 'Yes, I do want my mother to be happy, but I will not lie to her just because the truth is unpleasant,' or, 'Dad doesn't need to see me every day. If I went there less it might encourage him to go out more.' Nothing is to be gained by going over the events of the past years and feeling guilty or blaming others. There are really very, very few parents who actually try to harm their children. Most parents love their children and try to do what is best for them. However, as all parents know, when our children are small we are usually caught up in all sorts of difficulties so that we do things which later turn out to be mistakes, and we also do things which turn out to be very much for our children's benefit. The trouble is, at the time we have no way of knowing what will be a mistake and what will be a success. So often what we thought was good parenting turned out to have bad effects on our children, and what we thought we had done wrong and what we regretted turned out to benefit our children. So, waste no time going over the past searching for blame and guilt. What needs to be done now is to look at what is happening *in the present* and to try to understand it. *Understanding* means *seeing connections*.

3. Seeing connections

Jack came to talk to me. For the previous five years his wife Fay had been depressed, sometimes very badly, and she had been given many pills and some ECT. After all this she started coming to see me, and Jack found this confusing, since all along the doctors had been telling him that Fay was suffering from endogenous depression whose cause was unknown. So he came to talk to me, and, in the course of the conversation, we talked about Fay's parents. Jack said that Fay tried to do too much for her parents when they were quite capable of looking after themselves and they did not show much concern for Fay when she was ill. 'Fay's mother visits Fay's sister every week,' said Jack. 'We go and see them but they visit us no more than once a month, and when Fay was in hospital and very ill, they didn't visit her at all.'

I replied, 'When someone gets depressed it's always difficult for the parents. You know yourself, when the doctors were saying that Fay had endogenous depression, a kind of physical illness, while it was all very worrying for you, you didn't have to feel guilty about it because it wasn't your fault. But now Fay's coming here and we're talking about how she lives her life, and this involves you, since you have to ask yourself about what you're doing that's helping to make her depressed and what you should do to change. Now if you think about it, it's much harder for parents. If they think, "Fay's like this now because of what happened in her childhood", they feel very guilty, and helpless as well. You might feel guilty about what's happened in your marriage over the past ten years, but you and Fay are still together and still young, and you both can put things to rights and have a good life, but Fay's parents can't go back twenty, thirty years and change things. That's why many parents whose adult children get depressed like to insist that the depression is a physical illness, or that the child should pull himself together and get out of it – that way they don't have to feel guilty.

That's why, too, Fay's parents didn't want to see her when she was in hospital.'

Jack found my explanation very illuminating. He still thought that Fay's parents should visit her, but now he could see a connection between Fay being depressed and what her parents were doing, and this connection, this meaning, made the whole painful business slightly easier to live with.

A person may do something which seems strange or wrong to us, but if we are able to talk to that person and find out how that person sees the situation we shall find, first, that the person sees the situation differently from us, and, second, there is a connection between the meaning that the person has given to the situation and what he does. Of course, the meaning that the person has created is not an *excuse*. You may steal, or riot, or murder, or argue with your partner because you feel that you had a deprived childhood and you have never forgiven your father. Your reasons do not excuse your bad behaviour, but they do provide an *explanation* which can become the starting point for a change.

Unfortunately, we are not very skilled at finding another person's meaning. It is often much more satisfying to say, 'Wouldn't you think she'd look after her mother/dress better/put her children's welfare before her own', and so on, rather than to think carefully about why a person does what she does. In families people often ask for explanations, but do not phrase their questions very well. 'What do you think you're doing, bringing your bike in here?' 'Mrs Smith's little girl wears pretty dresses and she brushes her hair every day. Now why aren't you like that?' 'Why do you have to play golf *every* Saturday?' 'Why do you get upset just because I forgot your birthday?' Such questions do not inspire thoughtful answers, rich in explanation. Again, in families people do give explanations, but no one actually *hears* what they say. Finding explanations means asking careful questions and listening to the answers.

We give our world meaning and we act in accordance with that meaning. All our acts, all we say and do, have consequences. To live wisely we need to be aware of the consequences of our acts. We try to teach our children to look for the consequences of running headlong on to a busy road, or not obeying their teachers, or not cleaning their teeth every day. However, we are not very good at teaching children to be aware of the effects of their actions on other people. Perhaps this is because so many adults are not very expert at seeing the effects of their actions on other people. The most glaring example of this is those people who believe that by being violent to young people you can teach them not to be violent to other people. Beating children certainly punishes them, but what they learn from that beating is likely to be something that the person inflicting the beating neither wanted nor predicted.

Within families many examples can be found where one person does not see the consequences of his actions, the connections between what he does and what these actions mean to other people and how these people then act. For instance, a father may feel that he is not very successful and that he would feel more satisfied with himself if his son had a successful career. So as soon as the boy starts school the father encourages him to work hard and do well. At least, the father calls what he does 'encouraging'. His son calls it 'nagging', and comes to dread his father's interest in his schooling. The boy loses his joy in learning and looks for ways of escaping from school and from his father. The father's actions have more consequences than just upon his son. His wife sees the effect the father's passionate desire for his son's success has on the son and she tries to protect the boy. This divides the boy even more from his father, but the person in the family who feels the loneliest is the daughter who sees her father and mother so involved with her brother that they have no time for her. The father does not see what effects his actions have on his family, the mother does not see that she is alienating her daughter, the son does not see that he is set upon a life of escapes and failures, and the daughter does not see that, on the basis of her experience of her father and brother, she has concluded that all men are selfish and unlikely to be interested in her. Thus the father's actions, like a stone thrown in a pool, have consequences in all directions.

However, while the father's actions have *connections*

with the actions of the other members of the family, it is not correct to say he is *responsible* for those actions. Each member of the family is responsible for his or her own actions. They each make their own interpretations and they are not *compelled* by their father's actions to behave as they do. (When someone harasses you, it is always possible to deal with that harassment, at least in part, by being indifferent to it and by laughing at it. Alternatives can always be found through discussion, but not if you always practise Not Speaking and Keeping Things to Yourself.) We are free to make any number of choices, including the choice to see ourselves as not being free to make a choice. We create problems for ourselves and the people around us when we refuse to take responsibility for ourselves but expect other people to take responsibility for us (as in this family, the father expected the son to do for him what he would not do for himself – be successful), when we deny that we are free to choose but insist that we are compelled to behave as we do, and when we refuse to see the consequences of our actions.

Of course, the consequences of our actions are limitless, since everything in this world is connected to everything else (a family is part of society and in our small world every society is connected to every other society), so we can never be aware of all the consequences of our actions, but it is a good idea to be aware of the consequences of our actions which may rebound on us. I have come across some psychologists who have been convinced, rightly, that they are not responsible for their colleagues, but who fail to see the connections between what they do and what their colleagues do. Such lack of wisdom makes problems for people in groups, either working groups or families.

Seeing connections is part of wisdom, and living wisely means living harmoniously with yourself and with other people. Living harmoniously means avoiding the painful dead-ends of blame, fault-finding, guilt, revenge and not forgiving; it means being responsible for yourself, limiting and defining your responsibility for others, and seeing the connections between your actions and the actions of others.

So now let us go back to this question of living with someone who is depressed.

Mothers

The mothers of people who get depressed are extraordinary people – or, at least, so my clients would have had me believe. My depressed clients sat in my room and told me about their mothers, and, as they did, I realised that if any of these remarkable women had come to visit me none of them would have actually entered the room by the door. Instead I might hear the sound of golden trumpets as the room filled with heavenly light and up above I would have seen the mother slowly descending, her angel wings gently moving, and the glow of her halo revealing her compassionate, loving, beautiful face. Some mothers would have entered like this. The rest would have swished through the window on a broomstick. Having a mother who was an angel or a witch was very difficult, but some poor people had mothers who alternated, unexpectedly, between being angels or witches and that was even more difficult.

So I sat with my depressed client and we talked about this angel ('She'd do anything for me. I'd never do anything to upset her') or this witch ('I've only got to hear her voice on the phone and I'm upset'). Then one day I would happen to be shopping in town and run into my client, accompanied by an ordinary middle-aged or elderly woman who was introduced to me as 'My mother'. As we chatted about the weather and other trivial matters, I would try not to be observed as I peered to see if that carefully waved hair concealed a halo, whether there were huge feathered wings folded under her modest coat, or whether there was a black cat at her heels and cloven hooves tucked inside her neat, sensible shoes. Peer as I might, none of these signs were there, and I would have to conclude that my client's mother was just an ordinary woman.

It was not a good idea for me to say to my client, the next time we met, that I thought his mother was an ordinary woman. That would never do, because he did not want his mother to be ordinary. Ordinary people made mistakes, and he wanted his mother to be perfect. So he insisted that his mother was a Perfect Angel and All Criticism was forbidden. If his mother's deficiencies were too glaring to be denied, he expressed his disappointment that she was not a Perfect Angel by insisting that she was the Perfect Witch. But only he was allowed to criticise her. If you agreed with his criticisms he would get very resentful and if you tried to point out her virtues he knew that you were siding with her against him. ('You don't understand. You don't know her like I do.') Partners will be as familiar with these arguments as I am.

So being the mother of someone who is depressed is very, very difficult. You know that you are an ordinary person. You would not mind being a Perfect Angel, but you know that you have made mistakes, especially when your child was young and life for you had quite a few difficulties. You know that your child does not understand about these things, and you find it hard to talk about such matters. You know that you care about your child, and you always did your best in difficult circumstances, and still do, but somehow you cannot get through to your child. He (or she) seems to hang on to you, and yet every time you think the two of you could be close, he pushes you away. Sometimes he might hurt you terribly by saying cruel things to you, but even if he says nothing and is always polite to you, you know that he has a lot of resentment against you. You feel shut out, confused, helpless and misunderstood.

Val would tell me how much she feared her mother coming to visit, how everything her mother said or did upset her, how she was sure that gifts from her mother were offered not because her mother loved her but because she wanted to put Val under an obligation to her. Yet Val could not detach herself from her mother and treat her with that polite indifference we use for people we do not like but have to meet. Just why she could not do this can be seen in the poem which Val had written when she was twenty and so deeply depressed that she had been admitted to a psychiatric clinic.

Mother, Mother, why don't you come?
Can't you hear me crying for you?
I'm frightened and I'm alone.

I want to be comforted.
I want you to take me into your arms, like a child.
I want to cry myself asleep on your shoulder,
And relax warm and secure.
But nobody comes.
The pillow soaks up the tears,
The hostile darkness embraces me.
The blanket supplies impersonal warmth.
Only the spattering of icy snow on the window
Lulls me to sleep.

A year later and still depressed she wrote,

SOLITARY CONFINEMENT
You laughed at my weaknesses
– so I feared to show them.
You trampled on my dreams
– so I dreamed alone.
You were too busy to listen
– so I never spoke.
You handled my secrets indiscreetly
– so I ceased to share them.
You were insensitive to my needs
– so I hid them from you.
You never seemed to understand
– so I stopped trying to communicate.
You hurt me by your indifference
– so I bled inwardly.
You wouldn't let me near you
– so I kept my distance.
You cared for my physical needs
– so my soul became impoverished.
You drove me into myself
– so now I am imprisoned!

If you are the mother of someone who is depressed perhaps, as you read these poems, you felt, not just the shock of
such passion and the fear that your child feels like that about
you, but also some memories of your own mother and how
you got along with her. If you have read the first part of this
book you have found some things that apply to you, and to

your mother. Beliefs such as that anger is bad and that you should never forgive get handed down from one generation to another like the family jewels. There was one woman I had known for ten years, who had been depressed for longer, and who would tell me how, whenever she and her mother fell out over something, they would not speak for months and months. Neither would forgive the other. Setting such an example to the children, the grandmother and mother ensured that the three daughters never got on well together. Even at their father's funeral two of the girls would not speak to one another, and later one of the girls was completely estranged from the family. All this is to be expected in any family where the rule is 'Never Forgive'.

But of course it is not just mothers alone who make up these rules and see that they are obeyed. There are always fathers.

Fathers

Fathers, like mothers, become the victims of their depressed child's determination to have as parents Perfect Angels and not ordinary, fallible human beings. Of course, some fathers (and mothers) go along with this. They like the idea of being Wonderful Daddy, always there, caring for and protecting his little child, or being Famous Father, to be admired and emulated. However, most fathers are aware of the wall between themselves and their child, and they feel baffled and confused. In the confusion is the realisation, sometimes dimly perceived, sometimes known with startling clarity, that what is happening to your depressed child is connected with your own marriage and with the early years of your child's life. Your child's depression can seem like a threat to expose family secrets and a punishment for the misdeeds those secrets are hiding. Do you respond by blaming yourself and becoming depressed, or by denying that your child's depression has anything to do with you, or by being prepared to examine past events and what they meant to all concerned?

Married life is not easy. For a marriage to last both partners must compromise, and these compromises, while effective in holding the marriage together, can have implications for the children which they find hard to bear. It is often the case that in the early years of the marriage the couple have to survive some very difficult circumstances. For one generation of parents – now grandparents – it was World War II. For a later generation of parents it was the upheavals of the 1980s when whole industries collapsed and thousands of hard-working men and women were reduced to penury. Whatever the perilous circumstances, the young couple were concerned solely with surviving. They had neither the time nor the energy to examine how their relationship was developing. They agreed on one thing, that their children should have safe, happy lives.

In order to achieve this they made a tacit agreement to present the world to their young children as a pleasant, happy place, where bad things rarely happened, and then only to bad people. The father never spoke of the horrors he had endured, and the mother turned the home into a nest of domestic happiness. Thus the children enjoyed a happy childhood, and loved their parents for this, but when they at last ventured into the wide world they soon discovered that it was a harsh, cruel place. Disasters befell them, and, if they still believed, as they had been taught, that good people were rewarded and bad people punished, they blamed themselves when their partner proved to be faithless, or the fluctuations in the financial markets and world trade robbed them of their jobs.

The mother was bewildered by events and by finding that her methods of comforting and protecting her children no longer worked. The father, as ever, said very little. He did not invite his troubled children to talk to him because he had always held the view, a view which is held by many men, that, if you had a problem, you solved it, and, if there was nothing you could do to solve it, you did not talk about it. He and his wife never confided in one another but maintained a limited dialogue about practical matters. So each alone asked themselves that terrible question, 'I tried to do my best for my children. Where did I go wrong?'

Conversations about their children quickly turned into arguments. They surprised themselves when matters from the distant past emerged with a venom that had never grown stale. 'You were never here.' 'You mollycoddled them.' 'Your mother interfered.' 'Your father could have helped but he didn't.'

Similar arguments emerge when couples, long separated, meet to discuss their troubled adult child. Married or divorced, the couples find they are fighting old battles, with unresolved issues as bright and sharp as ever. Being told that their child's troubles are caused by a gene brings no respite or reconciliation. Instead, 'It's your side of the family', 'What about your father, he was an alcoholic', 'That uncle of yours, didn't he end up in an asylum?', 'You were never normal', 'Neither were you'.

Meanwhile, the children have their own view of their parents.

Good and bad parents

Most parents love their children and want to do their best for them. However, some parents, whether intentionally or not, are not interested in their child's welfare. All children want to believe that they have good parents, and many will deny the evidence of their own eyes and maintain that they have the best of parents. Accepting that, when it came to parents, you did badly in life's lottery, is very difficult. At the very least it undermines your self-confidence, and, at the worst, leaves you knowing that you are helpless and in great danger. So you try to make the best of a bad job. If you have one parent who beats you and another who comforts you after each beating, you see yourself as having one good parent and one bad parent.

Many people, depressed or not, believe they had one good and one bad parent, an angel and a devil. Actually this is not possible. If, as a child, you have a bad parent and the other parent does not protect you from the bad parent you have, in effect, two bad parents. As an adult you can say, 'My father was a brutal drunkard. If my dear mother opposed him he'd beat her' or 'My father was a sweetie to put up with my mother's nagging and wicked temper. He'd do anything to keep the peace', but when you were a child and in danger from your bad parent all you wanted from your other parent was protection. When the other parent did not do this you felt betrayed.

A journalist who had experienced suicidal depressions once asked me whether I had failed to take account of the effect of siblings. He said, 'My parents were great. I can't remember any bad times with them. It was my older brother who made my childhood a misery. He used to beat me up and destroy my things. I blame him for my extreme anxiety and lack of confidence.' I asked, 'Did your parents protect you from him?' He said, 'No, they didn't,' and with that came the realisation that his parents were not the Perfect Parents he wanted them to be.

Reconciliation between parents and children

Many of my clients, when they had reached a stage where they could see the connections between certain events in their childhood and the misery of their adult life, would consider talking to their parents about these events. Some did, only to find that their parents were greatly offended by the suggestion that they had been anything less than Perfect Parents. Some parents defended themselves by saying, 'You were a wicked child and had to be punished,' even though their adult child could now see that the cruelty of the punishment he had received far outweighed his childhood misdemeanours. However, some of my clients found that their parents had grown wiser and stronger. When their child asked them about past events they were able to say, 'Yes, that did happen. I'm sorry.'

That was all these adult children wanted to hear. They wanted to have their memories confirmed, both of the specific events themselves and of the suffering that these events caused them. 'I'm sorry' are the two words which can acknowledge pain inflicted and bring reconciliation. However, the 'I'm sorry' must be related to specific events and not be a general, all-purpose 'sorry'. To say, 'I'm sorry you were unhappy' is not an apology because there the person is not taking any responsibility for what he did. We can all feel sorrow for people who suffer without feeling that we were in any way the cause of their suffering. What needs to be said is,

'I'm sorry I hurt you,' but it takes great courage to do so. Parents cannot be certain that their child will actually accept the apology, and, even if the child does, the parent is left with the pain and sorrow and helplessness of having hurt someone they love. All parents who love their children and who acknowledge that they have made mistakes in bringing up their children know this anguish.

Husbands, wives and partners

My father, who was a commercial traveller and who spent much of his time listening to his friends and customers telling him about their problems, always said, 'Never interfere between husband and wife.' What he meant was that it was a dangerous business to get involved in any argument between a married couple. I often thought how right he was as I tried to find my way through the angers, fears, jealousies, resentments, loves and loyalties in order to discover the meaningful connections, not just in my client's marriage but the marriage of his parents. There are rules in every family about what can be said about each person in the family, and, if I carelessly infringed these rules, I was in trouble.

However, marriage must be talked about since depression is not some *thing* inside a person but it is the way that person relates to himself and the people around him. A partner is just as much involved in the depression as the person who is depressed. So, when a depressed person who was married came to see me, I would ask if the three of us could get together, at least occasionally, for a discussion. Through this request I discovered that I had as clients wives of the most important men in Lincolnshire. I knew this because when I asked if a husband could come along with his depressed wife, the wife relayed to me the message that, much as he wished to do this, if he absented himself from work for as much as an hour or two, thousands of acres of the best Lincolnshire potatoes would have stopped growing, wilted and died, or British industry would have ground to a complete halt, or the spiritual lives of all Christians would have been put in jeopardy, or the Nato forces of Western Europe would have been rendered defenceless, or international banking would have been brought to the verge of bankruptcy. I could not help but be so impressed with this that I was in danger of forgetting that saying which is so familiar to many family therapists, 'The craziest member of the family is the one who refuses to turn up for therapy sessions.'

So it is with all these Very Important Men, and with some of the wives of depressed husbands. It is not that they do not want to help their partner, but they knew that I, like all psychologists, had the power to penetrate directly into the inner recesses of their soul and see the hidden nasties there. They were afraid that their own depression would be revealed, or their murderous anger which was held in check by a smiling mask of kindly reasonableness would burst forth in disintegrating madness. They could not see that their depression or anger was no more than the pain of being an ordinary human being, since they did not want to be an ordinary, fallible human being. They wanted to be, and to be seen as being, a Perfect, Wonderful Person who looked after a partner who is ill. Such a posture fits neatly with the medical model of depression, where the depressed person is told that he is suffering from a mental illness, that he is a patient, not a person, and that pills and ECT will cure his illness. Partners who do not wish to inspect their own way of living believe in the medical model of depression.

However, not all partners are like this. They may not see a connection between their partner's being depressed and their own behaviour, but they are prepared to do anything which could help their partner. When this meant coming along to talk to me they would do this, and some of them made a few discoveries about themselves. Ron would bring Jackie to see me, and when I first invited him into my office along with Jackie he thought he was being asked to talk about Jackie in the way that relatives are asked to talk to the doctor about the patient. But he soon found that it was not so. Ron said, 'When I came here I thought I was an onlooker, but now I know I'm part of it.'

One set of connections which needs to be looked at is how aspects of our relationship with our parents become part of the way we relate to our partner. Sometimes we can see quite clearly that our wife is like our mother, or our husband is like our father, but it is not always easy to realise that our husband reminds us of our mother or our wife reminds us of our father, usually because we have conflicting feelings about these similarities. A man may be pleased that his wife keeps him in order in the way that his father kept him in order, but he may secretly resent her domination just as he secretly resented his father's. A woman may be pleased that her husband cossets her in the way that her mother cosseted her, but she may secretly resent the way he limits her independence in the same way as she resented her mother's restrictions. Sometimes we find ourselves re-enacting in our marriage scenes from our childhood. If such scenes made us happy, then such re-enactments can be quite joyful and pleasant, but, if such scenes in childhood made us feel frightened, helpless, angry, jealous or resentful, then replaying such scenes in married life can only create greater unhappiness.

Sometimes we do not perceive the similarity between the scenes from married life and those from childhood. When Fay and I were working out what were some of the things that made her feel down, she told me how nervous she felt when her mother visited her since 'an atmosphere' could develop between her mother and her husband, and so she had to try to prevent this and to keep everything smooth and peaceful. In another conversation she told me how, as a child, she had to act as a mediator between her mother and father whenever they quarrelled. Until I pointed it out she had not seen how she had been interpreting any difference of opinion between her mother and husband as being the same as the arguments between her parents. I went on to comment that probably her reaction to 'an atmosphere' between her husband and her mother was stronger than need be because she brought to the present the fears of her childhood. Quarrels between parents are always frightening to a child, since the child knows that he is dependent on his parents and that, if they fight, one or both of them might desert him. However, an argument between a woman's mother and her husband should not imperil a wife's security – not unless she sees herself as dependent upon her mother and husband as she was upon her mother and father when a child.

Just who is dependent on whom is another connection which must be looked at very carefully. In a culture where 'masculine' means 'strong and independent' and 'feminine' means 'weak and dependent' many married women have to keep up the excruciating position of trying to support a weak man while making sure he appears to the world as strong and independent. Any woman who has a marriage containing such a pretence knows how exhausting keeping up this pretence is. Not wishing to hurt her husband by exposing his weakness, the woman may collapse into a depression from which escape is impossible until she and her husband are able to face together the questions of weakness and dependency. In the play by Michael Wynne *The People Are Friendly* Kathleen, a middle-aged woman, tells how she gave up her cleaning job when her husband John lost his job when the shipbuilding firm where he worked closed. John defined himself by the work he did, so when he lost his job he felt that he had lost his identity. Kathleen said, 'I couldn't go out to work while he was sitting at home, it'd be rubbing his face in it. I'm not saying we couldn't have done with the money but it would have been more trouble than it was worth. I did miss it though, it was my little escape a couple of times a week.'[2]

Sometimes a man, or a woman, needs the partner to be weak and dependent for reasons other than appearing strong to the outside world. Sometimes what the 'well' partner needs is to be needed, and the 'ill' partner obligingly meets this need. (Some mothers, fearing the desolation of no longer being needed, can need their child to be ill, and the child, loving his mother, obliges.) When we need a person as well as love that person we can let our need influence us more than our love. We can say, 'I worry about you. I don't want you to be hurt,' and mean 'Don't do anything I don't want you to do.'

Here now is a story about a couple who loved one another. Put yourself in the position of the princess.

In the days of ancient Rome there was once an Emperor who had a beautiful daughter. Just as beautiful princesses are wont to do, she fell in love with a handsome man, and, just as powerful fathers are wont to do, the Emperor did not approve of her lover. So the Emperor's soldiers came and seized the man and threw him in the dungeon under the Colosseum.

During this Emperor's reign the most popular game that was played in the Colosseum was called 'The Lady or the Tiger'. In this game one prisoner, usually a wicked and admired villain or a noble who had offended the Emperor, was put in the arena alone and facing two locked doors. He was told that behind one door was a tiger and behind the other a beautiful lady, but he was not told which door was which. All he had to do was to choose the door to be opened. If, when he had chosen, the door was opened and out came the beautiful lady, the Emperor would pardon him and give him a farm far from Rome, and he would marry the lady and retire to his farm midst much rejoicing. But if the hungry tiger came out, he would die a horrible death.

When the princess heard that her lover had been seized and would be playing the Lady or the Tiger game she went secretly to the jailer and bribed him to tell her behind which door would be the lady and behind which the tiger. When the day of the game arrived she sat in the royal box and when her lover entered the arena and looked at her she signalled to him which door he should choose to have opened.

If you were in the princess's position and your lover/partner were in the arena, which would you choose. The Lady or the Tiger?

For some people the choice is easy. Some immediately choose the tiger, on the principle that 'If I can't have what I want then nobody else is going to have it'. Some people choose the lady on the principle that 'Much as I want my loved one near me, so long as I know that he/she is somewhere in the world, alive and happy I am content'. However, some people find the choice impossible because as much as they want their loved one to be well and happy, they cannot bear the thought of facing life without their loved one.

If you fear that you could not face life without your

partner then you will be inclined to do things to keep your partner with you and not let him or her wander. If husbands are allowed to go out to pubs and clubs, to spend their time in ways that you do not know about, then they could meet all kinds of people and they could lose interest in their wives and homes. If wives are allowed to go out to work, or to go out with other women, then they could meet all kinds of people and they could lose interest in their husbands and homes. So some of you feel it is much, much better if your partner is safely at home where you can keep an eye on him or her. And what better way to keep your partner safe than for him or her to be depressed.

For some of you (most, I hope) this is an extremely shocking and wrong thing to say. You do not want your partner to be depressed. You want to see your partner leading a happy normal life. But for this to come about you both need to look at your marriage to see how much you both relate to one another as adults in an equal relationship and how much you are both involved in a struggle for control of the other and of family life. If your marriage is more of a battle for power than a co-operative of equals, then being depressed can be part of the struggle for power, a way of one person controlling the other and preventing any change. Terrible though depression is, at least you know where you are with it. Your depressed partner will not be out and about, doing things and meeting people in situations out of your control; your devoted partner will not leave you, ill and depressed, while you need looking after.

Sometimes, when I am talking with a married couple, I say, 'There is no one single thing that you can do which will suddenly stop you being depressed, so what I am going to ask you is a purely hypothetical question. I would like you to tell me what you would say if I said to you that if you and your wife/husband stay together she/he will go on being depressed and if you separate he/she will be well.' Not every 'well' partner says, 'We'd separate.' When I put this question to a woman whose husband was in the constant pain of a deep depression, she, without the slightest hesitation said, 'He'll stay with me.' A husband who had been telling me how much his wife's deep and lasting depression and massive anxiety terrified him, said, 'If someone in authority said she would get better if I left then logically – straight away – I'd say I'd go – but then I'd wake up the next night, and I'd know I wouldn't go.' At the end of our discussion he thanked me for giving him the opportunity to talk things over at such length – 'I've been asking the psychiatrist for ages if we could have some psychotherapy' – and two days later I had a letter from him to say that his wife would no longer be coming to see me.

In the course of my work I have met many people who are suffering from terrible disabilities – mentally handicapped people who know they are not as clever as most people, people whose brains and spines have been damaged beyond repair in accidents, people who are dying slowly of multiple sclerosis or cancer – and who have not despaired. They know the implications of their disability, but they are able, in a sense, to escape from the prison of their damaged body, to separate themselves from their physical pain, and so to be interested in life, to care for other people and to enjoy their company, to take an interest in many things, to enjoy wit and humour and to laugh. But in depression no such separation of the suffering body and the free mind is possible. Body and mind are imprisoned, and the pain and suffering cannot be transcended. This is why depression is such a terrible affliction, and why doing anything to keep a person in the prison of depression is the utmost cruelty.

All too often family and friends find it impossible to understand how great the suffering of the depressed person is. The writer William Styron, skilled as he was in describing the varieties of human experience, called the experience of depression 'indescribable'. He spoke of 'anxiety, agitation and unfocused dread', and 'panic and dislocation, and a sense that my thought processes were being engulfed by a toxic and unnameable tide that obliterated any enjoyable response to the living world'.[3]

As the depressed person suffers the relationships the person has with his family changes. Some families have always been indifferent, even rejecting, of the person, and all the depressed person's suffering does is to increase their lack of concern. Some families become extremely concerned about their depressed relative. They offer love, comfort and support, but retreat hurt and baffled when they encounter the impenetrable wall of depression's prison. Being good people, they feel guilty, and this leaves them open to being manipulated by the depressed person. He, as he experiences it, is fighting for his life, and, in the way that we all do when in great peril, he uses whatever comes to hand in order to save himself. He fears another onslaught of the unnameable terror, and, since this often comes following some untoward action by a person close to him, he warns his relatives, 'Do not do anything which would upset me.' So his family tiptoe around him, frightened that the least thing they might do or say will provoke an outburst, or a deeper depression, or even suicide. Thus the depressed person becomes very powerful.

Powerful people find it extremely difficult to give up their power because being powerful gives a sense of being safe. Moreover, it brings many rewards. It can mean that your nearest and dearest will refrain from giving you news which may worry you, or they do your burdensome shopping, or they do not expect you to spend time with people whom you do not like. Often it is the rewards which follow being depressed which keep the depressed person depressed. Give up being depressed and you have to face the world's troubles, shoulder the burdens of daily living, and cope with people, pleasant and unpleasant.

Whenever we persist in doing something which causes us pain, or we persist in remaining in a situation where we are unhappy, there is something in that behaviour or that situation which rewards us. Sometimes the reward is that we avoid something we do not wish to do; sometimes the reward is that by suffering we can assure ourselves that we are good. To give up the behaviour which causes us a pain or to move out of an unpleasant situation we have to be prepared to give up those rewards.

We often forget that what gives us pleasure can also give us pain.

At some point in my discussions with a couple where one partner was depressed I would ask each why he or she married the other. By then I had heard a great many complaints. Now I wanted to hear of the virtues that each found attractive in the other, and what do I find? That the virtues, seen as so attractive in one light, could be experienced as pain-inflicting attributes in another. They are the very attributes about which the greatest complaints were made. Chalky married Rachel because she was strong, realistic, practical and organised (as well as pretty), but when he was depressed and she was encouraging him to be out and about and not let things get him down, he felt she was unsympathetic. Jackie married Ron because he was so gentle and calm, and then, when she got anxious and needed to talk and rush about, he infuriated her because he said nothing. 'Ron never worries,' she said. Chalky could not see that Rachel was expressing her love and concern in the ways that she knew best, and Jackie could not see that Ron was a silent worrier.

Sometimes the 'well' partner, hating to see the changes that depression has wrought says, 'I want you to go back to what you were' – a wish impossible to fulfil, for none of us can go back to what we were. The only way out of depression is to change, and this sometimes means that your partner has to make changes in things that you value. Like many depressed people, Tony despised 'ordinariness', but he knew that his wife did too, and that she loved him and clung to him because she saw him as extraordinary, even though she found much of his extraordinary behaviour quite painful. Later, when Tony had decided that it was not worth spending his life locked in battle with his wife, he wrote the couplet,

If you hadn't loved my devils so
I might have sooner let them go.[4]

Sometimes we cannot bring ourselves to make any changes in our marriage because we cannot bear to admit that our marriage is not everything that we want it to be. Most of us enter into marriage with romantic ideas that mean living happily ever after, and, when this proves not to be the case, we can feel cheated and angry, but we may hang on to the marriage and try to keep it as it is in the desperate hope that one day all our romantic dreams will come true. The trouble is that men and women can have such different ideas of what is romantic. Men who dream of coming home to a woman who is a happy wife and mother find it hard to accept that a woman can feel that looking after a home and family is boring, frustrating and unfulfilling. For many women the most important way of expressing love is not in sexual intercourse but in all those delightful, romantic gestures that anyone who watches the advertisements on television or reads women's magazines and romantic novels must know.

Yet so many husbands fail to realise this. Kay used to described how she dreamed of how she, dressed in a beautiful gown, would enter a room where her husband was standing, waiting for her. As music filled the room he would take her in his arms, kiss her, and then they would dance, slowly, beautifully, and so romantically. Kay's husband was a fine man, but he had no idea of how to fulfil Kay's dream of romance.[5] Fay would tell me of her romantic dream. She would say, 'If only I didn't have to arrange all our outings. If only he'd come home one evening and say, "Go and get dressed. I've booked our theatre seats, and a table for supper afterwards."' Had such a thought crossed her husband's mind he would have dismissed it because, had he announced that he had arranged such an evening, Fay would then point out to him that she was tired, that she'd heard that play was dreadful, and didn't he remember that she was on a diet?

All these problems that I have mentioned, and many more, could be resolved, or at least minimised, through frank and open discussion. But unfortunately this is the one thing that none of you is any good at doing. You are all experts on Saying Nothing, Not Wanting to Upset Anyone, Keeping Things to Yourself, Feeling That He Should Know Without Me Telling Him, and so on. You are all experts on Not Talking.

Not talking

In her study of love in our society, Jill Tweedie wrote of the silences between mother and daughter and between husband and wife. When a girl is young, Jill argued,

Out of insecurity and a wish to protect, the mother does her assiduous best to crush her little woman's selfhood

and turn her into one in a safe line of female nobodies . . .
She knows everything and tells us nothing or, worse, she
pretends. In the name of her loyalty to her husband, our
father, in the name of our best interests, she will not
breathe a word of what her life has been. Carefully she
constructs a painting-by-numbers, helps our clumsy hands
to fill the colours in. Fall in love – pink and red. Marry –
shining white. Dear little babies – pink and blue. Happily
ever after – silver and gold. Does she believe these are the
proper colours? She blurred them herself, of course, and
got them wrong, but is she hoping that we will be luckier?
When she comes round, years later, to cry over our kitchen
table smeared with the food spat out by our own infants,
sobbing of our father, what he has done, how she has lived,
what she has to put up with, what she really wanted to be,
it is too late. Why didn't you tell me, mother? Why did you
lie and lie?

Parents have good reason to lie to their children, and
wives to husbands and husbands to wives. Jill went on,

If you are to reveal yourself, warts and all, to another
human being – and this is an essential part of growth, as
well as being necessary for mental health – self-
preservation demands that that person has no reason to
use your vulnerabilities against you. Any inequality
provides an ulterior motive to do just that. An 'inferior',
whether by class, caste, employment or simply in the
world's eyes at the time, might be a true friend and
confidant unto death but there are many reasons why he or
she should not be; and if, for instance, a livelihood is
dependent upon a 'superior', the motives for using that
friendship are heightened.
    Between 'superior' men and 'inferior' women, the
same distrust occurs, foundation for the battle between
the sexes. Many a woman does not receive the full
confidence of her husband because he knows, however
much that knowledge be concealed, that the relationship is
a dependent one and that if a crunch comes, her economic
survival may oblige her to use her knowledge against him.
For the same reason, women conceal things from their

husbands – there is too much at stake for them to afford such intimacies . . . In any unequal relationship, the two concerned must devote a precious amount of energy simply to jockeying for position and the relationship devolves from a frank exchange to a tiring and constricting conflict of strategies. It is not easy to be honest with an equal who has no reason to use your weaknesses. How much more difficult when the motive is there.[6]

Jill wrote that in 1979. Since then there has been endless talk about relationships between men and women and what goes on in families but, in essence, little has changed. Life does change, but in many cases all the change means is that old battles get fought in new guises. What has not changed is that each us has to maintain ourselves as a person, and so we fear anyone who has the power to threaten our sense of being a person. My father was frightened of my mother because if she turned on him – or on anyone – she was utterly ruthless in what she would say and sometimes what she would do. When I look back over my life I can see how my life would have been markedly different had I stood up to my mother instead of retreating into silence, but then I remember how frightened I was of her. It seemed to me then that she held my existence in her hands and she could crush it if she wished. I have recognised that kind of fear in my clients when they were quite unable to defend themselves against their parents or their partner. I know from my own experience that it is not possible to give up such fear until your own self-confidence grows, and that self-confidence will not grow until such fear is relinquished. So it has to be a gradual process, little steps of increasing courage. Decrease the fear and the self-confidence grows: increase self-confidence and the fear decreases.

The more you see yourself as weak, bad, evil, unaccept-able to yourself and to other people, the less you can confide in anyone who you fear might want to use your confidences against you. No wonder George Brown in his survey of depressed women found that a significant factor in their lives was the lack of a 'confiding relationship'.[7] It was not just that they had no one who would listen; it was that they had no one they could trust enough to confide in.

Not Talking is an issue which all family members need to address. Just how you can do this, or anything else to help the depressed person, is not always easy.

What can I do to help?

1. Being there

Andrew Solomon wrote, 'So many people have asked me what to do for depressed friends and relatives, and my answer is actually simple: blunt their isolation. Do it with cups of tea or long walks or by sitting in a room nearby and staying silent or in whatever way suits the circumstances, but do that. And do it willingly.'[8] Gwyneth Lewis wrote, 'Depressed people are a pain, however much you love them. The best thing you can do is keep them company, try to keep cheerful yourself, and allow the patient be unwell for as long as it takes. I can't praise enough how Leighton supported me. He fed me, never reproached me for being ill, and, most importantly, never told me to get a grip.'[9]

It can be very difficult just to be there. Depressed people are not inclined to talk. Many people – including many therapists – find it very difficult to sit in silence with another person. Social chat about trivial subjects – the weather, football, television – often comes from a mutual but unspoken agreement to cover one another's fear of each other. If the other person is silent we can worry about what the person is thinking, most particularly what is he thinking about us. We wonder how we should sit and where we should look, whether to stare expectantly at the person or to gaze out the window and get lost in our own thoughts. It takes self-confidence just to sit quietly, accepting that the person does not wish to talk, and not knowing whether being there is a comfort to the other person.

Sometimes the depressed person is reassured just by having another person in the next room or working beside him, but sometimes the fact that the other person is working inhibits the depressed person even more. A client once told me about her visits to her psychiatrist, an important professor. Whenever she entered his office she was too shy and nervous to speak and would sit there trembling. The professor meant to be kind but he had no idea how to sit in silence, so he would say to her, 'I'm just going to sign these letters. You let me know when you're ready to speak.' He would soon be engrossed in his work, and so, even when she desperately wanted to tell him something, she remained silent because she did not want to interrupt his work.

You may try to greet the depressed person with a hug only to get a very chilly response. We all know that hugs are good for us, but you will soon discover that a depressed person does not always appreciate a hug or even a hand clasp or a gentle pat. Offered these, the person may sit there as unresponsive as a stone or even shrink away. Because the comfort of a hug does not penetrate the prison walls of depression the depressed person may feel nothing that requires a response. When a depressed person shrinks away from your touch it does not mean that he is rejecting you. Rather he is protecting you from the foul, destructive evil which he believes is the essence of his being and which he believes could injure you. It is best to respect the distance which the person wishes to maintain and show your love through your smiles and your voice.

Sometimes, when sitting with a depressed person you become aware that, although the person is slumped and silent in an attitude of despair, he is actually giving off wave after wave of silent rage. He may be directing the rage solely at himself or at the world at large, but it is hard not to feel that this rage is directed solely and specifically at you. We can usually endure bad temper from our loved ones if angry scenes are balanced with loving ones, but the depressed person is cut off from all other people. It is not just that his love cannot reach other people but that he does not actually feel any love for anyone. It is not that he has stopped loving others, just that the feeling of love is not available to him. As a result, if you are looking after a depressed person you can soon start to feel depleted of loving kindness, and discover in yourself an anger and impatience that you might never have felt before.

Staying with a depressed person is demanding and draining, and so it is imperative that you look after yourself, taking breaks, leaving the situation altogether and doing something you enjoy, something that help refill your well of human kindness and affection. You may feel that you ought not do this, but you must remember that if you do not look after yourself you will become unable to look after anyone else. Gwyneth Lewis advised, 'The best you can do is to allow someone else to go through the experience in the easiest way possible. Feed them, by all means, field their telephone calls, but don't follow them. You have to allow other people their pain. If you don't, you risk losing everything for absolutely nothing because anything you can do from outside will never work. You could end up throwing your life away, and your relative or partner, at the end of it, will still be ill: a double defeat. At least, if you look after yourself, you have a chance of living your own life and are much more likely to be of help to your loved one.'[10]

In caring for a depressed person you make the situation harder for yourself if, as in nursing a physically ill person, you look for daily signs of progress. The language of sickness and health does not reflect what actually happens in depression. A depressed person does not fall ill and then gradually get better. A person becomes depressed and remains so for a period of time. Some days the person may seem more cheerful or spend an hour or so doing something which suggests that he is getting back to normal, and then, in the blink of an eye, he is deeply depressed again. If you say to him, 'You did that yesterday. Why can't you do it today,' his only answer will be, 'I can't.' Depressed people use the language of sickness and health when they are with someone who sees depression as an illness, but they find what best describes what they are experiencing is that of a prisoner serving an indeterminate sentence. They say that they feel that 'it', the experience of depression, will never come to an end, and, when the experience actually does come to an end, they talk in terms of being a prisoner emerging from the darkness into the light. In reassuring a depressed person, do not say, 'I know that you're going to get better,' but instead say, 'I know that this bad experience will come to an end and you will be all right. Everything passes, nothing lasts forever.'

2. Accept that the person is depressed

People become depressed when they turn against themselves, hate themselves and blame themselves for the disaster that has befallen them. To help someone bring their experience of depression to an end you need to help them regain their sense of self-worth. You need to show through every word and deed that you value and accept that person.

Valuing and accepting a person means valuing and accepting everything about that person, even those parts of the person that you may deplore. You know quite well that if someone says to you, 'Of course I love you darling, but I wish you wouldn't . . .'. Whatever follows that 'wouldn't' shows that that person does not value and accept you completely. They are not prepared to take your good with your bad, your loving heart and your curious idiosyncrasies and personal habits. They see something wrong and unacceptable in you.

Thus, if you say to a depressed person, 'I value and accept you but you've got to get rid of that depression,' you are showing that you do not value and accept that person as he is. You will accept him fully only if he is happy. You do not accept that depressed is what he is.

Always remember that words are cheap. If a therapist tells a client that she accepts and values him, the client is likely to reply, 'You're paid to say that.' When children are small they accept praise from their parents, but they rapidly get to an age when praise from parents is dismissed with, 'They would say that.' So much for all the 'love-you-darlings' that nowadays parents are supposed to shower on their children.

When we do value and accept someone we treat that person as an equal. We do not look down on that person and patronise him either by demonstrating our superiority of being mentally healthy, or by pitying him for his inferiority as shown by his mental illness. Thus, when the depressed person talks to us we listen as an equal.

3. Depression equals difficult

Living with a depressed person is difficult, but even more so
when there are children in the household. Psychiatrists who
have taken no time to study what actually goes on in families
have concluded that, if the child of a depressed parent
becomes depressed, the child must have inherited a depression gene from the parent. Such a psychiatrist takes no
account of how children can interpret their parent's
behaviour in such a way that these interpretations years
later lead the child, now adult, into depression.

Gwyneth Lewis's account of one part of her family life
especially fascinated me because we both had mothers who,
after an outburst of anger, would retire to their bedroom, in
Mrs Lewis's case, for days, or, in my mother's case, for weeks.
She wrote,

> After the initial row and violent displays of frustration,
> Mam would crash out, retire to her bed for three days or so
> before gradually re-emerging to take meals with us and
> gradually slip back into family life. During this time we
> tiptoed around the house, whispered behind closed doors
> and generally put our own lives on hold until Mam was
> back in the land of the living. We'd watch television with
> the volume turned right down so as not to wake her. We'd
> jump if we heard her stirring upstairs or the bedroom door
> opening. We had no way of knowing what would happen
> next – whether we'd have to go through another round of
> bitter recriminations or whether we'd see her wandering
> around the house like a ghost. I don't know which was the
> more upsetting. I was always relieved when she went back
> to bed.[11]

Like my father, Mr Lewis did his best to deal with
his difficult wife and his two young daughters. However,
what Gwyneth learnt from her mother's behaviour was very
different from what I learnt from mine.

I learned to fear my mother even more, and I withdrew
further and further from her, with the result that, even when
she was pleasant and kind to me, I would respond very warily
with, metaphorically, an open door behind me through which
I could dash if suddenly she turned on me. I think that my

fear/run away response came from my earliest childhood when, as I know from what my sister has told me, my mother chastised me physically. A child's only protection from an adult's assault is to run away.

Gwyneth Lewis felt close to her mother, but 'it was usually me who set off my mother's rage and her plunge into despair.'[12] She wrote,

> One of the most heartbreaking things about depression is that, however much you love someone and whatever you're willing to do for them, you still can't save them. I know because I tried for decades. I thought that if I were a better daughter, my mother wouldn't fall into her pit of depression. This seems naïve now but it is still a deeply held belief of mine. It has made me do some very uncharacteristic things which didn't suit me, including writing a doctorate. I felt that if I dragged enough prizes back to our cave that she would be satisfied and not need to go through that hateful cycle again. In the end, my fantasy of rescuing my mother became a serious liability. It only ever did me harm and never did her any good.[13]

So, from our different interpretations of our mother's behaviour, I became irrevocably estranged from my mother, and Gwyneth Lewis, having become an expert in blaming herself, became depressed. However, as she said,

> There is another way of doing it though. The depressed person should be allowed all the space in the world and a safe place in which to go through the worst of their suffering. But they shouldn't take over the whole house any more than an incandescent two-year-old should be allowed to dictate to the rest of the family. Children, especially, should be encouraged to carry on as usual, told not to feel guilty about their mother or their father being ill and that, in fact, the best thing they can do to help is to remain cheerful themselves. I can't stress that enough. If depression is not to do a family more damage than it already does, the other members must be given permission to carry on with their own lives. They need to identify a cut-off point to enable themselves to maintain emotional

autonomy. This doesn't mean being unsympathetic or harsh to the patient but it does mean not giving your own life as a hostage to hell.[14]

Difficult or not, the depressed person is miserable. Do not try to cheer up the depressed person in the way that you would try to cheer up an unhappy person. When we are unhappy, being told that we should count our blessings can occasionally help. Concentrating on what advantages we have or comparing the disasters we have suffered with those of people in more tragic circumstances can help us get our ideas back into proportion. However, when we are depressed, being reminded of other people's suffering only serves to increase our self-hatred. We feel even more guilty because we are depressed. Moreover, when we are depressed we are desperately trying to survive *as a person*. In a situation where we are fighting to preserve ourselves *physically* we can still be concerned about others, but when we are fighting to preserve ourselves as a person we are utterly, utterly selfish. Other people's suffering means nothing to us.

Told of other people's suffering the depressed person is unlikely to say, 'I'll go and help them.' Instead he says, 'That bad news has upset me terribly. It makes me feel worse. I feel so guilty because I'm in this state.' Often the depressed person is quite unaware of the plight of those close to him. The selfishness shown by a depressed person can be to an onlooker quite breathtakingly selfish and also extremely irritating.

If you can understand why the depressed person is so selfish you are in a better position to accept what they do and to listen without being critically rejecting. You need to remember all the time that the person is in terror that he is about to shatter, crumble, even disappear, that the universe is falling apart around him, and that all that ever existed will disappear. This is the greatest fear of all. Depression is a defence against this fear, but it is not a complete defence. The fear threatens the defence all the time and sometimes it succeeds in breaking through. We all feel such fear whenever we discover that there is a serious discrepancy between what we thought our life was and what it actually is and we lack the self-confidence to deal with this situation.

When we see someone suffering we want to do what we can immediately to end their suffering. An unhappy person, if not lost in the depths of grief, can usually consider accepting advice, but a depressed person is likely either to ignore completely any helpful suggestions or to carry out what you suggest only to discover that your advice was wrong, and that you were at fault for offering it.

Suppose, for instance, you discover that the depressed person wakes early but does not get out of bed until noon. You suggest that he would feel much better if he leapt out of bed and got dressed the moment he woke, and not lie in bed dwelling on his misery. In saying this you mean well, but you do not know how, as he wakes, he is gripped by a nameless dread. He is too terrified to put foot to floor. He does not explain this to you because he expects that if he did you would despise him. Hence he might ignore your advice completely, or, to please you or perhaps to shut you up, he follows it just once, but in his rush to the bathroom and blinded by terror, he slips on the bathroom floor and injures himself. This might be entirely accidental, or it might be an example of the popular family game 'See What You Made Me Do, Ma' (i.e. by having an accident the child proves the parents to be wrong), or it might be one of those events where the person, hating himself and believing that he deserves to be punished, injures himself. Whether we are depressed or not, if we dislike ourselves, we do not take care of ourselves, and we are inclined to punish ourselves for our wickedness, all of which does not exclude the possibility of, at the same time, punishing the people who persecute us. There is more to being accident-prone than mere carelessness.

More frequently the depressed person, to save himself the trouble of actually showing you that your advice will not work, counters every piece of advice with, 'Yes, that sounds like a good idea, but . . .,' and produces a reason why your advice will not work. It is very easy to get involved in the 'Yes, but . . .' game, but it is an utterly futile exercise. If you find yourself caught in a 'Yes, but . . .' game start talking about something else.

4. Discussing the issues
As much as you want to help the depressed person, it is better to sit quietly with the person and, when he wants to talk, listen. Often what the person needs is to tell his story in his own way and in his own time. The listener does great service just by listening.

When we tell our story to an interested listener we feel that our existence is confirmed. We all need to feel that someone has acknowledged our existence and given it importance. This is why most people are so keen to tell their story to a journalist, even though the media can be far from kind to those people whose stories are featured.

Moreover, in telling our story, we have to turn our confusion of thoughts and feelings into sentences which the other person can understand. Thus we gain clarity. We feel more in control of our life. We take a step back and look at our life and, in doing so, we see anomalies which need to be resolved and conclusions which we have drawn and which now need to be changed. Our listener has held up a mirror to us and we can see ourselves more clearly.

If the depressed person has come to trust you, if he knows that you do not see him as being mad and bad and therefore will not reject him, eventually he will feel able to discuss certain issues with you.

The most fruitful kind of discussion is where the two participants consider alternative interpretations of the issues. You might have a conversation about your favourite books, or compare experiences of, say, your first kiss or the schools you went to, or your opinions about organic foods, but, whatever, you are comparing your contrasting views. When you present your views you do so, not in terms of how you are right and the depressed person is wrong, but in terms of comparing your interpretation, not just with that of the depressed person, but with that of other people you know. Through such a discussion it is possible to see how different interpretations led to different outcomes, and so the discussion becomes concerned with a comparison of desirable and undesirable outcomes. Of course, what is desirable to you might not be desirable to the other person, but this is just another example of how no two people ever see anything in exactly the same way.

This kind of discussion can help the person to understand that, while we control very little of what happens to us, we always have a choice of how we interpret what happens to us. Every interpretation has an outcome. Change your interpretation, and so change the outcome.

5. Practical help
The key to the prison of depression is coming to believe that you are valuable and acceptable. Changing how we feel about ourselves is a major change because how we feel about ourselves is central to our whole way of thinking and acting. Every decision we make depends on how we feel about ourselves. Depressed people who manage to find the key to their prison usually do so by creeping up on it, making little changes day by day. First they decide that, instead of refusing to look after themselves in any way at all, they will do some small thing for themselves. It might be no more than going for a walk or swim each day, or joining a yoga class, or talking to their doctor about the possibility of seeing a counsellor.

Often the depressed person needs some practical help to achieve such small steps, perhaps someone to mind the children or to provide transport. A walk, a swim, or joining a yoga class is much more enjoyable in the company of a friend.

These offers of help should not be presented to the depressed person as instructions, or even suggestions, as to what the person ought to do. Rather they should be offers of help, presented tentatively, after the person has said that he is thinking seriously of trying something new. Do not be wildly enthusiastic in case things go wrong, and when they go well do not say, 'I told you so.'

6. Allow the person to change
Families can stop a family member from changing, even when that person needs very much to change.

A family can provide stability in an ever-changing world. This is the blessing of families, but it is also their curse, because, if the family is to remain stable, its members must not change. However, individuals are always changing because every experience changes us. Thus, in a family there can be great tension between those family members who are changing quite markedly and those members who want everything to remain the same. No matter that a member is ill from being overweight, or unhappily married, or deeply depressed, other family members can refuse to let that person change. They visit the one who is dieting and arrive with cream cakes and the words, 'I made this just for you,' they talk about the importance of the sanctity of marriage to the one in wedded misery, and make the depressed person feel guilty for trying to become more self-confident.

There is more to this than simply preserving the stability of the family. Family members can oppose change because they themselves do not want to change. They do not want to make the effort to see another family member differently. Moreover, they may get some advantage from the person remaining the same. A woman may want her sister to continue being 'the fat one' so she can still pride herself on her slim figure. A man may feel unable to escape from his own unhappy marriage and so not want to see his cousin escape a similar misery. A husband may not want his depressed, docile wife to stand up for herself. A mother may want her daughter to stay with her at home and not take an interesting job overseas. The whole family may want to continue dumping their responsibilities on to one long-suffering member. Thus subtly or not so subtly they can try to undermine the depressed person's attempts to change.

This is one of the major limitations of therapy. As much as the client talks about his family, the therapist cannot possibly know all that goes on in the family. Only a family member or a friend who knows the family well can see how certain family members are continuing to undermine the depressed person's self-confidence and preventing that person from changing. It may be possible for you, as a concerned onlooker, to discuss these matters with the depressed person when he makes his first tentative steps towards change.

In all your interactions with the depressed person, whether in casual chat or deep conversation, do not use the language of sickness and health. The person is not ill but going through that experience which most people encountered at some period in their lives, sometimes very briefly, sometimes for lengthy periods. Terrible though it is, it is an experience from which great wisdom can come. Show in your every word and deed that you know that the person will get through this difficult time and will emerge from the darkness stronger and wiser.

Chapter 8

SUPPOSE I DID WANT TO LEAVE THE PRISON, WHAT SHOULD I DO?

---

1. Don't play the 'Yes, but . . .' game

For as long as you have been depressed, and probably for longer, you have been an expert in playing this game. This is how it goes:

You, to friend: 'I don't know what's wrong with me. I'm always tired, even when I wake up in the morning. I just drag myself through the day. I feel drained.'

Friend to you: 'Isn't it time you had your holidays? If you have a break right away from work you'd feel a lot better. Get away, have some sunshine and do nothing for a while.'

You to friend: 'Yes, you're right, I do need a holiday. But I can't get away. The new manager's only been with us a few weeks and he doesn't know his way around the place yet. He's always coming to me to ask how we do this and how we do that. And our secretary's off sick – usual vague sicknote from the doctor. Goodness only knows when she'll be back. And my eldest has got his finals coming up soon. I know he's not at home, but he rings us every week and I know he likes to know we're there, just in case something happens. Kids are like that, you know.'

Sometimes you play the 'Yes, but . . .' game silently. You to doctor: 'I've been feeling down, doctor, ever since my mother died. I know that's a year ago and I should be over it by now. I try to pull myself together but it's so hard. I dread waking up in the morning, and I'm not sleeping. I go off all right, in fact I can't wait to get to bed, but then

I have terrible dreams and I wake up and lie awake for hours.'

Doctor to you: 'Well, you have had quite a few worries over the past couple of years, haven't you? And it takes a long while to get over losing someone close to you. I'll give you something to make you feel a lot better. They take about a week or ten days to start working, but you'll soon find you're your old self again. And something to help you sleep.'

You to doctor: 'Thank you doctor.'

You to self, silently, 'The last time he gave me something to make me better I came out in a terrible rash. He said the rash had nothing to do with what he gave me, but I don't think he was telling me the truth. And those sleeping pills, they just make me feel dopey the next morning.'

Sometimes, when you play the 'Yes, but . . .' game, the 'but . . .' is not even consciously thought, since it is one of those Eternal Truths on which you have built your life. You to husband: 'Just look at the mess those kids have left. Clothes and dirty dishes all over the place. They think I've got nothing to do except pick up after them.' Husband to you: 'Leave it. They're old enough to clean up their own rooms now. If they don't they can just live in their own mess. You do too much for them, making their beds, doing all their washing and ironing. You slave after them and they just don't appreciate it. They're nearly grown up. It's time they learned to look after themselves.'

You to husband: 'You're just as bad as them. That's where they get it from. You just drop your clothes where you take them off . . .', and so on with the usual few words of domestic bliss. This is a diversionary tactic on your part so you do not have to present your 'but . . .' or even think it. For your unspoken 'but . . .' is your Eternal Truth that 'If I am not needed I cease to exist. I must do things for my family so they will go on needing me. If I make my children keep their rooms tidy they will go away and leave me and I shall be alone forever.' You do not have to say this to yourself. You just know it.

We all play the 'Yes, but . . .' game when someone foists advice on us that we do not want. Sometimes we point out how the advice is unacceptable, and sometimes we answer politely and express our distrust and rejection of the advice silently to ourselves, and sometimes we just change the subject of the conversation without even noting consciously that the advice runs counter to our Eternal Truths. We do all these things as such ordinary and regular activities in our conversations that we do not take special note of our doing so. However, here I am asking you, as the first step in finding your way out of the prison, to become aware of when you play the 'Yes, but . . .' game. (One popular form of the 'Yes, but . . .' is 'Yes, I'm depressed, but I don't want anyone to know.' As long as you are a closet depressive, hiding your state from yourself and the rest of the world, you can never find your way out of the prison.)

Some years ago I was introduced to Richard, a computer expert who had been unemployed for several years. Though we met only socially I gradually came to see how Richard had imprisoned himself with a series of 'Yes, but . . .'s. His friends would suggest he apply for this or that job. He would say yes, and then would come the buts. He wouldn't work for that firm, it had a bad reputation, or for another firm, he didn't like the boss. He was too skilled for that job, it was beneath him, the money wasn't good enough and if he took it he'd lose his housing benefit. Told of a well-paid job in Saudi Arabia, he explained that he couldn't leave his children who lived with his ex-wife, and he couldn't stand hot weather. He couldn't re-train, he was a computer man. When he talked of being depressed a friend recommended my books, but he didn't read books. Advised to go into therapy, he said that his ex-wife reckoned she'd been helped by therapy but he couldn't see any improvement in her, and anyway her therapy was just two women talking together and complaining about him. He thought therapy was a big con and he wasn't going to waste his time.

Frustrated by this impenetrable wall of buts his friends stopped offering advice and grew bored with his complaints about being jobless and miserable. His social life diminished, but, instead of understanding why and remedying the situation, his response to anyone who told him to get out more was another 'Yes, but . . .' – his friends were busy because they had jobs, he couldn't afford the fares, being unemployed he had nothing to say to people, and so on.

When Richard explained his 'buts' to his would-be helpers he spoke courteously but there was an undercurrent of intense anger. He was frustrated at every turn, and frustration breeds anger. Certainly the job situation was not good, but most of his frustrations arose not from his situation but from himself. He was angry with himself but he could not recognise this. He saw himself as being angry with his domineering father and all the father-figures who had plagued him in his career. His anger frightened him, and, as he was a man who did not introspect, he had difficulty in distinguishing feelings of anger from feelings of fear. He was an extravert, a people person, needing people, and frightened of being alone. Rather than recognise that the source of his fear was inside himself, arising from his way of interpreting himself and his world, he located it in people and places outside himself, and so he became too frightened to venture further afield than a mile or two from his home. A Berlin Wall built on the circumference of the circle around his home could not have imprisoned him as effectively as his own 'Yes, but . . .'s.

When you catch yourself playing the 'Yes, but . . .' game, ask yourself why you are doing it. Are you rejecting advice because it is of that useless and stupid 'Pull yourself together' kind or are you rejecting the ideas in the advice because such ideas threaten the edifice you have so carefully built around you? Have you become so clever at playing the 'Yes, but . . .' game that you play it with yourself and thus stop yourself from doing anything new? When you try something new, like going to a yoga class or taking extra vitamins, and you do not feel better *immediately*, do you say to yourself, 'That's no good' and cease your efforts? Have you made a rule of your life the well known precept 'If at first you don't succeed, give up'?

One reason we all play the 'Yes, but . . .' game is that it protects us from having to recognise and to think about new ideas. New ideas are always upsetting. They suggest that we might be wrong. They make the world a changing, uncertain place instead of being anchored on our Eternal Truths. New ideas are dangerous. That is why the peddlers of new ideas are often silenced by being sent to jail or murdered, and why newspapers are closed and books burnt. The 'Yes, but . . .' game is your form of censorship, and you use it all the time, especially when you come looking for help to end your pain.

'Please,' you say, each in your own way, 'take the pain away. Give me the magic pill or wave the magic wand or utter the magic formula or give the magic explanation and take the pain away, but don't change me.'

Some professional helpers actually accept this demand and try to meet it. They may give you pills which dull the pain or they may give you an explanation which you can use as an excuse for your depression. ('My brain has a chemical imbalance', or, 'Depression runs in our family. It's genetic.') The professional helper tells you, you are as you are because you had a difficult childhood, and he fails to make clear to you that what matters is not what our parents did to us but how we interpret what our parents did to us. So you blame your parents for your misery and refuse to recognise that, even though your parents' treatment of you led you to conclude that you were bad and unacceptable, you are free to change that assessment of yourself if you wish. However, eagerly though you might seize the pills or the excuse, you soon find that, though the pain may be dulled and you move more freely, the depression still lurks in a dark corner, like a sleeping tiger, and as much as you try to excuse your bad behaviour the memories of your childhood become even more painful.

There is no magic that will take away the pain and leave you to live your life *as you are*. You are a human being like the rest of us, and one of the facts of being a human being is that our actions have consequences and *we cannot escape the consequences*. (We may not be punished for our sins but we are certainly punished by them.) If you believe that you are essentially bad, evil, unacceptable to yourself and other people, if you fear other people, if your philosophy of life makes you fearful and pessimistic, if you are unreconciled to your past and you fear the future, if you believe that anger is bad and if you never forgive, then such beliefs and the actions that follow such beliefs will cause you pain. The only way to stop the pain is to change your beliefs. The only way to stop the pain is for you to change.

One way or another, this is what I would say to my clients the first time they meet me. Some clients leave and do not return but others stay and say, 'Okay, I accept I've got to change. But promise me that when I've changed I'll have no more problems and that I'll be happy.'

This request is based on two assumptions, namely:

1. Anyone who hasn't got my problems has no problems at all (therefore when my present problems disappear I shall have no problems).
2. Happiness is total certainty (therefore unless I know exactly what is going to happen I cannot be happy).

Both these assumptions are wrong. All human beings, rich and poor, young and old, wise and foolish, have problems and difficulties. As much as we might want to be secure and to be able to plan our future and see our plans come to fruition, no such security is possible since we are all members of a world-wide community and we are affected by matters far beyond our control. In 1980 in Lincolnshire the RAF bases were being closed and the Vulcan bombers which, carrying nuclear warheads, had patrolled the skies were being broken up for scrap. No one would have predicted that in 1982 the Vulcans would have been bombing the airstrip on the Falkland Islands. I would not have predicted that, instead of trying to help Fay deal with the uncertainties of Jack leaving the Air Force, I would be trying to help her deal with her fears that he would be sent to the South Atlantic. Twenty years later, on September 10, 2001, no one would have predicted that the next day the mighty World Trade Centre in New York would be a pile of rubble. Not even the terrorists themselves expected that.

So when my client said, 'I'm prepared to change provided you tell me beforehand exactly what will happen when I change,' I could only explain that I, being a mere human being, could not predict the future. Change creates possibilities, and every possibility more possibilities. Change is a journey into completely new territory. I cannot show you the way. I can only go with you, making my own discoveries as we go along.

Some clients were prepared to take this chance of risking change without guarantees. I guess if you have got this far through this book you are prepared to risk some changes. So we will proceed.

Having decided to give up playing the 'Yes, but ...' game, you need now to look at what you habitually do when you feel you are in danger. Now when any of us are threatened there are only two things we can do. We can stay and fight or we can run away. Sometimes we act precipitately and sometimes we stay to assess what is the wisest thing to do. If our house catches fire, should we stay and fight the fire, or should we rush out of the house? When our boss criticises our work, should we argue with him or be silent? Most people are quite flexible about when they fight and when they take flight, but some habitually do one or the other. Some people will never argue over anything. At the hint of a confrontation, they are off. Now, in the process of change, of finding your way out of the prison, you will come across many new ideas and be offered the chance of having new experiences. What is your usual reaction to what you see as the danger of something new? Do you take off like a startled hare, fleeing to something that you know is safe, or do you dig yourself even deeper into your entrenched position and fight off all change from there?

Try to work out which is your habitual response to change which you see as dangerous, so that, as you dare to explore, you do not suddenly find yourself running away to the safety of the old ways, or resisting the new ideas with old prejudices. If flight is your preferred mode of dealing with danger then you probably believe that self-inspection is dangerous and you say things like, 'I think I inspect myself too much.' The fighter from entrenched positions would never say this, since you inspect yourself frequently. Trouble is, you always find the same things. You say, 'I know what I am like. I like to keep myself controlled and orderly – I can't change.' Experiment with a new way of thinking.

New ideas and new experiences are not dangerous. They are *interesting*, *exciting*, *life-enhancing*, *good fun*, and *chal-*

lenges to be mastered. No fight, no flight. Just challenge and mastery.

Lao Tsu,[1] whose wisdom is as pertinent today as it was two and a half thousand years ago, spoke of the sage, the person who lives wisely and harmoniously. Where problems are concerned, he said,

> Because a sage always confronts difficulties
> He never experiences them.

The way out of the prison of depression is the way of learning how to live wisely and harmoniously. Such wisdom has always been known, but each of us must rediscover it for ourselves. All that I have put in this book has always been known, but what I have said strives to be *wisdom* and not just intellectual knowledge. I had to discover it myself and to know that I knew it. In writing this book I was trying to interpret and present it in a form which I hoped readers would understand and find useful. At some stage, my interpretation will be out of date. Other people will have to refashion and re-present for another society and a different time what human beings have always known about how to leave, and to stay out of, the prison of depression. When Vicky Rippere looked back over what has been written about depression since the sixteenth century she found that it is only quite recently that depression has been thought of as an illness. Instead, depression, or melancholia, has always been thought of as a lack of wisdom in living and a lack of self-knowledge. Over the centuries the cures for depression have always been the same. Vicky summarised them as,

> The basic notion of circumspect, temperate living, based on knowledge of one's own individual and constitutional susceptibilities, the focus on enhancing efficient biological functioning through attention to diet, sleep and exercise, the strategy of deliberately avoiding known physiological and psychological precipitants, the notion of the individual as a member of a supportive social network, the practice of systematically preparing to face adversity, and, finally, the concept of personal responsibility and initiative in choosing to live with care.[2]

Discovering how these ideas apply to you and how you can use these ideas is the way out of the prison. There is no magic key that unlocks the door. The door is always open, could you but see it. So to find the open door you have to set out on a journey. It will not be an easy journey. It will be rough going in some places, and sometimes you might despair of ever finding your way, but if you persevere you will reach your destination and recognise it when you are there. You may fear to start on a journey of unknown length to an unknown destination, but have courage. As Lao Tsu said,

A journey of a thousand miles starts under one's feet.

2. Treat yourself kindly

This is the hardest change to make. If you can manage this, the rest is easy.

Treating yourself kindly means looking after yourself. Yet this is the one thing you will not do. If you were physically ill, and not depressed at the same time, you would look after yourself. You would make sure that you did all the right things to get better. But here you are, enduring one of the most punishing experiences a body can take, and you do nothing to help your body to cope. Worse than that, you do the opposite. Instead of resting, you push yourself to do more and more. When you do lie down to rest, instead of deliberately thinking of pleasant things or indulging in a delightful fantasy, you lie there thinking horrible things and imagining the worst. Instead of making sure that, even though you are not hungry, you eat nourishing and attractive food, you starve yourself, or else gorge yourself on cakes and sweets and then, instead of enjoying the pleasant flavours and then feeling pleasantly replete, you feel guilty and hate yourself for being so greedy and uncontrolled. If you were tired and overworked, and not depressed at the same time, you would make sure that you took the time to relax, to do something pleasant and entertaining, to have a holiday. Instead, you refuse to allow yourself to relax, to take time off and do something pleasant and, if you do find yourself doing something pleasant and relaxing, you make sure you do not enjoy it. If you were tired, ill, and overworked, or even just living a normal life, and at the same time you were not depressed, you would look after yourself.

Or would you?

Perhaps when you were not depressed you did sometimes cosset yourself, but most of the depressed people I have known have never been in the habit of looking after themselves, and treating themselves kindly. They feel they must do everything the hard way, and every present they buy themselves and every pleasure taken must be paid for by extra hard work, or by some penance, or by giving something to someone else. If they have a bad cold, they struggle to work rather than staying in bed. They ignore all the signals that the body gives to show that something is amiss and they keep on going until one day they collapse with a burst ulcer or a uterine haemorrhage. Many women who get depressed have struggled on, refusing to seek treatment for menstrual disorders, yet every woman knows how wearying and debilitating menstrual pain is. (Yes, I know there are many male doctors who do not understand this and who trivialise or refuse to treat such disorders, so if your doctor is like this, either educate him or go to a woman doctor.)[3] All this neglect of your body and the effort to consider everybody else before yourself stems from the way you see yourself as essentially bad, and therefore you must always strive to be good, never daring to rest and take things easy.

But being depressed is a profound emotional experience, and all emotional experiences, whether pleasant or unpleasant, happy or unhappy, are accompanied by physiological changes. When we have a profound emotional experience, we then need a period of quiet to recover. When you are laughing, you can feel the changes going on in your body, and, pleasant though these changes are, you finally have to stop laughing and let your breathing and your heart rate go back to normal. To be angry or frightened means having strong physiological changes taking place in your body, and so if these emotions go on and on, as they do in depression, then further physiological changes will take place and come into consciousness as tremors, headaches, stomach pains, constipation and those sorts of strange, unpleasant feelings which, if you are so minded, you become convinced are heralding a brain tumour or a heart attack or a lethal cancer. Such pessimistic interpretations of the symptoms of tension simply make you more tense, thus producing more tension and more symptoms. Great and prolonged tension makes anyone's body more vulnerable to the various viruses that plague us, so it is no wonder that depressed people are more likely to pick up colds and influenza and other such diseases than are people who are not depressed. The wear and tear on the body of being depressed is very great, and so, to get out of the prison of depression, you must cherish your body and treat it kindly.

When you were not depressed you probably had some hobbies, sports or interests which you quite enjoyed but now you are depressed you will not do anything that might give you the slightest smidgen of pleasure. Since nothing holds any interest or meaning for you, you will not attempt anything from which the smallest enjoyment might come. So when someone says, 'How about coming for a walk? It's a beautiful day,' you say, 'Yes, but I know I won't enjoy it. And walking could bring on that pain in my chest. If the neighbours see me out walking they'll say, "Well, there is nothing wrong with him. Why isn't he back at work?"' So you stay inside and turn your face to the wall, and that chance vision of beauty which might have lifted your heart and given you courage goes unseen, that blessed tiredness which follows physical effort is not experienced, and that chance encounter where you felt the wisdom and love of another person is missed. And all because you will not give yourself pleasure and open yourself to the possibility of new experiences.

Mark told me about one chance encounter he had had which proved to be a happy one. I had first met Mark when he was recovering in hospital after taking an overdose. He had not lived in Lincoln for very long and knew few people, so I suggested to him that he should attend a day centre run by the Social Services. Instead of saying something like 'Yes, I know that would be a good idea, but being with all those people would make my headaches worse/I'm too frightened to go on a bus and I can't expect my wife to take more time

off work to take me/I'd meet other depressed people there
and that would make me feel worse', etc., etc., Mark went
along like, as he said, an obedient schoolboy doing a lesson
which he disliked but which he knew he had to do to pass an
exam. However, the dull, unpleasant lesson turned into
something else. At the centre he had met a voluntary worker,
John, who was preparing to enter the ministry of the Anglican Church, and in conversation with John, Mark was able
to discuss his search for meaning in his life and his fear of
death. John also introduced Mark to his church's Fellowship
group, where Mark felt welcomed and at home. When Mark
came to see me to tell me all this, he had not undergone a
sudden conversion and all his depression disappeared. He
was still a troubled young man, plagued by headaches and
stomach pains, but what he had gained was a measure of
trust which enabled him to say, 'I know I will get better one
day – perhaps not for months, or years, perhaps never
altogether, but I'll be all right.'

Perhaps part of your refusal to treat yourself kindly lies
in your belief, acquired when you were a child and at the
receiving end of activities of parents who held this belief,
that if you take notice of a child and give him things he will
be spoilt. This word 'spoilt' was around me a lot when I was a
child, since people, especially my mother, were always telling
my father that he was spoiling me. Since I did not know what
spoiling a child meant, I had to try to work it out. At first it
seemed that people were saying that Dad gave me too many
presents. Of course he was generous, but on what he earned
there was little money left over for gifts. But what he did give
me was time and attention. He told me stories, explained
things to me, read books to me, showed me what a beautiful
and interesting world I lived in. He listened to what I had to
say and he took me seriously as a person. Whereas the people
who believed that he was spoiling me let me know that I was
of no importance at all, or, worse, a nuisance, a blot upon
the landscape. My father was giving me the courage and
optimism to face life, to be myself, to speak up for myself
and what I believed in. The people who feared that I might
be 'spoilt' were saying, 'Go away. Be quiet. Nobody's interested in what you are or what you have to say. You are not

important. You are a nothing.' I was an adult before I worked out what 'spoiling a child' means. 'Not spoiling' a child means trying to break that child's spirit.

Well, your spirit has certainly been bent, if not broken, so now is the time to start putting it together again. You must begin by being kind to yourself and letting other people be kind to you.

Of course, you feel that you do not deserve the kindness and concern of other people. Very often my clients told me how they were wasting my valuable time and that I should really see some more deserving client. (I knew full well that these same clients would at some other time fend off any kindness and concern on my part with, 'She's paid to say those things.') When my clients claimed not to be deserving of my valuable time I just said, 'Don't be silly.' I used to go into long explanations of how everybody is deserving of help and how it is not right for me to judge one person as being better than another, but only to judge whether I might be able to help this particular person. I stopped giving this explanation when I realised that my depressed client would not appreciate the argument that all the people who come seeking help are equal in their right to be helped. My depressed client assumed that I was constantly judging, criticising, condemning others, because that is what he was doing – what you are doing.

And in this continual process of judging others, rather than accepting them, you work out careful sums of giving and taking. If anyone gives you something – a present or love – you feel that you must give something back in at least an equal amount. Presents, or their equivalent, can be quickly returned with the excuse to yourself that you do not want to be beholden to anyone. When someone offers you love, in any of the many forms that love can take, you are in trouble. You see relationships as a constant balancing of the books and you fear making a debt, the repayment of which is beyond you. However, if you want to get out of the prison of depression you have to learn that a loving relationship is not an exercise in book-keeping. A loving relationship is not one where each person says, 'If you love me then I shall love you.' 'If you are good to me then I shall be good to you.' 'How can you expect me to love you when you do things that I don't want you to do?' 'If you don't do what I want I shall stop loving you.' Relationships where these remarks are made are ones of commerce and blackmail.

When you are depressed you feel that all the love and kindness you once had has vanished, and so when someone offers you even the smallest modicum of love and kindness you feel that you should not accept it since you cannot return it in equal amounts. But now is the time to practise receiving. Practise just saying 'Thank you' when someone gives you something without adding 'You shouldn't have'. Saying that can make the giver feel that you do not like the gift. Even though it might not be exactly what was wanted, say how delightful it is. The most ordinary object takes on some glory when it is a gift. People like giving presents. Have the generosity to let them have the pleasure of giving. People like to be kind and helpful. Have the generosity to let them have the pleasure of being kind and helpful.

Practise, too, accepting compliments. Try to give up saying, 'This old dress, I've had it for years', or 'I'm such a fool with figures. I couldn't have managed it without Jim's help' and so on. Try, even, paying yourself compliments. Now I know this is very hard. I well remember one night, years ago, when the Lincoln Self-Help Depressives Group had a visit from a psychologist who was interested in co-counselling. He talked to the group about this and then set them some co-counselling tasks. All went well until he asked them, one after another, 'Say something good about yourself'. This request brought an embarrassed silence, and then the group leader burst into tears. Then there was much rushing to comfort her and much muttering about this psychologist who had upset everyone. He retreated, and nothing further was said about co-counselling for many months. Then, one evening when the group was together and feeling stronger, and no professional person was present, they decided to try this exercise again. Each person had to write down a list of his or her virtues. Afterwards one of the members told me that out of a group of eight people only five virtues were acknowledged and one of these was 'playing chess'! They were still all enjoying the pride of humility!

Treating yourself kindly means looking after yourself and accepting yourself in all your humanness. You are not the most perfect, wonderful person that has ever graced this earth. Neither are you the worst, most imperfect, wicked person that has ever dared to draw breath. Like the rest of us, you are a mixture of good and bad, and all your good and bad are mixed up together and belong together. You are not as bad as you think and you are better than you acknowledge. Treat yourself kindly, and when this is hard to do, perhaps you might like to say to yourself the words of Gerard Manley Hopkins:

My own heart let me more have pity on; let
Me live to my sad self hereafter kind,
Charitable; not live this tormented mind
With this tormented mind tormenting yet.[4]

3. Put pills in your power

Antidepressant drugs can be helpful. They can take the edge off your pain. They can have an uplifting effect, so that you feel an increased degree of energy and enthusiasm. You can use this change to make changes in your life, to look after yourself, to understand what has gone wrong, and to change and find your way out of the prison of depression. You should give serious consideration to taking an antidepressant.

Gwyneth Lewis said, 'I took the anti-depressants prescribed and am very grateful for the emotional space they gave me while I gathered my resources.'[5] She went on, 'After three weeks the antidepressants began to kick in. These affected the quality of my depression but without changing its nature. What they gave me was some psychic space, a small but crucial distance between me and the horrors. Like a line of crustacean riot police, they pushed back the nightmares clamouring for my attention. This gave me a narrow cordon sanitaire in which to move, some room to breathe.' Being a poet, she could find a good simile to describe the effect of taking antidepressants. 'It was exactly like when you're being tailgated at night by someone who has their headlights on high beam. You're on a narrow rural road so you can't let them pass (he's local and knows every twist of the road), so you flip the anti-glare device in your rear-view mirror. The bully depression hasn't gone, he's willing you to turn off or drive more quickly than is safe, but the edge has been taken off his main weapon – light.'[6]

However, there is no pill which can change the memories of an unhappy childhood into memories of a happy one; or turn an unhappy marriage into a happy one; or fill the person who takes the drugs with a permanent, unshakeable self-confidence; or persuade critical, unloving, ungrateful relatives to become accepting, loving and grateful; or turn badly behaved, or criminal, or addicted children into models of perfection; or provide a secure, enjoyable, well-paid job; or make the person you love love you; or create a secure, peaceful world; or banish death. If you have some of the problems that life can bring – and all of you do – then taking a drug which reduces your awareness of pain and fear can bring you periods of respite and help you rest, but such reduction in awareness cannot solve your problems. Only you in a state of keen awareness can do that.

People differ in how much pain they are prepared to feel. If I detect the first twinge of a headache I take an aspirin, but I have friends who suffer from migraine and yet take no painkillers. So it is that some people use antidepressants as an aid in finding their way out of the prison while others do this without any chemical assistance.

When a doctor offers you a prescription for an anti-depressant it is very important that you are clear in your own mind why you accept or reject them. Do not accept any drug just because you do not want to upset your doctor. Have a positive reason for taking this drug. Before you accept a prescription make sure you understand *all* the likely effects of the drugs. What doctors call 'side effects' can in themselves be distressing. For instance, common effects of the oldest antidepressants, the tricyclics such as amitriptyline and imipramine, are constipation and a dry mouth. If you already experience some bowel problems, or if your work involves a good deal of talking, these drug effects create additional problems for you, whereas if you are living quietly at home you should be able to deal with these effects.

The rushed nature of most GP appointments mean that hardly anyone emerges from the doctor's office remembering all the advice that the doctor gave. Before taking any pre-scribed drug always read the instruction sheet in the packet of pills. Ask your chemist about anything you do not under-stand, either on the instruction sheet, or in what your doctor told you, or about anything that has occurred to you after your GP appointment. If your doctor has not already done so, check with your chemist that the new drug does not con-flict with the drugs you are already taking, either prescribed drugs or natural health drugs. Herbal medicines contain chemical compounds which can conflict with or add to the effect of the chemical compounds in the prescribed drugs. For instance, St John's wort and antidepressant drugs, especially the SSRIs (selective serotonin reuptake inhibi-tors), contain similar compounds and should not be taken together.

Whenever we puzzle over why something happened we rarely say, 'No one knows', and leave it at that. Rather we make up some theory – a guess – about the cause of that event. This happens all the time in medicine and psychiatry, but unfortunately these guesses are often presented to patients as known facts. Many depressed people have been told that depression is caused by a chemical imbalance in the brain, and few doctors have gone on to explain that this is a theory, not a fact, because no one knows what a chemically balanced brain is. Some doctors will also say that anti-depressants put the chemical imbalance right. This clearly cannot be the case for, as the scientist Susan Greenfield[7] has often explained, antidepressant drugs have an immediate effect on the functioning of the brain, yet any antidepressant effect is not felt for ten days or so. Clearly something else is taking place, but as yet no one knows what that is. Some doctors tell patients that antidepressant drugs, especially the latest drugs, the SSRIs, target certain parts of the brain, but scientists who study the brain say that this is not so. Drugs which affect the brain affect *all* of the brain.[8]

The only thing that can be said for certain is that some

antidepressants help some people some of the time. Not all people are helped by antidepressants. Some people are helped by some antidepressants the first time they get depressed, but, when the depression returns a second or third time, the drugs do not always work. If you are helped by drugs you are fortunate. If you are not helped by drugs it is not your fault. Psychiatrists call patients who are not helped by antidepressants 'drug resistant patients' as if the patient is deliberately resisting the beneficial effects of the drug, when the truth is that there is no antidepressant – or any other drug, legal or illegal – which makes everyone happy all the time.

Whether an antidepressant helps an individual seems to depend to some unknown extent on what that person expects that drug to do. Doctors have always known that there is one drug which is helpful in all distress, whether physical or mental. This is placebo, the drug which the person believes will do him good. Recently researchers have been looking more closely at how placebo compares in effectiveness with active drugs. A large, five-year study compared the effectiveness of the SSRI Zoloft, the herbal remedy St John's wort, and a placebo. This study showed that Zoloft was effective with twenty-five per cent of those who took it, St John's wort with twenty-four per cent, and the placebo with thirty-two per cent. These are not brilliant cure rates – one in four chance of getting better on a prescribed drug and a herbal remedy, and one in three chances on the sugar pill you believe in, but at least with a sugar pill there are no side effects.[9]

A placebo does not have to be a pill. Many people find the key to the door of their prison by deciding to do something which is pleasant and which they believe will help them get better. People who associate their depression with the darkness of winter and so are diagnosed as having seasonal affective disorder (SAD) take time out to sit quietly and rest in a bright light. Some people resolve to care for themselves at least as far as changing their diet to a very healthy one, or they might allow themselves to be persuaded to indulge in the joy and comfort of aromatherapy. The change from 'I will not do anything pleasant for myself because I do not deserve it' to 'I will allow myself one small, pleasant activity' can be the first step in coming to value and accept myself.

These kinds of activities bring the depressed person into contact with other people who are kind and caring, and having contact with such people can be enormously helpful, something which can explain the glowing reports when the SSRIs were introduced. When the new SSRI drugs were being marketed they were advertised as being superior to the older antidepressants both in effectiveness and the number and degree of side effects. Now both these claims are being questioned. The American psychiatrist Arif Khan looked at ninety-six antidepressant trials between 1979 and 1996 and found that in fifty-two per cent of the trials the effect of the drug could not be distinguished from the placebo. Because the general physical health of the people taking the new drug needed to be monitored, they spent a good deal of time with their doctor, something like twenty hours over a two-month period. Compare what happens with the older anti-depressants – the usual ten-minute GP interview, or the repeat prescription month after month with no personal contact with the doctor. Andrew Leuchter, Professor of Psychiatry at the University of California, said, 'We don't actually know in any individual why they get better. However, one of the factors is undoubtedly the time we spend with people and the feeling of being connected which that gives patients.'[10]

All antidepressants have side effects, and the SSRIs are no exception. If you want to read about the effects of these drugs see David Healy's excellent book *Psychiatric Drugs Explained*.[11]

Right from the beginning Eli Lilly, the pharmaceutical company which makes Prozac, admitted that some five per cent of people taking the drug experienced a loss of libido, particularly men who found they could not get or sustain an erection. Now the figure for SSRIs is known to be more than fifty per cent.[12] Not being interested in sex may be the least of some people's worries, but for others sex is very import-ant. I have known couples who battle with one another through the day but who, in the comfort and safety of their bed, assuage the hurts and misunderstandings of the day, and re-affirm their commitment to one another. One of the main reasons for the popularity of sex is that it allows us close contact with another person without having to talk to that person. Human touch can be a comforter. Moreover, some people build their sense of being a person on the idea of being an effective sexual performer. This is what most young men do. Some young men get older and wiser and learn to pride themselves on a wider range of skills, but some continue to have as their closest relationship that with their supposedly unfailing penis. For all these different reasons an SSRI like Seroxat can be utterly devastating to the person who takes it.

William Skidelsky described what happened to him when he was at university but became depressed after glandular fever which left him with 'an all-consuming lethargy'. His GP prescribed Seroxat. William Skidelsky wrote,

> I started the course, and was quickly impressed by the intensity with which the pills kicked in. After just a couple of days I felt dizzy and excessively jaunty, as if I was on some kind of low-level amphetamine drip. A few days more, and it seemed as if I was being propelled upwards through the layers of my lethargy like a deep-sea diver returning from the ocean depths. Another week, and everything pointed to a glorious, miraculous future, one in which I could achieve anything, take on anyone. A month on Seroxat was enough to convince me of my invulnerability.

He returned to university and seemed to be happy, but 'it was all a sham. Things hadn't really changed; it just seemed as if they had. Worse still, the pills seemed to affect me in new and unexpected ways.' For him,

> The most obvious side effect was physical. I wasn't conventionally impotent. I could just about manage an erection, and orgasms were also sometimes possible. What came over me, rather, was a generalised desensitisation, a blockage of the usual channels along which the sexual juices flow. It was as if, in the mental ferment of Seroxat,

all the blood that had rushed to my brain to begin with couldn't be reclaimed for less cerebral purposes. Even from relatively early on, I was gripped by a devastating numbness in my groin.

He stopped taking Seroxat, but found that his feelings of tiredness had been replaced by 'ones more closely resembling depression'. His doctor gave him Prozac, and he found that his 'manic jumpiness was replaced by a feeling of unutterable calm'. He was unworried about his forthcoming exams, which he found to be 'the easiest thing in the world'. As soon as the exams were over he stopped taking Prozac. He explained, 'I didn't want to have anything more to do with antidepressants. Following my earlier experiences, I had come to believe that they are a false trail. Having taken antidepressants, I would urge anyone thinking of trying them to be extremely cautious. Because if the happiness they provide comes at the cost of not even caring whether that happiness is genuine or not, then they are not a solution – they are positively dangerous.'[13]

William Skidelsky wanted to enjoy life, and, as we all do from time to time, he longed for some magic pill which would restore his mental well-being. Doctors have always tried to meet this need. In the nineteenth century the happiness drug was opium until its addictive properties were recognised. From the 1940s to the 1970s the happiness pills were barbiturates and amphetamines, in the 1970s and 1980s they were the benzodiazepines like Valium and Ativan. The people who took these drugs reported feelings of calm, but it was an unnatural calm. They were not responding to what was going on around them, not responding to, or even being aware of, the people who mattered most to them. Later, when they were no longer taking these drugs, they mourned what they saw as the lost years of their life. Many people found that they were unable to stop taking the pills that had once produced a blinkered happiness. They no longer felt any kind of happiness, but their dependence on the drug was so great they could not stop taking it. Today there are some people still dependent on barbiturates, and there are many thousands of people still addicted to the benzodiazepines.

Perhaps our greatest universal failure is that we fail to learn from history, and so we are doomed to repeat it. The medical profession is no exception to this. The SSRIs were launched with great fanfare and promises, but by the 1990s the trickle of reports about worrying effects of these drugs turned into a flood. Many of these reports concerned the difficulties people had when they had tried to stop taking these drugs. The strange and difficult symptoms they experienced were diagnosed by their doctors as the return of their original problem, but actually what they were experiencing were the signs of a physical dependence on that drug. When they ceased to take the drug their body – and particularly their brain – protested. In the UK the drugs used in medicine are monitored by the Committee for the Safety of Medicine (CSM) and the Medicines Control Agency (MCA). The CSM has received a huge number of complaints about Seroxat while the MCA found that more adverse reports have been received about Seroxat than any other drug and that of the top six drugs most complained about by doctors five are SSRIs.[14]

All the drugs used for the treatment of depression, anxiety, mania and psychosis produce a degree of physical dependence, depending on the individual's physical make-up and the length of time the drug has been taken. **If you have been taking any of these drugs for any length of time DO NOT stop taking the drug abruptly**.

You have to come off the drug very gradually. Reduce your dose a *tiny* fraction, stay on the slightly smaller dose for a week or two and see how you feel. If you have no untoward symptoms, reduce your dose by another *tiny* fraction for another week or two, see how you feel, and so on. This process will take months, as many months or more as you have been on the drug, but slow and painless is better than fast and painful.

Whether you decide to take an antidepressant or not, you must get your body into as healthy a state as possible. What you eat is tremendously important – lots of fresh fruit and vegetables, cereals of different kinds, yoghurt, fish, and a limited amount of animal fats if you are not a vegetarian. Along with this every day, without fail, you must exercise.

Join a yoga class, get to know your body and learn how to relax. Go for a proper walk and not just a trudge around a supermarket. Put on some music and dance, run up the stairs, go up and down a set of kitchen steps until you are breathless. Exercise is reported to produce those hormones in our brain that cheer us up. Moreover, it makes us tired. When you go to bed at night you may want to lie awake and worry, but your body will overrule you because it needs to sleep.

A small proportion of people suffer severe and very deleterious reactions to the SSRIs. You need to know about these so that, if you prove to be one of those unlucky people, you will know that what you are feeling is the effects of the drug and not the signs of incipient madness.

Some people, perhaps even shortly after they start taking an SSRI, find themselves gripped by a feeling of intense physical restlessness or turmoil along with a severe tenseness and an inability to rest or to sleep. This extremely painful state is called *akathisia*. Akathisia seems more likely to affect people who are extremely anxious, especially those who experience periods of panic.[15]

Anyone who has been a psychiatric patient for some time is likely to have been prescribed a number of different drugs, perhaps taking several different drugs at once. Such a cocktail of drugs can produce some very unpleasant reactions. If a doctor feels that a certain drug is not working he is likely to switch to another one, and this change in itself can produce deleterious effects. These symptoms are called *serotonin syndrome* and include confusion, hypomania, agitation, shivering, tremor, diarrhoea, incoordination, and fever. The symptoms can be mild but they can be more severe and even fatal.[16]

Life is not easy and all of us, from time to time, think, perhaps fleetingly, of killing ourselves. Sometimes we feel an urge to kill those people who frustrate or persecute us. Some people, believing that the world is an incorrigibly evil place, think of not just killing themselves but also their children to save them from the terrible world. When we think about murder and suicide most of us know that we could never put our thoughts into action. We have logical reasons as to why we would never do this, and these reasons serve to inhibit our actions.

However, certain drugs can be effective in removing inhibitions, as anyone who has been drunk or high on an illegal drug knows. It seems that the SSRIs, Prozac and Seroxat particularly, can have the same effect with a small percentage of people. Tragically, some people taking these drugs have killed themselves, and some have killed their family before killing themselves. Perhaps, if you have been prone to outbursts of anger, or if, with every reversal in your life, you thought of suicide, and, if you are thinking of taking an antidepressant, it could be wise not to take an SSRI.

If you are taking an SSRI and you experience intolerable symptoms, or if you find your thoughts being dominated by impulses to suicide or murder, you must see your doctor immediately and ask to be taken off these drugs.

Antidepressants at their best do no more than ease our pain, help us rest, and let us feel moderately cheerful. However, the drugs which ease physical pain always come with a warning that points out that when we are in pain something is wrong with us. We need to heed this warning. *Pain is our truth*. We need to understand our pain, not just try to get rid of it.

Many people cannot tolerate the sight of another person's pain, and some such people are in the medical profession. Some doctors prescribe antidepressants without recognising that there are times when it is appropriate to be in pain. A health visitor told me how she had been to see a woman whose two-week-old baby had just died of a brain tumour. She said, 'It was her first baby. She told me that her GP wanted to put her on an antidepressant. I told her she was right to cry – and to scream and shout and kick things.'

Burying pain does not eradicate it. It just festers and poisons us. When our heart is breaking and we cannot breathe for the pain in our chest we need to cry and scream and shout and protest at the sheer unfairness of life, and, when we have no more strength to cry and scream and shout and protest, then we can begin to recognise our loss and see that sadness, now our lifelong companion, is our friend, for it is a constant testament to the love and value we gave to that which we have lost. How can we be human if we cannot let ourselves be sad?

4. Create a peaceful place within yourself

When Chalky first came to see me he told me of the pains he had in his chest and arms – sometimes a dull ache, sometimes a sudden stabbing pain in his chest or a darting pain down his arm. I asked him what he thought was causing the pain.

He looked even more anxious. 'I think it's – it's my heart. The doctor just dismisses it. Says it's just tension. He might be just telling me that so I won't worry.'

He sat stiffly, forward in his seat, hands clenched on his knees. I tried to get him to relax. You could have cracked walnuts on his chest and arms. He smiled apologetically at his failure to follow my instructions to relax and, as I explained how prolonged tension in the muscles produced pain and other strange sensations, he looked politely disbelieving. Nothing I could say would take his suffering away from him.

So we talked of other symptoms of his depressed state – how he could not think clearly, how he dreaded every day, how meaningless life had become, how he struggled to keep going because if, for a moment, he faltered, he would plunge into a far greater, deeper depression.

'The bottomless pit of chaos, madness and death?' I asked.

'Yes,' he said.

So much for my attempts to get him to relax.

This is why depressed people cannot manage to relax. It is not that they are in some mysterious way prevented from relaxing but that they fear that, if they do stop struggling and let themselves relax, something far worse will happen to them.

But it will not. If you stop struggling, if you seek ways of relaxing and finding an area of peace within yourself, you will not fall down into the pit of depression. You will not become mad or die.

Being depressed is like being thrown into a pool of deep water. If you struggle and splash around helplessly you keep going under the water, the water gets in your eyes and nose and mouth, and you get tired and feel sick. But if you stay still, the water itself holds you up and you gently float. If you want to get out of the prison of depression you need to let your own natural resources buoy you up. Stop struggling and you will be all right. This may sound crazy, but no more so than that advice about what to do when your car goes into a skid. Turn the steering wheel in the direction of the skid. That advice always sounds wrong to the novice driver, but experienced drivers know that it is true.

So how do you learn to stop struggling and to create a peaceful place within yourself?

First, learn the techniques of relaxation and practise them regularly. The basic principle is simply to choose a set of muscles in any part of the body, clench these muscles and then let go. You can work systematically through every part of your body, and finish in a state of complete relaxation, or you can become aware of an area of tension – the muscles of your face set into a frown, or shallow breathing and a tightness in your chest – and consciously you tighten and let go and take some slow, deep breaths. It is a good idea to have some skilled instruction first. You can join a relaxation or yoga class, or buy one of the many relaxation tapes that are readily available now. If possible listen to the tape before you acquire it. Check that the voice on the tape sounds pleasant to you and, if the full relaxation is accompanied by a guided fantasy, that the picture you are expected to imagine suits you. In my yoga class our teacher during the full relaxation exercise would take us for an imaginary walk beside a lake and through a forest. All goes well for me until he mentions fir trees. All my forests contain eucalyptus.

It is a good idea to have some lessons with an experienced teacher of relaxation methods because you are probably so tense in some parts of your body that you have lost all awareness that those parts of your body can be relaxed. When I first started yoga my teacher would say, 'Now relax your shoulders,' and I would think, 'How stupid. How can you relax your shoulders? Your shoulders are just there.' It took me a while to discover that I was holding my shoulders 'just there' and that I could relax them. Then I came to

realise how stiff my shoulders were and how tight the ten-
dons were around my armpits, shoulder blades and upper
spine. One friend, greatly experienced in yoga theory as well
as practice, pointed out that I was holding myself in a
'flinching away from pain' posture, even though life was no
longer dealing me the blows which required such a reaction.
I practised my yoga diligently, and now I flinch only at the
appropriate times, and, when I do, I practise relaxing my
shoulders.

Once you learn the knack of relaxing your body you can
practise it quietly when you have a spare half hour or when
you are faced with a difficult situation and you can feel the
tension rising. However, relaxing the body does not always
relax the mind. The old worrying thoughts can keep scurry-
ing about there like noisy rats. You have to find ways of
quietening, relaxing your mind.

Richard is a young man who has had a very difficult life.
One evening at the Lincoln Depressives' Group, when we
were playing our favourite records, Richard told me that he
had brought along his record of the Toccata from Widor's
Fifth Organ Symphony. 'Every time I hear it,' he said, 'it
fetches me out of depression.' This is what you must discover
– what sights or sounds take you out of the worrying round
of immediate reality and into something more real, more
beautiful, more important and more than yourself. I look at
the sky, or trees, or birds, or usually all three together. I have
had three homes in different parts of England, and each one,
though full of many imperfections, gave an immediate vista
from each window of sky, trees and grass. My garden calms
and sustains me. When we take the time to look at nature, or
to listen to music, or to read a poem, we move into that quiet
and concentrated state which is the essence of meditation,
and meditation is all about finding that peaceful place
within yourself and using it as a source of courage and
strength. Meditation is not about sitting cross-legged for
days and going into a trance and becoming very strange.
Meditation is about discovering for yourself something that
has been known by all peoples, all cultures and all religions.
Le Shan, whose excellent book on meditation is well worth
reading, wrote,

We meditate to find, to recover, to come back to something of ourselves we once dimly and unknowingly had and have lost without knowing what it was or where or when we lost it.[17]

This is in effect what Krishnamurti teaches, 'There is nowhere to go. You are already there.' He said,

Wander by the seashore and let this meditative quality come upon you. If it does, don't pursue it. What you pursue will be the memory of what it was and what was is the death of what is. Or when you wander among the hills, let everything tell you the beauty and the pain of life, so that you awaken to your own sorrow and to the ending of it.[18]

Meditation has a long Christian tradition,[19] beginning with Jesus' vigil in the wilderness. The early Christian monks who withdrew to solitude in the desert meditated by using the repetition of the prayer, 'Lord Jesus Christ, Son of God have mercy on me, a miserable sinner.' St Augustine taught that contemplation was essential for the soul to find God. The religious houses which grew up in the Middle Ages provided a retreat for meditation, and such retreats are still available today, not only for those men and women who join a religious order but for those people who wish to withdraw for just a few days. A friend of mine went to a Quaker retreat for several weeks after her husband had died suddenly. There, she later told me, she had time to be alone, to sit in her room or to walk in the garden, or to be with people when she needed to be with people. If you want to find within the context of your Christian beliefs your way out of the prison of depression, you should consider making a retreat or joining one of the informal groups who get together for a few hours' meditation and communion.

If you would like to make a retreat but not necessarily a Christian one, there are now in Britain, America and Australia a number of communities of followers of the Eastern philosophies which offer the experience of a retreat and meditation. Such an experience can be very much like psychotherapy, since the ways of life in Buddhism, Taoism, Vedanta and Yoga very much resemble psychotherapy.[20]

Yoga has become so popular now that there should be a class close by to you which you could join. If you are worried about looking funny in a leotard and tights (everyone looks funny in leotard and tights) get a track suit or loose-fitting trousers and top. You will also need a piece of carpet about as long and as wide as you are and a small cushion. In class there is no competition. Each person works at her or his own pace and own level. As my teacher always said, 'Go as far as you can – then a little bit further.' You learn to stretch and bend your body, to control your breathing, to relax, to pay attention to yourself in the here and now (what is called centring) and to meditate.

Whether or not you join a meditation class, learning to meditate is something you have to do for yourself. You have to find what is the right way to meditate for you. Other people will make different suggestions and you can try each one out to see what works for you, but, whatever meditative path you follow, it must be your own.

To start, you have to find or create some space and time for yourself. This may mean ignoring the work that needs to be done or telling the family to leave you alone for an hour. Then you need to work out what is the most comfortable way for you to sit. Lying down is not recommended, since you tend to go off to sleep instead of keeping watchful attention. You can sit cross-legged on the floor (a small cushion under your buttocks helps to maintain a more comfortable posture) or you can sit in a chair which supports you comfortably. Some people cover their heads with a shawl; some people close their eyes; some people focus on a small object like a stone or a flower. Then you begin the process of centring, of bringing your thoughts back into yourself and becoming aware of where you are, how you are sitting, how your body is feeling. You breathe deeply and slowly, and as you do you attend to one thing. It may be your breath which you observe going in and out. You may count your breaths, and each time you find your attention wandering, you go back to one. You may think of a colour, and watch it with your inner eye. Or you may take a word or phrase and say it over and over with complete attention. It might be a mantra taken from Eastern literature, or a phrase which carries special meaning for you, like 'Love and hope', or 'Peace and light', or a verse whose meaning grows with familiarity like Julian of Norwich's

All shall be well and all shall be well and all manner of things shall be well.

As you do this, other thoughts will come into your mind. You just let them come and go while you pay attention to your breath, or your colour, or your mantra or your verse. At first you may find this very difficult, but you must persevere. At first you may manage to sit for only a few minutes, but as you come to discover that not only is sitting in meditation pleasant, but it leaves you with a continuing sense of peace and relaxation, so you will naturally lengthen the time that you sit. Of course there are bad days when worrying thoughts will intrude and distract you from the immediate present, but do not give up. Let those bad days come and go too.

When you come to realise that nothing, not even the blackest, most terrible day of your life, goes on forever, then you are able to let things come and go and to pay attention to the present. In meditation we are practising the art of *mindfulness*, of *paying attention to one thing at a time in the here and now*. Like looking at a small child's face and thinking how beautiful she is, instead of regretting the circumstances of her birth, or fearing that you are too inadequate to be a parent, or envying her security as a child, or dreading what may happen to her in the years to come. Like preparing a meal and paying attention to the food itself and what you are doing, instead of worrying about whether it will turn out all right, or whether your family will like it, or being angry because no one appreciates you, or thinking about what job you must do next and the one after that and how on earth will you get it all done. Mindfulness means paying attention to the here and now and not worrying about results, paying attention to what is and not to what might be. Learning how to be mindful is learning how to be. The Zen arts[21] have specialised in teaching how to be mindful and how to discover the beauty of your own spontaneity. You may decide to study one of these arts in order to learn how to live in the present, the only place where we can live.

But to relax, meditate, be mindful and spontaneous, you have to learn to trust yourself, and that means trusting others.

5. Risk putting some trust in yourself and others

If you see yourself as bad, evil, unacceptable to yourself and to other people, then you cannot trust yourself. If you fear, hate and envy other people, you certainly cannot trust them. If your religious or philosophical beliefs render you fearful and pessimistic, then you cannot trust God or whatever you see as the powerful forces which contain the universe. Trusting nobody, you must be constantly afraid.

There was a time when you trusted others and the world you lived in. But then other people abused your trust, and the world dealt you some unexpected and terrible blows. Some of these things will have happened in your adult life and some in your childhood.

In depression you are defending a position which you adopted as a child when you were under very great threat. We like to think that children are innocent in the sense that they are not responsible for their opinions and actions but produce their opinions and actions as a result of the treatment they receive from the adults around them. Yet, what happens to all of us in childhood is that we are placed in moral dilemmas which offer us several courses of action. Being young and uninformed we may see only two possibilities when, in fact, other choices are available. Nevertheless, as children we have a choice and we make a choice. Jackie's story of the Noddy Clock shows a child being placed in a moral dilemma no different from that which many adults have to face – whether to tell the truth and to go on suffering and to allow others to suffer, or to lie to prevent the suffering of others and risk being found out as a liar.

A stark choice between two grim alternatives leaves the child with the questions of how much courage he can summon to his aid. Faced with the choice between seeing your parents as wicked or yourself as wicked, one child might decide to be brave, to recognise that the people on whom he depends are incompetent or malicious, and so he has to look after himself, while another child might be too frightened to depend on himself and so decides that he must be the wicked one and his parents good. Thus in the same family with the same parents, one child may grow up rebellious and independent, and another child conforming and dependent. As children we made certain choices. As adults we are free to change these choices. Let me repeat, *what matters is not what our parents did to us but how we interpret what they did to us.*

If, as children, we decide that we must conform to parental demands, we can try to make this easier for ourselves by telling ourselves that our parents are always good and wise and they know what is best for us. Yet the evidence of our own eyes and ears shows us that this is not so. Parents are fallible human beings. Even the best and wisest of parents make mistakes. Parents may love their children but they rarely understand them. All children want their parents to be all-wise, all-good, all-protecting, all-understanding. Discovering that their parents fail on every count is a disappointment all children find hard to bear. If, added to that, the child has defined himself as being bad in order to see his parents as being good, he cannot bear to think that his sacrifice was useless, a foolish waste. So he tells himself that this was not so. He lies to himself and tells himself that his parents are perfect.

The greatest damage you can do to yourself is to lie to yourself. It always leads to suffering, your own suffering and other people's suffering. A wife who insists to herself that her selfish, alcoholic husband 'really does care' usually ends up sacrificing her children for her husband. A man who tells himself that his competitive devotion to his work is 'really all for the family's sake' closes his eyes to his wife's distress and his children's anger. If we lie to ourselves long enough we lose the ability to distinguish between truth and falsity. When we cannot tell what is true for us we lose touch with who we are. One depressed person will say, 'I feel as though I don't exist.' Another will say, 'I am not in control of my mind.'

This, one way or another, is the path you have taken into the prison of depression. Not trusting yourself has rendered you helpless. Lying to yourself has made you lose touch with

yourself. Les Murray is a famous Australian poet and someone who knows depression well. When Gwyneth Lewis asked
him what was the cure for depression 'the truth' was his
instant reply. Gwyneth Lewis discovered that depression
'thrives on secrecy'.[22] A lack of truth requires secrecy.

Not trusting yourself and lying to yourself are terrible
ways of living but not irreversible. You can choose to trust
yourself and to take responsibility for yourself. You can find
yourself simply by accepting yourself. You have not gone
away or ceased to exist. All you have to do is to *be yourself.*

When one of my clients tells me that he has decided to
be himself I know that our meetings will soon come to an
end. Val announced one day that she had decided to give up
worrying that she was not the perfect mother, wife and
daughter. She had decided to be herself. 'They will all have
to accept me as I am,' she said, 'I'm not going to stay in just
because the children think I ought to be there to wait on
them. I'm not going to expect that my husband and I should
have the same interests. If I want to garden or work on my
photography I'll do it. And I'll try to accept mother as she is.
If she wants to give us presents, I'll let her.' On her next visit
to me she said, 'What I'd like is to have a three-month break
from seeing you. I'd like to see if I can get on all right on my
own.' I knew she would be all right, just as I discovered Nick
would be.

Nick was a very handsome, witty young man, and I found
his company a delight, but he considered himself the most
boring person in the world, a blight on any company. It was
important, he said, to make a worthwhile contribution in a
social group. His childhood experiences had taught him
that this was the way his parents judged people and he
accepted this as an axiomatic truth which he applied to
himself and others. The trouble was that he did not feel
that he could make a proper contribution to the group.
The social life of his family and friends centred on a pub
where they would meet regularly on a Friday and Saturday
night. Nick would spend a long time getting himself
properly dressed for these occasions and he would become
increasingly tense as he tried to prepare himself to have

plenty of witty things to say to his friends. Once there, he felt himself to be grossly awkward and tongue-tied, and the misery set in. But he could neither avoid these social evenings nor devalue their implications. So he stayed depressed, until one day he arrived at my office beaming with happiness. He said that on the previous Friday when he was getting ready to go to the pub, he suddenly decided that, 'I was going to relax and try to be myself. I did this – I didn't try to crack any witties and get in with the group, and as I did this I started to enjoy it. Funnily enough, something did come to me that I really wanted to say, when I didn't try to. When I tried to say something, force myself, I'd say something that was alien – it didn't make sense. But at the weekend things started coming to me that I wanted to say and people were listening. It was Friday night and I went through the same things – the washing hair routine, all that jazz, and it came to me in a flash that I could stop if I wanted to. I was dreading going out, and I thought, why, if this makes me feel that bad, why should I worry about other people. I'll just go out and make sure I enjoy myself, and as soon as I did that I wasn't worried. I felt like a different person in a way. I was like a different person to myself. With my parents, I've always felt that if I wanted to say anything to offend my parents I shouldn't say it, and in the end you don't have anything to say. It was like a sudden enlightenment. We went to the same pub we normally go to on a Friday night, but it seemed like a different place to me, it seemed fresher, seemed to be more exciting, everything was great.' Such a discovery rendered me superfluous, and Nick no longer came to brighten my Monday mornings.[23]

Not trusting other people affects what we do in a multitude of ways. You want to go on holiday but you cannot fly because you cannot put your safety totally into the hands of other people. Or your social life is extremely constricted because you cannot use a public toilet or even a toilet in a friend's house because you do not trust another person to keep a toilet properly clean. Distrusting oneself and others makes life very complicated, as Jean described in one of her letters to me.

> I find myself in states of raw red rage for days on end. I can find all sorts of reasons for my rage – the main one being my childish inability to accept the fact that the world is not perfect, and I realise it is going to take an awfully long time before acceptance of that fact is totally absorbed. Now the question is – what the Hell do I do with all that anger in the meantime? I think I know the answer. Jack pointed out that anger is emerging and can be channelled, but I have been finding it tricky, because I have to keep my life paced to meet a lot of Emily's demands, which means containing a great deal of anger until I can find an appropriate outlet – tricky to release blind fury in a controlled manner whilst playing picture dominoes. I can hear you saying, 'Who said it would be easy?' . . . Where did all this anger spring from? It's been going on and building up for weeks – since the beginning of the invasion of our house by all sorts of friends and relations. I find it hard to relate to people honestly because of the Should and Ought in my head. Until I married my mother criticised out of existence every friend I ever had, consequently I prejudged all people I met by her standards, and of course never found anyone to like at all! I still suffer from this, and find it hard not to over-react and allow the free run of my heart and home to everyone. Or to find out what my true feelings about people are.

Sometimes not trusting others means expecting gratitude. You cannot take your family's and friends' love on trust. If you give them anything – presents, affection or your time and effort – you expect them to make their gratitude quite explicit, on the principle that seeing is believing. When such gratitude is not forthcoming you feel neglected and you complain. 'After all I've done for you' has alienated more children from their parents than any act of parental cruelty.

Usually not trusting others means keeping secrets and not confiding in others. That way you can both protect yourself and control other people since they can act only on limited information about you. You feel that you must try to control people, especially the people you love and depend on, and thus you create a power struggle where there should be love freely given and received.

Trusting other people should not be an either/or situation – either you trust someone or you don't. Each of us can be trusted in different ways and in different situations. To work out whether you can trust another person to behave in a certain way, we need to understand that person to the best of our ability. Sometimes a person appears to be untrustworthy but is, in reality, responding to the demands of a situation of which we are ignorant. A mother may be horrified to discover that her son is stealing money from her purse and spending it on sweets. What she does not know is that he feels that he has to purchase his popularity at school and he does not trust her enough to tell her.

Risking trusting others means learning more about other people and more about yourself. Then your acts of trust and mistrust are informed decisions and not the outcome of blind prejudice. Remember, trusting means hoping, and hoping means uncertainty. Trusting yourself and others means accepting uncertainty.

Rather than accepting uncertainty, when you were a child you constructed a simple view of the world, possibly with a predictable God, where virtue was rewarded and vice punished. When you discovered that the world does not work in this just and fair way you felt betrayed. My friend Jeffrey Russell who, as a mediaeval historian and a devout Christian, has studied the concepts of evil down the ages,[24] wrote to me to comment on my book *The Courage to Live* and said,

Another aspect of facing death is the sense that it's not fair if we've been nice girls and boys. Do you recall one of the most striking pictures to come out of the Warsaw ghetto? It's a small boy, perhaps ten years old, cowering against a wall as four heavily-armed Nazis approach him. The look on his face might as well be in writing: 'But Mummy told me that nothing would happen to me if I was a good boy.' So long as we hold to the illusion that God, or the cosmos, or whatever, will not harm us if we are good little children, we will not be able to construct death (and

therefore, as you show so clearly, life either) in any
meaningful way.[25]

Your lack of trust in God, or the cosmos, is the mistrust
of someone who has been betrayed, and not the acceptance
that life is a chancy, unpredictable business. You are trying, still, to hang on to your belief that if you are good
everything will be all right. Sheldon Kopp calls this state
'pseudo-innocence'.

Unwilling to tolerate life's ambiguity, its unresolvability,
its inevitability, we search for certainty, demanding that
someone provide it. Stubbornly, relentlessly, we seek the
wise man, the wizard, the good parent, someone else who
will show us the way.
    Surely *someone* must know. It simply cannot be that
life is just what it appears to be, that there are no hidden
warnings, that this is it, just this and nothing more. It's
not fair, not enough! We cannot possibly bear having to
live life as it is, without reassurance, without being
special, without even being offered some comforting
explanations. Come on now! Come across!
    You've got to give us something to make it all right.
The medicine tastes lousy. Why should we have to swallow
it just because it's the only thing we can do? Can't you at
least promise that we will have to take it just once, that it
won't taste that bad, that we will be just fine immediately
afterward, that we will be glad we took it? No? Well then,
surely, at least you have to give us a lollipop for being good.
    But what if we are talking to ourselves? What if there
is no-one out there listening? What if for each of us the
only wise man, the only wizard, the only good parent we
will ever have is our own helpless vulnerable self? What
then?[26]

What then indeed. Are you going to spend your life
looking for someone to protect you? Are you going to go on
hanging on to your parents, trying to make them into good
parents? Are you going to go on trying to make your fallible
partner into the perfect partner? Are you going to go on
expecting God to answer your prayers and to reward you

when you are good? Are you going to go on looking for the doctor who will take away your pain with a magic pill? Are you going to go on looking for the therapist who, with a magic wand, will abolish all your misery? Perhaps there is a guru who can do the trick. If only you could find him. But then when you do meet a guru, this is what he is likely to say,

> He who is in search of a guru should first seek the guru within himself. If he seeks a guru outside without seeking the guru within, then he is consciously and unconsciously stupefying himself. He who has no faith or confidence in his own inner guru and is trying to have faith and confidence in an outer guru, such a person may enjoy his illusions for a while, but ultimately he is forced to be disillusioned.
>
> Guru consists of two syllables gu and ru; gu (darkness) and ru (remover). He who removes darkness from our understanding is the real guru, and such a guru and his 'office' are always open in our hearts . . . if one cannot contact directly with the inner guru, then one must seek for an outer guru. The outer guru is he who guides the true seeker into this inner journey for the intimate contact with the inner guru.[27]

So, to find your way out of the prison of depression you have to trust yourself. But how can I do that, you ask, when I am so helpless and despairing? Just the right state to be in, said the philosopher Joseph Needham.

> It's in weakness there's strength. If we can stay weak and keep open, keep moving around and come to the point where we just give up and know that what we are doing, where we are going is hopeless, really hopeless, and not grab on to something else and try to build a structure out of it, then we reach a state which in the traditions of the West is called Despair. Another word for this Despair in this sense is Deep Openness. When you're in Despair, when you come to the end of the rope, only then can help come.[28]

6. Find someone to talk things over with

Help comes in two ways – from yourself and from other
people. But help cannot come from other people unless you
are prepared to find it and to accept it. You have to find the
people to confide in, and you have to overcome your habit of
keeping things to yourself. Perhaps you are ready to confide
in someone, but there is no one available. Your family
will not listen, and your doctor prefers to write you a
prescription rather than give you his listening attention.

So you need to find someone who will listen. Someone
outside the family and, possibly, outside work, is usually best
– someone who has no interest in keeping you as you are or
who has no reason to feel guilty about what you might dis-
close. It need not necessarily be just one person. On your
journey out of your prison you will meet many different
gurus, people who throw light on your darkness. A nurse
might listen to your fears about your health and the drugs
you take, and may find the words to calm your fears. A friend
may share with you the burden of family responsibilities. A
parson or priest might listen and acknowledge your religious
doubts and fears and impart the courage and trust which
enables you to deal with these. Of course, not everyone you
hope to confide in will respond in a helpful way. Many nurses
will tell you that doctor knows best and hurry up and take
your medicine. Friends may have so many concerns of their
own that they do not want to know about yours, while some
parsons and priests have all the sensitivity and understanding of an old boot and so always resort to their 'religious'
language whenever they have to face real suffering. Nevertheless, 'Seek and ye shall find' or 'When the pupil is ready
the master appears'. When you are prepared to set out on
your journey without maps, you will find some friends who
will listen and accompany you for part of the way.

You might like to consult a professional listener of some
sort. You may find someone in the Health Service, or you
might go to a private therapist. Talking to people who have
been depressed and are now coping is tremendously helpful.
Tony Lewis in his articles in the *Guardian* on his experience
of depression, during which he tried to kill himself, said,

I would like to make a few suggestions for those finding themselves in my situation. First, accept and believe in the fact that you will recover, however hopeless everything seems. Secondly, make sure that your food is good and wholesome. Emotional problems use up a lot of energy, and if you don't eat properly you feel tired. Again, the stomach reacts quickly and sensitively to stress (this is exemplified by the sensation produced there when someone sees a horrific sight) and if you are anxious your stomach produces a lot of acid which should be neutralized.

Equally important, try to keep fit. I always feel better after exercise, and therefore take part in yoga, walk a lot and swim a great deal. (It was only this year, by the way, that I overcame my ten-year phobia about water.) Another useful fact was the creation of a daily routine. Without some kind of time-table the day may seem endless and even the smallest decisions become difficult. So when you get up write out on a piece of paper all you intend to do and keep to it. This helped me. I was also grateful to have a lifeline with other people in the form of a club I belonged to. In that friendly, support atmosphere I felt relatively safe.

Talking to people was a great help. I found it especially comforting to have the counsel of people who had been through the same kinds of experiences I suffered.[29]

In looking for someone to talk to, inspect your friends and acquaintances. Many of my depressed clients, when they first came to see me, gave me the impression that they did not have a friend in the world. They spoke only of their families. Of course they knew people who were not family but they would not dream of talking to friends and acquaintances about personal matters. They would certainly never talk about being depressed. They felt it was shameful to be depressed, and that their friends would despise them even more than they already did. Then one day something happened and the truth could be no longer hidden from a friend. Lo and behold it turns out that this friend had been depressed, and so was able to say many helpful, courage-strengthening things about the experience.

Friends are wonderful people. I always regret that I do not devote more time to my friends – write them longer letters more frequently, visit them more often, invite them here more often – but in my mental map of my world my friends stand like giant statues of themselves. My friends are the people with whom I have a continuing conversation. There may be long gaps between exchanges, since many of them live in Australia or America, but the conversation is never interrupted or concluded.

To turn an acquaintance into a friend you have to give that person time and attention. If you have no friends it is because you are so wrapped up in yourself that you do not give other people your time and attention. One part of not giving time and attention to other people is fearing that if you do they will reject you. The other part is feeling that other people are boring and you have better things to do than talk to them. However, if you want to find your way out of the prison of depression, you need friends.

Carol Parris once interviewed a group of forty women who live in Lambeth, London, and asked them about their health and about their friends. She found that out of the forty women only thirteen had not 'visited the doctor and received a prescription for tranquillizers or antidepressants at some stage in time as wives and mothers.' To the question, 'Do you have any friends that you are particularly close to?', she found that ten of them had no close friends at all, while most had only one close friend. She found that many women had strong relationships with their families. One said, 'We do a lot around the family, all of us. We don't do anything without phoning each other. We speak to each other every day on the phone. I can confide in my sister almost anything. But Mum still rules the roost and we don't do anything without telling her.'

Another woman said, 'When my mother was alive she was with me every day. I suppose that I didn't think I needed anyone else. I was very hurt when my mum died. I could talk to my mum about anything and I don't think even my husband and I have such a close relationship. A lot of men, I don't think they have the closeness, somehow.'

The value of friendship with another woman was seen as being linked to shared experience. A woman said, 'If I stopped seeing my friends I'd be back on the lonely trail, wouldn't I? If we all stopped being friends, I'd be back to how I was before, back to the depression stage. I find talking to my friends can be a lot easier than talking to my husband. Let's face it, he's a smashing bloke but he can't understand. He can't understand. He's at work all day so he can't understand the situation. Where if you speak to the girls they're more sympathetic. They're in the same boat as me. They've all got young children at home, and if I feel a bit down about something I can talk to them about it and I find I feel a lot better.'

Carol Parris commented, 'The women I interviewed spoke enthusiastically of the way in which friendships with other women eased their personal worries and frequently became substitutes for visits to the doctor.' One woman said, 'My relationship with my friend Jean is probably the strongest one because we can discuss anything with each other, you know, and if I've got any worries I'd come and talk to her and get it off my chest. I suppose it's why I don't go to the doctor's so much. Things are not so bad once you have spoken about them, and we laugh about them and in a couple of days' time it's all right.'[30]

A friend is someone whom we know and love and who knows and loves us. Even though you fear that if someone knows you that person must certainly reject you, you must risk rejection (not everyone will reject you, really) since, as Sheldon Kopp said, 'Who can love me if no one knows me?'[31]

In confiding in another person we are, in effect, telling our tale. Each of us has a story, the story of our life, and as we tell that story, or just part of it, we know that our life has significance, at least in our eyes and the eyes of the person who listens. One of the saddest things I found again and again in my work, was that so many of the troubled people who came to see me had never had the chance to tell their story. No one in their family had listened. In the person's sorry round from doctor to doctor, in and out of hospital, no one had ever sat down with the person and let him tell his tale in his own way. Of course case histories had been taken, but in those the doctor or the social worker asked about what they thought was important and not what the person suffering thought was important. And you cannot tell your story to someone who can only spare you a few minutes of his precious time. So when the person finally got to me and realised that I was prepared to listen (Prepared! My idea of heaven is being in a garden with people who tell me stories), the relief of telling the story was sometimes all the person needed to find his way out of his troubles.

In listening to another person's story we are, in effect, bearing witness to that person's existence, courage, suffering and pain. Nancy Banks-Smith, who for many years has reviewed television programmes for the *Guardian*, is often asked how she can bear to watch so many news reports and documentaries about gross cruelties and immense suffering. To this she always replies that the sorrows and suffering of people must be witnessed. By witnessing we are saying, 'Yes, this did happen.' We open ourselves to the anguish of witnessing another person's suffering, and perhaps, when we suffer, someone will be prepared to witness our suffering and acknowledge that it did happen. We confirm one another's existence as a person by mutual witnessing. Sometimes we can relieve our own anguish by hastening to cure the person's pain and to put right what has gone wrong, but so often there is nothing we can do. Then we have to be able to face our own helplessness and not preserve a glorified image of ourselves and reduce our pain by denying the other person's truth. For if we do this we wound the sufferer even more. As Jill Tweedie wrote,

> Ex-depressive as I am, with only the occasional lapse, I cannot dismiss the idea that the vision of life seen in depression has the truth in it, the bare-boned skeletal truth, and an intrinsic part of depression is knowing this and being told that it is not so. Reality, however terrible, is bearable if others allow its reality. When they refuse you that, when they skip around you pretending you've got it wrong, that's rock-bottom time.[32]

7. Discover that there's nothing wrong with seeing the funny side of things

What's funny about being depressed, you might ask. Of course, some depressed people do laugh. Some of you keep up a smile and a joke so no one will know how you really feel. Some of you laugh and feel what T.S. Eliot called

> the conscious impotence of rage
> At human folly, and the laceration
> Of laughter at what ceases to amuse[33]

Some of you never laugh and joke, not because you have no sense of humour (everyone has a sense of humour) but because you believe that life is a serious matter and to be a good person you must always take things seriously. You would never dream of laughing at anyone, because if you laugh at anyone that means you do not love that person.

What rubbish! As anyone who manages to cope in any way with his life will tell you, one thing that makes life bearable is that it is funny, and that when we laugh at people we love we are showing that we love them for what they are, that we accept them as they are. One mark of the closeness of a group of people is the way they tease one another. They tease, not to exclude the person from the group, but to show that the person is special and unique. When we laugh at ourselves we show that we accept ourselves. We all have our pretensions to exceptional greatness and goodness, and we will not give them up, but we know that they are pretensions, and therefore ridiculous, and we laugh at them, not in bitterness but in love. Laughter puts sensible limits on our pride.

One of the reasons that your parents, especially your mother, looms so large in your life, is that you dare not laugh at them. You want to see them as superhuman, larger than life and you do not want to risk upsetting them. All children laugh at their parents, but some parents punish their children severely for this and insist that the child must accept the parent's evaluation of himself or herself as a dignified, important person. Some parents want to insist that their way of seeing the world is the only true one, so of course they must forbid their children to laugh at them. What humour shows is that there is always another way of seeing things. Humour exists only because there are always alternative ways of seeing things. If we all saw things in the same way there would be no humour.

Yet, what else can you do about your parents, but laugh at them? Most parents, by the time their children are grown up, are too old and set in their ways to change very much, and most of what they do which upsets you, upsets you simply because you see it that way. Laughter is your way of seeing things differently. Laughter means that you can love your parents for what they are, that you can accept them and no longer be afraid of them. Laughter casts out fear.

Harry Williams said of laughter,

God, we believe, accepts us, accepts all men, unconditionally, warts and all. Laughter is the purest form of our response to God's acceptance of us. For when I laugh at myself I accept myself and when I laugh at other people in genuine mirth I accept them. Self-acceptance in laughter is the very opposite of self-accusation or pride. For in laughter I accept myself not because I'm some sort of super-person, but precisely because I'm not. There is nothing funny about a super-person. There is everything funny about a man who thinks he is. In laughing at my own claims to importance or regard I receive myself in a sort of loving forgiveness which is an echo of God's forgiveness of me. In much conventional contrition there is a selfishness and pride which are scarcely hidden. In our desperate self-concern we blame ourselves for not being the super-persons we think we really are. But in laughter we set light to ourselves. That is why laughter is the purest form of our response to God. Whether or not the great saints were capable of levitation, I have not the evidence to decide. What I do know is that a characteristic of the great saints is their power of levity. For to set light to yourself is true humility. Pride cannot rise to levity. As G.K. Chesterton said, pride is the downward drag of all things into an easy solemnity. It would seem that a heavy seriousness is natural to man as falling. 'It was by the force of gravity that Satan fell.' Laughter, on the other hand, is a sign of grace.[34]

Whether or not we believe in God, we know that laughter brings the grace of peace and sharing with others. It also brings courage.

8. Dare to explore new ways of thinking and doing

It is all very well for me to talk about courage and exploring, but, if you feel so down and hopeless that you can barely get through each day, you are not in any state to go rushing about and doing all sorts of new things. Perhaps the only new thing you can contemplate doing is going into hospital. *Deciding to go into hospital* is one of the biggest decisions you can take (don't tell me other people make that decision – you decide to let other people make that decision for you) since it means transferring yourself into an environment very different from your own. When in 1983 I wrote about going into hospital the way in which psychiatric patients were cared for across the UK was very much uniform in format, although there were big differences in how well the care was given. In the years that followed there were major changes in the NHS. The large psychiatric hospitals were closed, general hospitals opened one or two psychiatric wards, and the emphasis was on care in the community. Multidisciplinary teams were set up consisting of a psychiatrist, a psychologist, a social worker, a psychiatric nurse and a manager, and the power was shared more equitably among these professionals. Much more emphasis was placed on psychotherapy, but the belief that there were mental illnesses which were caused and could be managed by changes in the biochemistry of the brain remained as strong as ever. However, along with the closure of NHS psychiatric hospitals an increasing number of private psychiatric hospitals were opened and more people were seeking private psychiatric care. In the USA most patients will go to a private hospital and what treatment they have will depend very much on what their insurance companies will pay for. As a result many depressed people still have to ponder the question, 'Should I go into hospital?'

The problem about deciding whether or not to go into hospital is that it is like buying a pig in a poke. It is very hard to find out what you will be getting. If you decide to buy a house, you can do the rounds of the estate agents, and if you decide to buy a car, you can read about the results of road tests in the car magazines, but if you decide to buy a stay in hospital, finding someone who can give you the necessary information can be very difficult. Most psychiatric units have information pamphlets about the activities and therapies on offer, but in some places these pamphlets are not so much information sheets as wish lists of what the unit would have if there were the funds to do so. Usually all you can do is to consult your general practitioner who then suggests that you go to hospital. Few GPs have had spells as psychiatric patients in their own local hospitals. When a doctor is admitted to hospital it is usually at some place which is a decent distance from his home – thus supporting the still prevalent belief that it is a shameful thing to be a psychiatric patient.

So all your GP may know about the psychiatrist he is sending you to is that he is a good chap – very helpful (takes troublesome patients off his hands) and very reliable (will visit the patient in a crisis). The GP may know very little of just how each psychiatrist practises psychiatry. Psychiatrists come in many shapes and forms. I can refer to them as 'he' because there are in Britain relatively few women psychiatrists, especially at consultant level. Each has his own idiosyncratic way of working, and so I can list only some of the varieties here. Some are wonderful – kind, understanding, sympathetic, wise, supportive and patient. Some are very strange, and leave you wondering who is the crazy one here. Some hold strictly to the medical model of depression and will give you pills and ECT and expect you to get better. Some try to give as little medication as possible and always have time to listen. Some visit their wards regularly and see their patients frequently while others make fleeting, irregular visits to the wards and appear to have abandoned their patients there. Some are trained therapists and some think psychotherapy is a waste of time. Some are skilled behaviour therapists while others think that if you reward a patient for anything you are only encouraging him to be manipulative and demanding. An increasing number use cognitive therapy, some sensitively, some crudely and simplistically. Some psychiatrists have a profound empathy with fellow human beings while others think that psychiatric patients are weak, inferior and stupid people. This last kind of psychiatrist often divides his patients into the 'deserving' and the 'undeserving' or frequently expounds his belief in 'penis therapy', i.e. 'All she needs is a good fuck'. Any woman who is given the currently fashionable diagnosis of Borderline Personality Disorder is likely to have this said of her.[35]

If you find yourself with a psychiatrist who offers you nothing but pills and electroconvulsive therapy (ECT) find another psychiatrist. Antidepressants have been around now since the 1950s, and ECT even longer. Studies conducted by psychiatrists of what happens in the long term to people treated only in the traditional way with drugs and ECT show that a large proportion of these people do not recover. Some people get depressed, get over it and never get depressed again, but many go on enduring one episode of depression after another until these episodes merge into one life-long misery.[36] Psychiatrists do not see depression as a curable illness but as an illness similar to epilepsy or diabetes. They talk of 'managing depression', not of curing it.[37]

ECT is still widely used. Many psychiatrists argue that ECT is necessary in certain cases where the person is considered to be 'unreachable' by any other means, and that the memory loss which ECT causes is negligible. Those massive amounts of what special nursing called tender loving care which can get through to people withdrawn into silent misery are not available on a psychiatric ward, not just because of staff shortages, but because of a general philosophy within the psychiatric system which can be summed up as, 'If you make this place too nice people won't want to go home.'

ECT affects memory quite badly. It does not select bad memories and wipe them out. It knocks out good memories too. People who have had ECT talk about not remembering even that they went on a family holiday, much less that they enjoyed it. Photographs of these happy events do not restore the memory. Some people speak of how they no longer remember their adult children as children, or how they cannot remember why their garden meant so much to them.[38] If your television broke down would you employ a TV repair man who opened the back of the set, threw in a few spanners, and then shook it violently? So why employ a psychiatrist who wants to do something similar to your brain?

Still, you can ask your GP which psychiatrist he recommends. He may offer you a choice and he may even be able to tell you something about the psychiatrist. However, if you come into hospital as a result of a crisis (usually a suicide attempt or a family dispute) you have no choice about the psychiatrist whose patient you become.

So, you enter hospital and you are given a bed on a particular ward. Now, not only does one psychiatric hospital differ from another, but within a hospital one ward will differ from another. You are not likely to be put on a long-stay ward or a geriatric ward but on some kind of admission ward. Some wards may have just one consultant in charge while two or three consultants might admit patients to another ward. One ward may be a very quiet place, where patients are arranged in still-life poses around the walls, while another is all hustle and bustle where patients and staff (indistinguishable through the lack of uniforms) are busy doing all sorts of things. You may be surprised to discover that the ward has both male and female patients.

The old asylums were designed to keep men and women apart. Ugly and cruel though these places were, they did give women patients protection from assault by the male patients. The suffering of many of the women had arisen from the cruelty they had received at the hands of their fathers, brothers, husbands and other men, so to be protected from men must have given them some measure of relief.

However, in the 1980s the managers of psychiatric hospitals were required to cut costs. They discovered that having separate wards for men and women was 'uneconomic', and so they created wards where men and women had separate sleeping areas but shared living quarters. This change was advocated by the managers on the grounds that such 'socialisation' would be therapeutic. The managers did not explain how, say, a frightened, depressed woman would be helped by being close to a large psychotic man, nor a gentle, depressed man would be helped by being close to an angry, distraught woman. Managers, I noted, rarely if ever encountered a psychiatric patient. I also discovered to my cost that if a member of staff raised any objections to such mixing of men and women all that person achieved was to bring scorn and opprobrium down on his or her head.

As more and more hospitals closed and patients returned to the community the remaining or new psychiatric units took in only the more difficult and disturbed patients whose ages could range from the teens to the sixties. Such diverse people with diverse problems did not form a community. Moreover, there was a quick turnover of patients because for economic reasons treatment had to be brief. In the old admission wards in a psychiatric hospital a good charge nurse or sister could establish a consistent ward ethos because patients stayed on the ward for several months and most of the staff were permanent. Now many of the staff are likely to be agency nurses. With such a rapid change of staff and patients these wards can seem to be more like a transit camp than a therapeutic community.

Some things, however, never change. Under the old system a senior nurse and a psychologist would work out a therapeutic programme for a patient, only to have it destroyed by a psychiatrist who ignored such plans and discharged the patient or made radical changes in the drugs the patient was taking with the result that the plan could not be put into effect. This still happens on the new psychiatric wards.

However, under pressure from women staff, women's groups, patients' advocates (people who have been psychiatric patients and who act as advocates for psychiatric patients who have difficulty in expressing their views) and MIND, a number of Mental Health Trusts have opened women-only units. Some of these, such as the Camden and Islington Mental Health Trust's unit, Drayton Park, are true therapeutic communities where the staff mingle with the residents (not 'patients'), where every interaction has the possibility of being therapeutic, and where there is a wide range of therapies available, such as individual and group therapy, yoga, massage and aromatherapy.

So, before you decide to go into hospital, find out all you can about what is on offer.

What, then, is a good ward?

First of all, it has a consultant in charge who takes the time to listen. Before you come into hospital you should have a long talk with him so you can feel reasonably sure that he understands, at least in outline, if not in depth, what you are feeling and that you can trust him enough to put yourself in his care. Once in hospital you should see your consultant regularly, and not just in case conferences. You will be told that you should talk regularly with your 'key worker' who will be another member of staff, but you may feel that there are certain matters you wish to discuss only with your consultant, particularly any health matters or the drugs you are prescribed.

You may be told that case conferences are for the patient's benefit, but it is only an indirect benefit. Staff have case conferences so they can communicate with one another, and occasionally the communication will be about you. The only immediate benefit you can get from a case conference is to be able to ask for weekend leave. Case conferences can be very upsetting for you if you have to go into a roomful of people where the only familiar faces are those of your doctor and nurse. On a good ward you should know all the people at the case conference.

Beware the consultant who sees your family separately from you to gather 'facts' about you and your illness. (Apart from facts like your date of birth and educational achievements, there are no facts, just different interpretations by different people, some of whom are very biased.) This only serves to mark you out as the 'ill' one in the family and lets the other family members congratulate themselves on how well and sane they are. Beware, too, of the psychiatrist who likes to see your husband on his own so they can be chaps together talking about what a problem the little woman is, and aren't all women like that, especially at that time of the month or when they reach a certain age, ha ha ha. A good psychiatrist has studied the methods of family therapy and marital therapy, as well as individual psychotherapy, and though you are the one in hospital he knows that there are problems in the home to which every family member contributes and which must be made explicit and, if possible, solved, if you are to cease to be depressed.

If your GP refers you not to a consultant psychiatrist but to a community team, the first person you meet could be any member of that team. One member of the team will be appointed by the team to be your 'key worker'. While every member of the team can have a part in your care your key worker has the duty to build up a good relationship with you and, with the rest of the team, to create a therapeutic programme for you which is usually a combination of some kind of psychotherapy and a course of antidepressant drugs.

Psychiatrists are medical doctors, and in the tradition of medicine they place great emphasis on arriving at a diagnosis. This allows them to decide what drugs to give you. If the psychiatrist thinks you are psychotic (out of touch with reality) he will prescribe major tranquillisers such as chlorpromazine. If he thinks you are manic, you are likely to be given lithium. If he thinks you are very anxious, you are likely to be given a minor tranquilliser such as Valium and if he thinks you are depressed, he will give you one or two of the many antidepressant drugs.

Arriving at a diagnosis in psychiatry is somewhat different from arriving at a diagnosis in general medicine. If you go along to your GP to complain, say, about a pain in your chest, receiving a diagnosis can be comforting ('It's indigestion') or worrying ('I think it's a heart condition'), but you know that your GP can usually get some tests done to check whether the diagnosis was right. Unless your psychiatrist gives you a diagnosis such as 'It might be a brain tumour' there are no physical tests to check whether the psychiatrist has made the right diagnosis. Psychiatric diagnoses are simply a matter of opinion, and psychiatrists rarely agree on a diagnosis. This is why, if you remain a psychiatric patient for long enough to be interviewed by several psychiatrists, you will acquire a whole collection of diagnoses, which can be extremely confusing if you are still expecting that psychiatry operates in the same way as physical medicine. Psychiatrists have no way of testing their diagnoses except by asking the patient questions, and thus the process becomes circular, and hence very different from diagnosis in physical medicine.

For instance, if you met me you might hear me coughing and ask me what was wrong. I would reply, 'I have a chronic lung disease called bronchiectasis.' You might then say, 'How do you know you've got bronchiectasis?' I would answer by talking about a number pf physical tests – X-rays, CT scans, lung function tests, sweat tests, all of which serve to confirm the presence of the disease and the extent of the damage it has caused. By contrast, you might say to a psychiatrist, 'I feel hopeless, terribly guilty, not interested in anything. I cannot make a decision and I feel utterly isolated.' From this the psychiatrist would diagnose you and say, 'You have a major depressive disorder.' You could then ask, 'How do you know I've got a major depressive disorder?' and the psychiatrist would reply, 'Because you have the symptoms of major depressive disorder – hopelessness, guilt, indecision and a sense of isolation.' Which is what you told him. All he has done is to give you a word which lumps together your different feelings and experiences. There is nothing outside of what you told him that will confirm his diagnosis.

The GP Terry Lynch wrote,

In twenty years of working as a doctor, I have never heard of any person having a diagnosis of depression, schizophrenia, manic depression or any other psychiatric condition confirmed by a blood test or any test. Dosages of psychiatric drugs are not adjusted according to blood-test results, as happens with all biochemically based illnesses. When doctors decide to stop treatment in cases of 'mental illness', no blood test is done to confirm that the supposed biochemical abnormality has been eradicated. This would not happen with any known biochemical abnormality. Why no tests? Because no such tests exist – because no biochemical abnormality has been demonstrated in any psychiatric illness . . . Manic depression is the only psychiatric condition where regular blood tests are carried out. These tests are not done to check the level of any body chemical. Rather, they are done to check the blood levels of the treatment drug lithium, a drug with highly toxic side effects.[39]

Although many psychiatrists talk about how in depression there is 'a chemical imbalance in the brain' and how antidepressant drugs put this imbalance right, such talk is based on faith, not proven research. At the Tenth Anniversary Conference of Depressed Anonymous in the USA in 1995 a psychiatrist gave a lecture on the chemical imbalance in depression. He said that a test for this chemical had been discovered but it was so expensive few patients could afford to have the test done. I challenged him on this by pointing out that if ever such a test had been discovered the drug companies would have rushed to buy the test and mass-produce it cheaply. The psychiatrist then admitted he told his patients they had a chemical imbalance in order to comfort them and give them hope. His audience did not feel comforted.

Psychiatrists rarely give a one-word diagnosis of 'depression'. After all, they have scores of different kinds of depression to choose from. The *Diagnostic and Statistical Manual*, drawn up by American psychiatrists but increasingly used in the UK, lists thirty-nine different kinds of depression.[40] (Always remember that the fact that a word exists does not necessarily mean that something exists in reality to which the word refers. Consider the words 'Father Christmas'.) The words for depression most commonly used in the UK are 'clinical depression', 'reactive depression' and 'endogenous depression'. 'Clinical depression' means that you are very depressed, 'reactive depression' means that your psychiatrist thinks that an identifiable event in your life has made you depressed, and 'endogenous depression' means that your psychiatrist thinks that you are a normal person leading an ordinary life and the depression has arisen without any external cause. Traditionally the treatment for endogenous depression is drugs and ECT, rather than psychotherapy.

The diagnosis of depression depends so much on

cultural values. If 'endogenous depression' means a depression for which no cause in the patient's life can be found, and if the doctor doing the diagnosing believes that all a woman needs to make her happy is a husband, a home and children, then a depressed married woman is likely to be diagnosed as having an endogenous depression and treated accordingly, which means a greater likelihood of receiving only drugs and ECT and little psychotherapy. Research shows that many more women, particularly older women, receive ECT than men.[41]

If you decide to go into hospital you will soon know if you are on a good ward. On a good ward your therapeutic programme is drawn up soon after you are admitted. It lays down all the activities in which you will be involved, and these activities are actually carried out. As you progress you work out with the staff how your programme should change. Very likely you will attend the ward group which is held regularly. This is a meeting of all staff and patients on the ward and it is intended to improve the way the ward functions as a community. Some of the things discussed are practical ('Whose turn is it to do the washing up rota?') and some of the things discussed are personal but affect the community as a whole ('Why does Bill disappear every time he has promised to organise a table-tennis tournament?', 'Why is Dr Smith always late for the ward meeting?'). Then there may be other, smaller groups, led by one of the staff where the members of the group are encouraged to help one another. Some kind of individual therapy should be available, perhaps talking with a counsellor, perhaps a course of cognitive therapy. There should also be relaxation classes, art therapy classes, occupational therapy classes, perhaps music and drama therapy classes, and a variety of recreational activities. At some stage in your stay on the ward you will be involved in most of these as part of your therapeutic programme. No chance to sit and moulder in a corner on this sort of ward. Moreover, the ward is kept clean, and there are rooms where silence is respected.

But suppose you do find yourself on a ward where the only sound is the rattle of the drugs trolley? If you are in a terribly run-down and ill state or if you are exhausted and need a break away from your family, then a short stay on such a ward can be helpful while you regain your strength. However, once you do regain your strength a ward which offers no more than pills, ECT and nursing care will do nothing for you. There is no therapeutic miasma which seeps out of the walls and makes you better.

When you are depressed it is hard to think clearly and it is easy to become even more confused. It is often very difficult to work out the identities of all the different people you meet and what they are supposed to do.

Your consultant will have working with him one or two junior doctors. These may be a medical student doing a psychiatric placement, a senior house officer who has just graduated as a doctor, a junior registrar who is studying for the qualifying examinations for entry into psychiatry (in the UK this is the entry to the Royal College of Psychiatrists), or a senior registrar who has passed the qualifying examinations and is waiting to obtain a consultant post. The junior doctors are responsible for the day-to-day care of the patients but they are also involved in training in psychology and psychotherapy.

Clinical psychologists hold degrees in psychology, which is the study of why people behave as they do. They have had experience in a wide range of therapies but usually specialise in one. These therapies include group therapy, individual therapy, family therapy, and cognitive therapy which helps people become aware of how the way they think leads them to become miserable and depressed.

Most of the nurses who work in psychiatric wards or in the community teams have trained as psychiatric nurses (which includes some training in psychiatry and psychology) and many have also done courses in therapy and counselling. They run groups and talk to patients individually.

The social workers, as well as having social work qualifications, have usually had training in therapy and counselling. As well as helping patients with practical problems they run groups and talk to patients individually.

The team might also contain an occupational therapist whose work covers a wide range of skills. If you have some kind of physical handicap the occupational therapist, sometimes along with a physiotherapist, can help you improve your home to meet your needs. Very often an occupational therapist can teach you new skills which can increase your self-confidence. In all these interactions the occupational therapist will be using the skills of a therapist and counsellor.

Well-equipped teams include an art therapist and a music therapist who are skilled in using the arts to help people gain a greater understanding and so be able to change.

Finding a therapist or counsellor
Nowadays many people, in order to sort out their unhappiness or depression, set out to find their own therapist or counsellor. Therapy and counselling are burgeoning professions, and although there are many excellent therapists and counsellors there are also many therapists and counsellors who are at best useless and at worst damaging.

In the course of my work I meet many therapists and counsellors, and I cannot see any significant difference between them in what they do. So here I shall use the word 'therapist' to refer to both, and I shall use the pronoun 'she' because, apart from psychoanalysis and cognitive therapy, the majority of therapists and counsellors are women. Research into the benefits of therapy shows that, while different therapists work in different ways, what determines the success of the venture is not the method which the therapist uses but the quality of the relationship between the therapist and the client, and whether the client is prepared to change.

It is possible to tell right from the beginning whether you have found a good therapist.

(a) At the first meeting, as well as asking about the arrangements for your sessions and, if the therapist works privately, about the way the costs are worked out, ask the therapist about her professional qualifications and the theory in which she works. If the therapist is very vague about qualifications and theory or if she turns your question back on you and asks, 'Why are you asking me that?' find another therapist.

(b) Whatever your problems, the reason you are in difficulty is because you have lost confidence in yourself
and have turned against yourself. The aim of therapy
should be to help you rediscover your self-confidence
and for you to become your own best friend. This can
come about in many different ways, but, however the
therapist works, she should show you in everything
she does and says that she values you and is on your
side. You might not leave every session feeling happy
because often the session will have brought back painful memories and shown you some hard truths, but you
should never feel that the therapist has deliberately
set out to hurt or belittle you. Therapists are no more
than human and so might inadvertently say something which hurts, so you might occasionally need to
overlook an unintended mistake, or discuss what happened with the therapist, but, if you find that the
therapist is consistently putting you down, leave and
find another.

(c) You go along to a therapist hoping that this person
will wave a magic wand, say a magic word and all your
pain will disappear and you will live happily ever
after. A good therapist rapidly makes it quite clear
that she does not have a magic cure but that she is
prepared to accompany you on the journey where you
will find your own solutions. If instead the therapist
gives you to understand that she is in possession of
some great secret which, if you are a good patient, she
will impart to you and so make you well, you are in the
presence of a charlatan. Leave and search further for
an honest therapist.

(d) While the relationship between the therapist and the
client can be thought of as a special kind of friendship, it is not a friendship in the sense that you have to
meet the therapist's needs. The therapist is there for
you. You do enough for the therapist by allowing the
therapist to have an interesting job and perhaps earn
some money while doing it. You do not have to look
after the therapist, and you certainly do not have to
meet the therapist's sexual needs. Sex with your

therapist is never a cure for your misery, no matter what an unscrupulous therapist might say.

(e) We get into difficulties when we think that we are as we are and we cannot change. If you say, 'I've got a depressive personality,' or 'I'm a Gemini so I can't help doing what I do,' or 'I inherited depression from my parents,' you are in effect saying that you are fixed and unchangeable, and therefore doomed to suffer for the rest of your life. It does not matter if you find the best therapist in the world, if you do not see yourself as capable of changing and if you are not prepared to change, then there is nothing that therapist can do to help you. A good therapist will not be saying to you, 'The way you see things is wrong. My way of seeing things is the Right Way and so you must see things as I do.' Rather, a good therapist will help you discover that what you call 'I' is a collection of ideas, attitudes, opinions, beliefs, memories and feelings which have built up over your lifetime as you interpreted what was happening to you. You created these interpretations and, since you created them, you are free to change them. A good therapist helps you discover that you have choices. You can choose to see yourself as bad and unacceptable or you can choose to see yourself as valuable and acceptable. It is always tempting to hang on to your old choices on the principle that the devil you know is better than the devil you don't know, especially when seeing yourself as bad and unacceptable can have such good rewards. For instance, if you did decide to think of yourself as valuable and acceptable, would that mean that your friends and relatives would stop telling you what a wonderful person you are?

Finding a good therapist can be difficult, but you also have to get some idea of all the different kinds of therapies there are. One way of sorting out the different therapies is to divide them into exploratory and prescriptive therapies.

In exploratory therapy the therapist and you explore your thoughts and feelings by talking about what has happened to you in your life. For instance, you might say, 'My mother died last year.' You might go on to describe the circumstances of your mother's death, and then the therapist asks you, 'How did you feel about that?', thus inviting you to talk about your feelings, especially feelings that conflict with one another, say, sorrow at losing your mother yet relief because in some ways she was a burden to you.

Or you might say, 'When the doctor told me mum mightn't live more than a few days I tried to get all the family together. Some of them couldn't – or wouldn't – come, and I was upset by this.' The therapist might then ask, 'Why was it important to you that all the family should be together when your mother died?' To answer this question you need to talk about an important principle by which you live your life – perhaps the principle that family members should support one another.

In prescriptive therapies the therapist gives advice about what a client should do. This may be general advice, such as, if you start to feel panicky, breathe deeply and slowly, and relax your body, or it may be specific homework where you have to carry out certain tasks or keep a diary of your thoughts.

Some therapists use either exploratory or prescriptive methods, and some use both. Exploratory therapies can be based on the theories of psychoanalysis (in the UK there is Freudian, Jungian and Kleinian psychoanalysis) or existentialism, or person-centred therapy, or dynamic therapy, or humanistic therapy, or personal construct therapy, any one of the many kinds of exploratory therapies, too many to list here. Different therapies have different jargon, but what all these therapies are based on is the understanding that what determines our behaviour is not what happens to us but how we interpret what happens to us.

The most popular prescriptive therapy is cognitive therapy, sometimes called cognitive behaviour therapy. If you are referred to a clinical psychologist, or if you come under the care of a community psychiatric team, you are likely to be given cognitive therapy, while many psychiatric wards have nurses or psychiatrists who have trained in cognitive therapy.

Cognitive therapy was invented by a psychiatrist in the USA, Aaron Beck, but, as it is a psychological method, it has been developed by psychologists. Cognitive therapy is similar to personal construct psychology (this book is an example of personal construct psychology) in that it is concerned with our ideas, but, while personal construct psychologists know that we have good reasons for holding certain ideas, cognitive therapists simply condemn certain ideas which they call 'maladaptive' or 'dysfunctional'. Cognitive therapists see the idea that 'I am bad and have to work hard to be good' as being dysfunctional, and do not pay any attention to the fact that, when we first acquire that idea, it was the best idea available to us at the time. It allowed us to survive. When we are small children we know that we are dependent on our parents. If our parents mistreat us in some way we have the choice of seeing ourselves as being completely alone and helpless, or of seeing ourselves as being capable of pleasing our parents and keeping ourselves safe. A child who sees himself as being completely alone and helpless suffers and dies, as the pictures from famished, AIDS-ridden or war-torn countries show. The child who tells himself that he can save himself by trying to be good may not be able magically to produce food and shelter out of emptiness, but within a family he has a chance of keeping himself alive.

Cognitive therapy is helpful in that it is an effective way of becoming aware of how you talk to yourself, how you constantly denigrate yourself and create self-fulfilling prophecies such as 'Everybody hates me' or 'Everything will turn out badly'. Cognitive therapy has some effective methods of showing how we can choose the way we talk to ourselves, how we can praise and encourage ourselves, and how we can make discriminating statements, such as, 'Some people are impossibly difficult, but I can win most people's interest and liking by being interested in them,' and 'This new job could be difficult but I'll give it my best shot.'

Cognitive therapists set their clients homework. It can be extremely useful to have a written account of your efforts to change your day-to-day living, or of your success in encouraging yourself, or of working out alternative ways of interpreting certain events. However, it seems that much of the research on cognitive therapy, of which cognitive therapists are very proud, is based on people who were mildly depressed and not on people who were in the grip of a devastatingly incapacitating depression.

One of the current leaders in cognitive therapy, an internationally renowned teacher of cognitive therapy, is the American psychologist Christine Padesky. She is a charming, friendly woman who undoubtedly has helped many people, both clients and therapists. I attended one of her lectures to a large group of counselling psychologists. She began by talking about those problem clients, the ones who would not carry out the homework set by their cognitive therapist. She asked the audience to consider a client who, in the first session with the therapist, reveals that he lies in bed late every morning, brooding on his woes and disinclined to make any decisions about what to do that day. Accordingly, the cognitive therapist sets the client the homework, to be carried out every morning, of leaping out of bed at first light, showering and dressing, and so ready to face the day. However, when the client returned for the second session, he reported that he had not carried out the homework. Christine Padesky asked the audience to comment on this dereliction of duty.

The audience sat silent. Most of them were experienced counsellors and they were probably as stunned as I was at the notion that someone should instruct a deeply depressed person to rise with alacrity on waking. Did Christine not know that in deep depression we awake in terror. The defence of depression dissolves in sleep and so, as we enter into wakefulness, the terror of annihilation, the unnamed dread, comes upon us. To get out of bed, to face the turmoil of the day, would only increase the terror. The bed offers an illusion of some safety as we huddle under the covers.

Gwyneth Lewis spoke of being 'dug into your duvet snow-shelter', and advised,

The crucial thing is not to listen to your mind. What's going on in there is: 'Shit! I'm in trouble, I knew it would always come to this, there's nowhere to go, no rest. This is terrible. They're bound to sack me, if only I hadn't . . . Why

can't I get up? Get up! I can't. I must get up and climb a
mountain then bake a cake then go to the gym, that would
show them that I'm OK. Everyone else is fine; it's only me
who's mad. I've lost it. This is the end of me. Oh my God, I
can't bear this . . .'.

Your best bet is to keep very close to the ground, don't
raise your head an inch into the wind. Expose yourself to
this onslaught and you're lost, even though it is your own
mind that has created this gale, what Les Murray calls a
'head-storm'. Stay still and even these enormous,
terrifying powers will pass.[42]

Getting up and getting dressed immediately on waking
may be a sensible task to undertake when you are making
your way out of the prison of depression but it is not a
sensible task while the 'head-storm' is still raging.

Over the years I have met a vast number of therapists
and counsellors, and so I know that the majority of them
went into that work after they had encountered loss and disaster in their own life. They know what it is like to go
through a period, possibly a long period, of uncomprehending misery and fear. By going into therapy they came to
understand their misery and fear, and from this they decided
to become therapists themselves. While they may refer to
themselves in terms of the particular training they under-
took, what they value most is what they learned from their
own personal experience. In contrast, most cognitive
therapists do their training as a postgraduate course. In such
training there is no requirement that the student seek self-
understanding through personal therapy. Thus many cognitive therapists have not lived long enough to encounter
major loss, disaster or disappointment, nor have they struggled with and meditated upon the far-reaching consequences
of loss, disaster and disappointment. Consequently, clients
are sometimes astounded by the naivety of their cognitive
therapist.

Aaron Beck, the founder of cognitive therapy, specifically ordered his disciples not to discuss religious or philosophical ideas with their clients. Yet it is in depression
that all the major moral issues present themselves in a very

personal way. These are issues over which theologians and philosophers have argued for centuries, yet never arrived at any universal answers. All the questions about a virtuous life, about truth, responsibility, loyalty, forgiveness, shame, guilt, sin, redemption, about the meaning of death and the purpose of life, are the questions over which the depressed person ponders and to which some satisfactory answer must be found if the person is to relinquish the prison of depression and all the suffering that state entails. Finding such answers is best carried out in conversation with other people, but all too often our friends and family do not want to have to discuss such matters, or they try to foist their answers on us and not let us find our own. A good therapist is one who knows that the task of the therapist is to accompany the client on a journey without maps to an unknown destination where, on reaching it, the client will know it for the first time.

Finding other help
Help is usually only a telephone call away. The Samaritans are always available and you do not have to be suicidal to phone them. In the USA, Australia and many other countries there are similar organisations. Their telephone numbers are usually listed at the front of the telephone directory.

Relate and other marriage guidance organisations offer counselling to individuals as well as to couples. In the UK the National Association for Mental Health (MIND) has numerous local associations, many of which offer group therapy, counselling and drop-in centres for those in need of a chat and company.

In the 1970s many people realised that they could help themselves solve all sorts of problems by forming self-help groups. Your health centre, your community psychiatric team or your local mental health association should be able to tell you what is available in your area. You can also contact the Fellowship of Depressives Anonymous[43] and/or Depression Alliance,[44] while in the USA Depressed Anonymous[45] offers considerable support. There are a vast number of mental health websites, most of which, or so it seems from my searches of the web, are based on an uncritical acceptance of the theory of mental illnesses and of the DSM, but you may find some which are useful.

If there is no *self-help group* available in your area, why don't you put a notice in your local paper or on the notice board of your health centre, asking interested people to contact you? You will soon have the nucleus of a group. If you let the social workers, psychologists and community nurses at your psychiatric hospital know what you are doing, they should be able give you support. Not only are they likely to send people to join your group but they may be able to help you find suitable rooms for your meetings. The Social Services, the Health Service and the Probation Department usually have space in their buildings available in the evenings for self-help groups. Churches, too, often have a convenient room.

What should a self-help group do?
This is up to the group to decide. Some groups decide to be a kind of friendship club where people meet for a chat and to do social things together. Some groups decide to run as a therapy group. Self-help therapy is quite possible. You do not need a professional therapist to run a therapy group. If you would like to try this, but do not know where to start, get hold of a very useful book by Sheila Ernst and Lucy Goodison called *In Our Own Hands*.[46] This book tells you, very clearly and simply, how to set up and run a therapy group and what kinds of therapeutic exercises can be undertaken. The jargon of therapy (Gestalt, encounter, bioenergetics, psychodrama, etc.) is explained in a simple but critical way. Joining a self-help group will be one of the most valuable things you can do. You will meet a group of people who know what it is to be depressed. You do not have to explain it to them, or apologise, or pretend that you are happy when you are not. In a self-help group you give and receive friendship, and in sharing the responsibility for the group you build up your confidence and self-respect.

Those are some ideas about where you can get help, provided you are prepared to go out and find it and to work hard with what you are offered.

What can you do quietly, on your own?
You can read. There are hundreds, perhaps thousands, of books like this one where the writer gives advice. Some of this advice you will find useful, but no one book has all the answers for you. A book can be a signpost, pointing you along the way. Some of the most helpful signposts are not in books of advice but in literature, in poetry, novels, plays and biographies. You are not the only person who has found life to be difficult. This is why people write. Of course, there is fame and money but the main reason for writing is to master our life, somehow to take our experience and create something of it, and by taking it out of oneself and putting it on the page we change painful confusion into poignant clarity.

One person who understood this perhaps best of all was the poet Rilke. When a young friend, Wolf Graf von Kalckreuth, a poet, shot himself, Rilke wrote a requiem, where he chided him, not just for being impatient, but for failing to use his art to save himself.

Why could you not have waited till the point
where hardness grows unbearable: where it turns,
being now so hard so real? Look,
this might perhaps have come with your next moment;
that moment, maybe, was already trimming
its garland at the door you slammed for ever.

. . .

O ancient curse of poets!
Being sorry for themselves instead of saying,
for ever passing judgment on their feeling
instead of shaping it; for ever thinking
that what is sad or joyful in themselves
is what they know and what in poems may fitly
be mourned or celebrated. Invalids,
using a language full of woefulness
to tell us where it hurts, instead of sternly
transforming into words those selves of theirs,
as imperturbable cathedral carvers
transposed themselves into the constant stone.
That would have been salvation. Had you once

perceived how fate may pass into a verse
and not come back, how, once in, it turns image,
nothing but image, but an ancestor,
who sometimes, when you watch him in his frame,
seems to be like you and again not like you: –
you would have persevered.[47]

Gwyneth Lewis started writing poetry when she was seven years old. She found that 'The project of getting the real world into a pattern that sounded beautiful thrilled me deeply.' Alas, she was not allowed simply to enjoy writing poetry. Her mother, a teacher, would 'correct' her work and insisted that she compete in the eisteddfod. Gwyneth did well in these competitions and at school, but soon attracted the envy and scorn of some of her classmates. Hurt by this, she stopped writing, and thus, in denying herself, damaged herself. Now she knows that writing is an essential part of her. Moreover, 'Poetry is my lie-detector test, the best way I have of detecting my own bullshit. It's better than therapy, than conversations with friends, and is comparable in accuracy only to prayer. If I'm unsure of what I think of a situation and try to write a poem about it, I'm able to make sense of it. Any lies in my thinking, any self-indulgence simply won't scan and I have to abandon them and move on to what will work practically, both in the poem and in my life. Poetry represents the minimum amount of reality that I require to live well. Without it, what I'm living isn't my genuine life but a forgery. It may be plausible but it wasn't meant for me.'[48]

So, what you must do is turn your fate into a verse – or something similar. It does not have to be good poetry or prose. Most, or all of it, is for your eyes only. Just how and when you write you will decide. In the first year that I came to England, in 1968, the second depressed patient I met was Jean Brumpton. It never occurred to me that I had said anything to Jean which might have been of any use to her, but years later she got in touch with me to let me know that life was going well for her and she sent me this poem

TO DR. DOROTHY
To me you suggested the written word,
Just about ten years ago,

And when the appropriate time occurred
Seemingly without effort did the writing flow.

Anytime during day or night,
With jumbled thoughts that made no sense,
On any scrap of paper within my sight,
They were scribbled down and sorted hence.

A very real effort your guidance bore
Also your calm and gently humorous way
So, using the written word once more
May I, my gratitude to you convey.

Every December Jean sends me a birthday card and a
Christmas card along with a letter to let me know that her
life continues to go well.

You can do what Jean did, write on scraps of paper as
the thoughts occur to you, or you can do what Philip Toynbee did, keep a diary, a sort of log of your spiritual journey.

I have often asked people what for them was the worst
part of being depressed. The answer most commonly given
was 'isolation', the prison experience itself. The second most
common answer was 'lethargy'. This was more than simple
tiredness, or even a sense of being unable to do anything or
feel anything. It was an all-encompassing vacancy of energy
and spirit. Gwyneth Lewis discovered that this peculiar
lethargy was extremely valuable. I would call it a time when
the meaning structure was re-building itself, but the meaning structure *is* our own sense of being a person, and our
sense of being a person *is* our life story, something that the
poet knew. She wrote,

Something important was changing inside me. Lethargy
isn't the opposite of energy, but its predecessor. I felt like a
computer that was trying to catch up with itself,
swallowing new information, discarding the old.

People in the middle of depression are beings who
have to live, for a while, without a story, which is why it
feels as though you've lost your soul. But this period is a
dark room where you're developing the next chapter of
your life before living it. The work will be all the more
vivid if you're patient and let it take its own course.[49]

When you have the energy you can work on the reconstruction by thinking about, and sometimes writing about, certain aspects of your sense of being a person.

First there is writing what we call a *script*. This can be a self-description, or part of a biography. If you feel that you are completely bad and useless, then write a description of yourself as if written by a sympathetic friend. This will make you look at yourself in a different way. You could choose some event in your life which you feel was a turning point and write your biography going backwards and forwards from that point, trying to get very clear what was significant about that event and trying to capture the half-thought, usually quickly repressed ideas, which that event symbolises.

Another script to write begins with you answering very quickly this question, 'How old will you be when you die?' and then decide

(a) why you chose that age, or why you dared not think of an age (that is, lied to yourself. We all have some notion of when we expect to die, even if it is only an average of the ages at which our parents or grandparents died);

(b) what you *hope* to do between now and then;

(c) what you *expect* you will do between now and then;

(d) why there are differences between what you hope and expect and how these differences can be overcome.

Then there is writing a script about that relative who causes you the most pain and concern. Only, instead of saying 'She is like this' or 'He does that', say 'I am like this' or 'I do that'. You write the script as if you were that person. If you and your partner are working on this you can write scripts for one another and then compare results. Don't fight over it. Try to help one another deal with the shock of discovering how little you know of one another.

There is also the *writing of letters*. These are letters that you do not necessarily post. They may be letters to people dead and gone but to whom you still have something important to say – 'I didn't have a chance to thank you,' 'I never told you how much I love you,' 'I'm so angry that you went and died and left me all alone.' Or they may be letters to people about old, but still strong, angers, resentments, jealousies, guilts and fears. There is no point in sending such letters to a little old lady who was once a fierce giantess who terrified you. But writing to that ferocious figure who denied you what you needed can turn that figure in your mind into an ordinary human being, especially if, in return, you write yourself the letter you wish you had received from her but didn't. You need to write to both your parents, so that you can arrive at a point where you can recall your parents in the way that Sheldon Kopp recalled his in the dedication of his book.

> For my dead parents, whom I often miss. My Mother whose strength and ferocity nurtured me, almost did me in, and taught me how to survive. And my Father whose gentleness and passivity showed me how to love, let me down often, and freed me to find my own way.[50]

Now we come to *laddering* which shows how the simplest, most prosaic decision we make is linked to the way in which we experience and value our existence. This exercise seems like a party game, but I must ask you not to use it as such. Many people find it distressing, for even if they do not give you truthful answers to your questions, the answers that do come into their minds can be unexpectedly revealing. I do this laddering exercise only in workshops with people who have had some experience of self-exploration, and even they sometimes find it a shock. I would not give this exercise to a client, although I do frequently ask the question, 'Why is it that important to you?'

So, the laddering exercise. Take any three things – three makes of car, three kinds of food, three types of music, three famous people – and ask, 'In what way are two of these the same and the other different?'

Suppose we took three kinds of food, say, cream cakes, apple pie, grilled steak. In what way are two of these the same and the other different?

We could answer, 'Cream cakes and apple pie are the same because they are comforting foods and steak isn't.'

Or, 'Cream cakes and apple pie are soft and mushy and steak isn't.'

Or, 'Cream cakes and steak are because they are luxurious and apple pie isn't.'

Or, 'Cream cakes and steak are because they are extravagant and wasteful and apple pie isn't.'

Or, 'Apple pie and steak are because that is what my mother used to cook me.'

Or, 'Apple pie and steak are because that's what I used to eat when I was in the Army.'

You might be able to think of some more similarities and differences, but the one that is important is the one that applies to you. Decide what it is and follow it through here. Suppose we decide on 'Comforting foods as against non-comforting foods'. Now ask, 'Which do you prefer, comforting food or non-comforting food?' and the answer comes, 'Comforting food.'

The next question is 'Why is it important to you to have comforting food?' The answer might be, 'Because it makes me feel better and makes me feel comfortable.'

'Why is it important to you to be comfortable?'

'I don't like being uncomfortable.'

'Why is it important to you not to be uncomfortable?'

'I don't know. Nobody likes being uncomfortable. I don't like being uncomfortable – it makes me feel I don't belong.'

'Why is it important to you to belong?'

'To belong – to feel you're part of a group – you know, being with people who know you and accept you. Really that's what life's about.'

'What would happen to you if you could not be with people who know and accept you – if you were completely on your own?'

'I'd get myself with a group as quickly as possible.'

'But what if you couldn't do that – if you had to be totally alone.'

'That would be the end of me, I guess.'

Another person might say, 'Comforting as against non-comforting food', but choose 'non-comforting food' as his preference.

'Why is non-comforting food important to you?'

'It, well, makes you stronger. Comforting food, sort of holds you back.'

'Why is it important to you to be stronger and not held back?'

'Well, to achieve, to make something of yourself – I don't mean becoming famous – I mean developing yourself.'

'Why is it important to you to develop yourself?'

'Because – well – I want to find out who I am – who I could become – kind of knowing myself.'

'What is the opposite of knowing yourself?'

'Not knowing yourself – living in a kind of chaos, I suppose.'

'What would happen to you if you had to live always in a kind of chaos?'

'I couldn't – that would be madness – I'd die.'

So, from the choice of food we go by the way of the question 'Why is that important to you?' to how each person experiences his sense of existence and sees the threat of his annihilation. Some fifty per cent of people experience their sense of existence in relation to other people and the threat of annihilation as being completely rejected and abandoned. I call these People Persons or extraverts. The other fifty per cent experience their sense of existence in terms of the development of themselves as individuals, achieving and gaining clarity and organisation. They see the threat of annihilation as losing control and falling into chaos. I call these people What Have I Achieved Today Persons or introverts.[51]

Remember what I am describing here is not *how* people act but *why* people behave as they do. It is vitally important to know *why we do things*. If we do not know why we do things we live our life driven helplessly by unknown and unseen motives and passions. If we do not know why we do things we are not in charge of our life.

Do not confuse my use of the word 'extravert' with the more commonly used word 'extrovert'. We often use the word 'extrovert' when speaking of a person who is very sociable. Such a person might be sociable because he wants to have lots of relationships in order to maintain his sense of existence (my idea of an extravert) or because he has realised that he had been concentrating so much on his sense of individual achievement that he had not learned social skills, and so he set about acquiring them (my idea of a successful introvert). We often use the word 'introvert' when speaking about someone who is shy and withdrawn. Such a person might be, in my terms, an ordinary introvert little interested in social skills or a shy, unconfident extravert. Some shy extraverts think that they are introverts, and do not understand the huge difference between introverts and extraverts in the way they experience their sense of existence and in how they order their priorities.

It is important to know how you experience your sense of existence and see the threat of annihilation because then you will know what is your top priority and what you fear the most. People Persons or extraverts get into difficulties whenever they feel they are in danger of being rejected and abandoned, while What Have I Achieved Today Persons or introverts become very unhappy if their lives allow them no sense of achievement, and they feel in danger of being overwhelmed by chaos.

Of course we all want to have good relationships *and* a sense of achievement, but unfortunately life often presents us with situations where we cannot have both. Suppose, as an introvert woman, you are persuaded by the argument that if a woman wants to have children she should not pursue a career, even though you could have had a career where you could have achieved a great deal. Sooner or later you will discover that raising children and doing housework are not activities which yield a satisfactory sense of achievement. Or, suppose, as an extravert man, you are being pressured by your firm and your family to relinquish your job as a much-loved team leader and accept a job as a senior manager where you make policy and hire and fire. You know how much the previous manager, a man who always put duty above popularity, was disliked. Situations such as these frequently arise in one form or another, and, if you do not know what is of prime importance to you, you are likely to suffer. If you do understand what is vitally important to you, you will put into such situations certain life-savers. As the introvert woman you organise your family life so that you have some time to yourself to do something that gives you a sense of achievement. (This time to yourself should not be an alternative to getting a night's sleep.) As an extravert man who knows that he must not let his need to be liked overshadow his career, you take some extra training in management skills – after all, there are some effective bosses who are not disliked by their employees – and come to discover that it is possible to survive even though you are not liked by everyone in the world.

Extraverts and introverts are often drawn to one another. Opposites attract, and, although I have searched far and wide, I have yet to discover a couple which is not made up of an introvert and an extravert. However, what draws us together can also push us apart. When Gwyneth Lewis, an introvert, went to university she soon fell in love with R. However,

> After about five months of unquestioning bliss, and of doing no academic work whatsoever, second-year exams were looming and I wanted to do some studying. R poured scorn on anybody who worked consistently as a 'plodder', someone who had opted out of the challenge of living. But for me, reading and understanding, say, the work of George Eliot or Milton was a crucial part of who I wanted to be. In order to write you have, first, to be a reader. R was sociable, always at the centre of a group; I needed to spend time alone. Our conflicts hardened into fixed positions – he said I was ambitious, calculating, puritanical, afraid of real life and under my parents' thumb. I soon became bored with the drifting life of pubs and chat, but I could not do without his approval.[52]

Understanding how extraverts and introverts think and feel could help you sort out some of the issues you have with your partner.

There are some other exercises you can do to find out more about yourself.[53] Some I have mentioned before, like *The Lady or the Tiger*. Which would you choose and why? Find out whether your need for your partner is greater than your love. And there is the journey to *Planet A and Planet B*. Would you prefer a place where you were safe, but everyone ignored you, or a place where people took notice of you but only to be hostile? Discover how much you need your paranoia.

Find out, too, how you feel about being liked or respecting yourself. Ask yourself, 'Suppose I was placed in a situation where I could act in only one of two ways. First I acted one way, people would like me, but I would not respect myself. If I acted the other way, people would not like me but I would respect myself. Which would I choose, respecting myself or other people liking me?'

When you have answered, then ask, 'Why is it important to me that . . .?'

What this exercise might reveal is an important conflict. Perhaps you want to be able to respect yourself but people whom you see as powerful (by seeing them as powerful you have given them this power) force you to do things you do not want to do, or perhaps you want people to like you but in your job you should make decisions which other people would not like, and so you try to sit on the fence (so everyone thinks you are weak) or you try to avoid making decisions (so everyone thinks you are indecisive) or you try to find solutions which suit everyone (thus proving the old adage 'Try to please all and you shall please none'). You will have to work this out if you are going to be able to live at peace with yourself. You have to know yourself in order to be true to yourself.

Another exercise is to write down a list, in order of importance, of the virtues you most value and the vices you most despise. Then ask for each one, 'Why is this important?' and see where your enquiry leads. See how the answers to these questions link to your answers in the other exercises. If you and your partner do this exercise together you will discover some more clues to what is unspoken in your disagreements.

Another question to ask yourself is, 'Which frightens me most, fear or anger?' Both frighten you, but one frightens you more than the other. You might find that you prefer fear, on the grounds that a little anxiety gets you going and makes you feel alive, while anger you find completely abhorrent. You might be married to someone who will never admit he is afraid but who uses his anger to try to make his world into what he wants it to be.

Suppose there is some event looming and you are frightened of what is going to happen. Your mother may be coming to stay or you are required to go to the firm's ball, or your daughter expects you to go to her graduation or your son wants you to take him fishing – all fearfully dangerous events, of course – and you cannot see any way of avoiding them other than by being very depressed. Try something else. Write down what it is you are expected to do and then say, 'If I do this, what is the very worst that could happen?'

Write down your answer and look at it in the cold light of day. If you have said, 'I'll die,' then perhaps you should rejoice, your troubles will soon be over.

If you have said, 'I'll make a fool of myself,' ask yourself, 'What is the worst thing that could happen to me if I made a fool of myself?'

Is your answer that, if you made a fool of yourself, everyone in the whole world would reject you, or that you would lose control and everything would fall into chaos? That is, if you risk doing something quite ordinary you will be annihilated as a person.

You may feel as if you are going to be annihilated as a person but can this actually happen? If you could actually disappear as a person then you will not be there to know that you have disappeared as a person. If you are there to know that you have disappeared as a person, then you have not disappeared as a person.

To fear disappearing as a person is to fear an illusion – something which cannot happen. Whenever we feel that we are falling apart and are about to be annihilated what actually is happening is that part of our meaning structure is falling apart as it has to because it no longer fits what is actually happening. It may be that a significant part of your meaning structure is falling apart, say, that bit of your meaning structure has to do with your plans for your future. If the person with whom you planned to spend the rest of your life is no longer prepared, or able, to do that, then your plans have to be scrapped and new ones created. However, *you* are still there, knowing that the future is not going to be what you wanted it to be, and feeling the pain and sadness of that loss. You need to ride out the storm of your ideas crashing around you, knowing that the storm will pass and things will fall into place.

However, the less self-confidence you have and the less you value and accept yourself, the more frequently you will encounter situations where you feel that you are going to fall apart. So you need to build up your self-confidence. Since it takes a little time to do this when it has been dangerously diminished you have to do what most people do in tricky situations – they pretend to be self-confident. Acting is a skill we all can learn. You might not be able to become a great Shakespearean actor but you do have the ability to treat a roomful of strangers as a stage where you are going to act a role which is defined by self-confidence, warmth and friendliness. Any competent actor can teach you how to do that, but, if you do not know any professional actors, simply watch what other people do. Watch closely how one person deals skilfully with introductions, how another person is good at small talk, and how another is extremely good at getting people to talk about themselves. Copy what they do. This last is the easiest way of overcoming shyness, and people will love you for encouraging them to talk about themselves.

Acting *as if* you are self-confident, acting *as if* you value and accept yourself slowly, imperceptibly changes to actually *being* self-confident, actually valuing and accepting yourself.[54]

Consider now the things that you feel compelled to do. No strange force is compelling you, nor any person other than yourself. When you see your own values clearly you can ask, 'Do I do this because I believe it is right or do I do it because the parent in my head tells me to and I'm too scared to disobey?'

You are you; you are the parent in your head; you are the child who is scared to disobey. You can choose to spend the rest of your life going around as three squabbling people, or you can choose to make yourself into one whole person. Gwyneth Lewis told how she came to realise that 'Far from being a victim of other people, I'd been doing nothing but bullying myself.' She asked, 'How many "shoulds", "musts" and "oughts" are in how you talk to yourself? If there are several, you are hounding yourself with a pre-ordained agenda, rather than calmly observing to yourself, "I don't really feel like doing it but I'll consider myself a terrible failure/wimp/bitch if I don't." '55

More women than men get depressed. There are many reasons for this but an important one concerns the way most of us came to believe that, to be acceptable, we have always to put other people's needs before our own. Gwyneth Lewis discovered that this belief prevented her from being happy. She wrote,

> Very often the problem isn't the content of our thoughts but in the links we make between them. Often my second thought presumes too much. The first thought is not only more accurate but usually more humble than its brainy but tricksy successor. For example, as I was feeling a lot better one day, I found myself thinking, 'I'm so happy today,' followed closely by, 'If only Mam were this happy.' I was shocked when I noticed how automatically I was willing to compromise my own well being by making it conditional on someone else's. Besides, how do I know that at any given time my mother is not happy? And if she isn't, what business is it of mine? Once I told my mother that all I wanted was for her to be happy. 'What if I'm not a happy type of person?' she said, perfectly reasonably. If I want the freedom to live my life for myself, then I have to allow it to everyone else.[56]

If you are a woman then you must spend some time thinking and writing about what it means to you to be a woman. The women's movement has produced an extensive literature. Whether or not you read some of this, or join a women's group (in some places there are Women's Therapy Centres) you must consider the fact that *two-thirds* of psychiatric patients are women, most of them with the diagnosis of depression. The diagnosing has been done by men. Many women denigrate themselves without realising that they have learnt this from a society where men have political and economic power and wish to keep women in subservient roles. Of course there are men who do not behave like this, but their numbers are relatively few and as yet they do not have the power to change the political and economic institutions.

Women should take into consideration the fact that the days have long passed when all a woman could fit into her lifespan (no more than forty or fifty years) was marriage and children. Now, when a woman's children can take care of themselves, she still has half of her life or more to live. Home and family cannot be an occupation for a woman's full lifetime, not unless you want to devote your time to being an interfering mother-in-law or to being ill.

So you have to find something more to do. If you found when you did your laddering that your experience of existence is to be a member of a group, then join one of the helping professions or become a voluntary worker, alongside the helping professions, or join an acting group, or take up a team sport. If you found that your experience of existence is to seek clarity, then go back to studying, or take up one of the creative arts. Or perhaps you would prefer to create a balance. Having spent your life being part of a group, try something on your own, and find that solitariness is not so terrible after all. Or, seek clarity by learning to tolerate chaos and join a group of some kind. What you discover about yourself will be liberating.

When I was researching for my book *Time on Our Side: Growing in Wisdom, Not Growing Old* [57] I asked a large number of people of all ages what they felt about time passing and growing older. Everyone said that they feared this, but what they feared was much more than simply fearing that old age would mean being incapacitated and then dying a painful death. What people feared were changes in those aspects of themselves on which they had built their sense of being a person. Men who had built their identity on being sexually active, or on the particular job they did, feared the loss of sexual potency with age, or the inevitable retirement from the one thing that gave their life meaning. Women who had built their identity on being sexually attractive, or on being needed, feared the loss of beauty with age, or the loss of the ability to look after others. They did not understand, much less accept, that life has its seasons and each season has its own qualities which can be enjoyed, provided we let ourselves do so. Most of the people who feared growing older had no understanding that what they feared most were just ideas in their head, and that they were free to change those ideas.

When you think about taking up some new activity, and then feel frightened, you have to work out just what it is you feel frightened of. It may not be just fearing to make a fool of yourself. You are probably still carrying round in your head parental prohibitions like 'Don't mix with strangers', 'Those kind of people are common', 'No child of mine would ever do a thing like that', and, especially where sport is concerned, 'Don't do that, you'll hurt yourself'. Such prohibitions put a barrier between you and the rest of the world. You need to identify these prohibitions and decide whether you want to go on obeying them or whether you would prefer to be free. When you do manage to overcome your prohibitions and try something new, do not say, 'That was a fluke. I'll never manage it again.' Think back over what you did and write down the things that you learned from it. Then next time you can decide how, if necessary, you will alter what you did.

To live at peace with ourselves we have to come to terms with death. Somehow, we have to accept that our death is inevitable. Running away from death is no solution. But it is very difficult to accept our death when we feel that we have not lived a satisfactory life. It is tremendously important that, year by year, we put something into our life which we feel is satisfactory.

However, it is impossible to feel that our life is satisfactory if we feel that we have to work hard in order to earn the right to exist. As long as you regard yourself as bad, evil, unacceptable to yourself and other people you will be unable to accept your death and the thought of death will frighten you. Running away from death is no solution because we cannot run away from our own knowledge that death contains that which we fear the most, that is, the conditions which most threaten our existence as a person. No matter how many people gather at our bedside, we have to enter the valley of the shadow alone. No matter how clever we are at keeping things under control, death is a process beyond our control. We cannot evade our fears but, by acknowledging them and talking about them with others, our fears become more manageable. When you accept yourself you can accept your death. It is not until you possess yourself that you are able to face losing yourself.

Accepting yourself can mean resolving the grief left over from earlier years. Then you had lost somebody – or even something – and you were not able to show your grief, perhaps not even admit it to yourself. There is nothing brave or wise in denying grief, in pretending that you feel no pain or anger or sorrow. The road out of your prison must take you through this grief. Perhaps someone will help you through an experience so crudely called 'grief therapy', but so effective. Here you have to enact a scene, perhaps the funeral where you did not cry, and now you do cry, or perhaps you pretend that the person you have lost is back with you, and you can talk to that person and say what should have been said and hear in return (you say it yourself) what you should have heard. Grief therapy is deeply moving, so it does help if someone is with you, but you may prefer to do it on your own by talking and writing – and probably crying. Remember, tears are good for you. Tears wash the eyes.

Accepting yourself means giving up all that nonsense about self-sacrifice. Leap in front of a bus and save someone's life if you must, but do not devote your life to domestic sacrifice. No good ever comes of it. All you achieve is to encourage your family to behave badly – to be selfish and inconsiderate, to expect the world to be the way they want it to be, and to be unaware of the needs and feelings of others. If you wait upon your children and never expect them to do their own washing and get themselves a meal or to look after their own belongings, you rob them of the chance to learn, as they grow up, the skills of living, and thus you undermine their confidence in themselves. If you are sacrificing yourself to your family so as to make them need you and so they will not go away and leave you, then your self-sacrifice is dishonest. You are looking after others for your own sake, not theirs. Your family will know if this is why you are being so self-sacrificing and they will resent and despise you for it. If you are sacrificing yourself because you expect love in return, then all you achieve is to make others feel guilty when they do not live up to your expectations. Do you want to get a little affection for what you do for people or to be loved for what you are?

So you must ask yourself, 'Am I sacrificing myself so as to overcome my feeling that I am a bad, worthless person?' 'Does being a self-sacrificing doormat do anything for me except confirm me in my belief that I am a bad, worthless person?' 'Do I do things for other people, not because I love them, but because it is my duty, that is, because I am too scared to refuse to do things for them?' 'Am I doing good because it bolsters my pride/ensures that I shall go to heaven?' 'Does my self-sacrifice encourage others to continue being badly behaved?' (Some people get away with the most outrageous behaviour all their lives because their children and partners are too frightened to complain, much less to demand that an adult behave as a responsible adult.)

You must also ask yourself 'In my need to do things for other people, am I so busy doing things for them that I don't really know what they want?' 'Does my sensitivity to my own feelings blind me to what other people are really like?' 'Do I really know the people I love?' 'Can I truly love someone if I do not know who that person really is?'

Finding out about yourself always means finding out about other people. Accepting yourself for what you are means accepting others for what they are. Accepting yourself means forgiving yourself for being what you are. Accepting others means forgiving them for being what they are – or what they were. In forgiving ourselves and others we gain the courage and strength of true humility.

'Humility,' said Philip Toynbee, 'must mean trying to see ourselves as we really are. And pride is always a denial of the (painful yet exhilarating) truth about ourselves.'[58] Humility is not a constant harping on your faults and errors and general worthlessness. When you find yourself doing this (like being unable to say anything good about yourself, or constantly apologising, or feeling quite unable to do anything even moderately well) remember what Archbishop Fenelon wrote to one of his parishioners,

It is mere self-love to be inconsolable at seeing one's own imperfections; but to stand face to face with them, neither

flattering nor tolerating them, seeking to correct oneself
without becoming pettish – this is to desire what is good
for its own sake and for God's.[59]

A humility which is not fuelled by pride, along with self-
acceptance and forgiveness are all aspects of the one process
whereby we come to see ourselves as we are and other people
as they are. Since we no longer have the pride and arrogance
to try to control ourselves and our world so as to make ourselves and our world into something which they are not, we
can now be spontaneous. Since we no longer have to hide
ourselves from other people, to put a barrier between ourselves and our world, we can be open and vulnerable, and so
feel ourselves to be alive. Since all desire leads to suffering,
ceasing to desire that the world be what we want it to be
reduces our desires and so our suffering. We then know,
along with Lao Tsu, that,

It is more important
To see the simplicity,
To realise one's true nature,
To cast off selfishness,
And temper desire.[60]

Learning to accept yourself and others, to accept that
what you have lost is well and truly lost forever, and that
sadness is now your trusted companion, to be courageous,
loving, humble and forgiving, and to face death with equanimity is no small task. But this is what you must undertake
if you are to find your way out of the prison of depression
and never return to it. This is what Philip Toynbee found. He
wrote,

Partly through my reading and partly through some
independent but slow and heavy process within my mind
and heart, I gradually began to think of this depression in
quite a new set of terms. Instead of looking for its causes
and thinking about how to get rid of them, I began to look
for its purposes and to wonder how I could fulfil them. I
couldn't and still can't tell whether God sends us such
acute afflictions to bring us to some new understanding
through our pain. But I am now as sure as I can be that

depression is often a sign, whether human or divine, that the life of the victim needs to be drastically changed; that acts of genuine contrition are called for; that the dark block within can be dissolved only by recognizing that something like an inner death and resurrection is demanded of the sufferer.[61]

Death and resurrection – or a journey without maps. Good luck!

Chapter 9

LEAVING THE PRISON

As you work at understanding and accepting yourself and understanding and accepting other people, you may come to the conclusion that there are things about yourself that you cannot change. You have to live with the consequences of past ignorance and past mistakes. You may now see clearly that you are engaged upon work which has little meaning for you, and that to leave the prison of depression behind you forever you need to find some other work which you would find interesting and important, but making such a change may not be easy, and you have financial commitments. You may now see clearly that your partner can never give you the marriage that you want, and that staying in this marriage will mean that you will often be lonely, but you do not want to abandon someone who loves and needs you. Searching your past for clues about your present you have stumbled upon long-forgotten memories whose poignancy and sadness are nearly unbearable. How much easier it would be to stay in the prison whose dimensions you know so well! There you might not be happy but you are safe.

However, once we know something we cannot unknow it, although we can lie to ourselves that we have. The prisoner who has glimpsed freedom cannot rest easy in his cell. Once you have seen the open door of your prison you have to go through it.

So you gather together every shred of courage and step through the open door. Outside you find freedom and a new kind of happiness, a happiness tinged with sadness. Now you can see clearly that you had brought from your childhood a burden of anger, resentment, guilt and grief. You may have forgiven yourself and your family and resolved the anger, resentment and guilt, and allowed yourself to grieve, but the sadness remains. You know that on certain grey days ghosts of the old, bad feelings might return.

You have not achieved a life of undiluted happiness. What you have achieved is to change uncomprehending, guilty depression into wise and gentle sadness. You are a survivor who has rid himself of all unnecessary baggage. You know that depression is not something visited upon you, but is a moral dilemma, the terms of which you now comprehend.

You have learned that what you feared the most cannot happen. When you discovered that there was a serious discrepancy between what you thought your life was and what it actually is you felt yourself falling apart, shattering, crumbling, in danger of disappearing altogether. You were terrified. Now you know that what you feared cannot happen because you know that what was falling apart was some of your ideas, ideas which had been important to you but which now had to change because they no longer fitted what was actually going on. You are you and you cannot be annihilated as a person.

You know too that there will be times in your life when some of your ideas will no longer fit what is going on, and that, instead of being frightened that you will fall apart, you will recognise that what you are feeling is simply your ideas falling apart. You know that you will have to go through a period of uncertainty, but uncertainty no longer frightens you. You know that this period of uncertainty will pass. Everything passes. Nothing stays the same.

However, in the future, when you encounter difficulties and loss, you can be tempted to retreat into depression and hide away from the crises, the turmoil and the challenges. Once we have learnt a skill we never forget it completely. You have learnt the skill of being depressed. You need to remember the thoughts and the kinds of circumstances which can call forth your use of this skill, and work out how to avoid them. Becoming depressed always begins by devaluing yourself, not accepting yourself, and assuming that other people do not value and accept you. In the dialogue you have with yourself you negate and criticise yourself. You tell yourself that you are useless, you are a failure, everything will turn out badly and so on.

The moment you hear yourself start on this tirade tell yourself STOP! Such a tirade against yourself is actually a self-serving ploy to avoid confronting a current difficulty or disaster. You are denigrating yourself in order to hide away from something that must be faced. Hiding away will only make things worse for you.

To stop yourself being seduced into going down the path of depression strengthen yourself by reminding yourself that you value and accept yourself. If other people do not value and accept you they are all fools, and why should you be impressed by the opinions of fools? Enjoy your successes, and, when thinking over events, remind yourself of your successes and satisfaction just as Philip Toynbee did. One day he went for a walk, and later wrote,

> A free and purposeful man!
> And a changed world.

> For years all visual beauty has been tangled up with nostalgia. 'Tears at the heart of things'; poignancy: carried back by a tree to some half-memory of a childhood tree, so *freshly* seen so long ago. A florid and deeply satisfying melancholy. Or the tree was a *memento mori*; my melancholy softly expanding into a future with no trees at all.

> But now, on this walk, I stopped several times and looked at a single tree as I haven't done for years. No; as I have never done in my life before. The tree was there and now, in its own immediate and peculiar right: *that* tree and no other. And I was acutely here-and-now as I stared at it, unhampered by past or future: faced from the corruption of the ever-intrusive ME. Intense happiness.

Later he wrote,

> But it is important to get rid of the disastrous Christian notion of 'merits' to be acquired; like so many good conduct marks collected through a term at school. If there are stages on this journey and if I have reached even the

first of them, then I know that whatever is new seems much more like a gift than an achievement.

He concluded that

I recognise more and more that if I have any godly function on earth – and of course I have; everybody has – then it is to act as both a warning and an example on the very lowest rung of the ladder. The present account of my hopes and fears; large failures, small successes; humiliations and perceptions (perceptions often from the heart of humiliation) is meant for the spiritually backward – who nevertheless know enough about the Spirit to be in a state of often subdued but never extinguished hope.[1]

Hope, and an armoury of things to do when grey days threaten, are what you now possess. Jill Tweedie recorded what she did.

Now when I glimpse depression shuffling in the wings, waiting to come on, I have tricks up my sleeve to forestall it. I think, for instance, of optical illusions. That box, drawn on paper, that seems to project its closed end towards you but, at a shifting of the mind's gears, becomes suddenly open, hollow, so that you can look inside. Those pencilled lines of identical length, one with arrows at its ends pointing outwards, the other with arrows pointing inwards, the first seeming half as long again as its apparently shrunken twin. Marks on paper that serve as reminders of some possibility of control over reality, if only in the mind's eye.

I have other remedies, too. I no longer allow the blanket to fall without a struggle – instead, I force myself to track that fall to its source. The mind veers away, reluctant to reveal the awesome pettiness, the huge egoism that often sparks mild depression, the bloated baby that screams in all of us and blackens our horizons with its bawling for attention. Once the baby is discovered, though, the blackness lifts. Also, I attend to my body, something I once thought far too undramatic and suburban a thing to do. My soul in upheaval and you talk of a tonic or

Vitamin C? Cold showers? Walk round the block? Would anyone have dared suggest such cures to Byron? Still, the links between body and mind are indissoluble and the banal fact is that forcing oxygen through the lungs does, sometimes, set the mood afloat again. Other people have their own methods of rupturing the dark circle. One woman goes away, anywhere, if only for a day. Another, reasoning that while she feels like death she might as well do the deathliest chores, does so and recovers. Yet another, drained of all energy, reads *Moby Dick* for the umpteenth time and forgets herself in Ahab's chase.[2]

Kay, whom I wrote about in *Choosing Not Losing*, worked in a department store in town. So I saw her fairly often. Sometimes we chatted and sometimes there was only time to smile and say hello. She had her down days. I could see the tired strain behind her immaculate make-up and quiet smile. But she had changed. She now had good friends, including her daughter, Penny, and her daughter-in-law, her son Steven's wife, and a much loved grandchild. She had always been beautifully dressed and groomed, but before her way of dressing had seemed to create a barrier behind which she would hide. Now the barrier had gone. She was open, gentle and wise.

It was during the Falklands crisis that Kay and I met for a chat. That was the week the *Coventry* was sunk off the Falklands. The Ministry of Defence had announced that a frigate had been sunk but it was over twelve hours, a long night, before we were told which frigate it was. We talked, and Kay said, 'Did I tell you that Penny's baby was stillborn? She had a terrible time. Steven's on a frigate, down there in the South Atlantic. Now I know what worrying really is.'

1995

Over the years I have kept in touch with a number of people who used to be my clients. Usually we exchange Christmas cards but some visit, write or telephone. None of them lead perfect lives, but then nobody does. All have encountered difficulties, some very great, but they have coped. They take joy in their family and friends. What they have achieved would have been unimaginable when they were depressed. Let me tell you about three of them.

When I first met Tony he would say, 'Out of the jaws of success I snatch failure', and his life certainly followed that pattern. He had talents galore, especially in music, and he threw these talents and his relationships away. We met and talked for many months but there was never a point where I felt that Tony was changing. Yet he must have been, because a friendship he had formed turned through some dramatic times into a stable, steady, loving relationship. No longer despising himself for failing to be the greatest composer and classical guitarist ever, he found great satisfaction as a music teacher and choirmaster. Now able to carry a creative project to fruition, he composed a requiem for his choir which they performed with great distinction. Tony was not simply snatching success out of the jaws of failure. He was securely, steadily creating his own success.

When Val first came to see me she was frozen in her depression, barely able to move or speak. Eventually she did decide to treat herself more kindly, but she had many more betrayals to endure before she said, 'Enough is enough'. Her decision to end her marriage was brave, but even braver was her decision, after many months of trying to support herself and her children on social security, to take a six-month job which had a chance of turning into a much longer job but which also held the chance that, in the crazy way that social security works, she would be left without an income. She risked everything and she won. Now she talks about her work with wry, pessimistic humour and, though sometimes disheartened as all social workers are, she enjoys her satisfaction and success.

My picture of Jean when we first met was of a heap of grey, trembling jelly. She was anxious about everything. We met for only a few months because Jean and her family returned to Scotland but she kept in touch, usually by letter, brilliant accounts of the dramas that befell her. One day, when she has the time, she will write her autobiography and what an amazing story that will be! Divorced, she married again, thereby more than doubling the number of children in her care. She and her husband have splendid arguments, much to the amusement of their children. How she has changed! She is a countrywoman, solid, dependable, funny, life-affirming, a blessing to all who know her.

2002

Tony, Val and Jean continue to flourish. They and other ex-clients whom I hear from occasionally have had their difficulties and disappointments, but they now distinguish clearly the real problems of life from the problems that they created for themselves when they did not value and accept themselves, and when, as a result, they feared other people and the world they lived in. Best of all, they enjoy life.

Since 1983 when this book was first published, many readers have written to me. Some want advice about finding a therapist, some want to tell me about a good and/or terrible experiences they have had with therapists, some simply want to tell me their story, and some want to thank me for my books. However, none of those who thank me for my books ever say it was simply the magic power of my books which changed their life. Rather, they say that what they read set them thinking, and their thinking changed what they did, and now their life is richer and happier.

None of these people say that changing was easy. In her letter Clare said that she hoped that other people would be comforted by *Depression: The way out of your prison* as she had been, and then she queried what she had written. 'Comfort? Your message is anything but. You offer no easy solutions, but the result is self knowledge and being able to live with one's self – comfortable living.'

Clare told me of the event when she was nine years old which had robbed her of her self-confidence. She wrote,

> My parents had a small farm. One of the fields was situated by the river and always known to us children as the river field. My father owned a small rowing boat and would take us for boat rides. I loved it, especially in the summer. The dragon flies flashed near the surface of the water – brilliant blue and turquoise – and brilliant yellow

king cups grew near the bank. Sometimes my father took me on my own and gave me the oars. He taught me how to row. Sometimes he would let me take over and I would row unaided. I loved it!

He had a friend called Bob who rented out punts to the fishermen. He looked like an uglier version of King Henry VIII in his green army jacket and waders.

I felt confident as only a child can. I wanted to show my brothers and my sister that I could row a boat.

As the oldest child I had to spend a lot of time looking after the younger ones. My mother said I had to keep them away from the river, but it was a beautiful day. The sun was shining and I wanted to take them out for a special treat. So I loaded John, Sophie, Phillip, Martin and Neil into the boat and took them down the river. I felt totally in control and happy. I took them down a stretch of water and back, and then, having delivered them safely to the shore, told them not to mention it to mummy. I knew she wouldn't approve.

It was when we were back in the house that my sister told my mother that I had taken everyone down the river in the boat. My mother's reaction was white fury. She told me to go to the breakfast room and wait for my father to come back.

I knew I was going to be punished. I was very frightened. When my father got back they both came into the breakfast room and shut the door. I had to bend over my mother's knees. She held me down and I could not move. They pulled down my knickers and thrashed me. *For your own good.*

After that the river ceased to exist. It was not that I was forbidden to go to the river. I must have been traumatised by what had happened.

Last year, I was visiting my parents and they had a slide to show me, taken by my mother's younger sister over thirty years ago. There we were as children. My mother looked identical to how my sister looks now. I was holding baby Neil in my arms. As I looked at the picture I was struck how confident and pretty I looked then. For most of my life I have felt odious. I asked my mother to get out other photos, and there was a photo of my father's friend Bob. Suddenly I couldn't stop crying. The memory of the boat ride and the beating suddenly resurfaced.

Clare remembered how 'at about fifteen feeling terribly sad – an unbearable aching – and being told I "should be ashamed of myself – you've no right to be miserable at your age".' She went on, 'When I suffered from depression I was forced to endure this unbearable aching pain. Many a time I wanted to die to escape it. I didn't notice my surroundings or derive pleasure from anything.'

Clare reminded me that, in my book *Breaking the Bonds* I had written 'If we do not go back and check our conclusion that "I am bad" we make this and the constant feeling of guilt into our whole way of living.'[3]

Clare went back and checked the conclusions she had drawn from her beating and from the many occasions when her mother had made it clear to her that she was the bad child in the family. Now Clare could write,

My depression is a result of my interpretation of circumstances. It isn't an illness, though it is a ghastly experience. I feel as if I've been shut up in a high security prison all my life since childhood, since I was nine years old. In middle age I feel free.

Chapter 10

THE PRISON VANISHES

T.S. Eliot wrote,

> We shall not cease from exploration
> And the end of all our exploring
> Will be to arrive where we started
> And know the place for the first time.[1]

To 'know the place for the first time' means seeing a place keenly, fiercely, intensely, in the here and now. This kind of knowing is the closest we can ever come to seeing reality as it is.

Knowing the place where you started, knowing the life you lead and the world you live in, knowing yourself – all this is being truly and completely alive. Most people live their life in a dream, taking themselves and their world for granted, reacting to circumstances, not thinking about the consequences of their actions, not understanding that what they take to be reality is in fact the pictures their brain has created. Many people live like this but in the dark prison of depression. Coming to understand that what we take to be reality is actually a set of meanings which each of us has created in our own individual way is what the Buddha called enlightenment. To become enlightened does not require hours of meditating while sitting cross-legged, nor do you have to chant and eat vegetarian food, nor even shave your head. All you have to do is to know in your heart as well as your head that you see the world, not as it is, but as you are, and that you do what you do not as a result of what happens to you but as a result of how you interpret what happens to you.

Understand this and you become one of the happily enlightened.

Knowing yourself and your world in this enlightened way means that you are always discovering and learning something new. In the most ordinary of places you see things that you have never seen before, see connections where before you saw only rifts and gaps. The world and all the people in it become intensely interesting. You discover in yourself talents and abilities you never dreamed you possessed. Every new experience strengthens you.

The path the enlightened tread is not without its difficulties. The people around you may be pleased that you are no longer depressed, but they may not be pleased that you have your own ideas about what you do, that you stand up for yourself and no longer try to fulfil their needs and wishes without demur. If you are not careful you can return to the unenlightened state where you spent your time worrying about the future, resenting the past, feeling bored, angry and envious in the present, and believing that in the overall scheme of things you are bound to suffer. To stay on the path of enlightenment we must be mindful of what we are doing.

Being enlightened does not mean escaping into some great philosophical and religious way of life where you no longer have anything to do with the mundane world. On the contrary, you become more aware of the real world in *the present*. Instead of thinking about the present in terms of the past (how I was deprived, was cheated, have suffered) and of the future (how I must do this perfectly, won't get it right, shall be blamed, shall be punished) you pay attention to what is happening now – the flavour of the food you are eating, the sound of a bird outside your window, the story someone is telling you, the task you are doing now. And as you are mindful of the present you are also aware that you are part of everything which exists. Although this is mysterious and unknowable in an intellectual sense, it can be comprehended in a way which supports and sustains you. We can feel we are part of everything which exists when we are in a garden, or walking in the mountains or beside the sea, or listening to music, or watching children play. People use different names for everything which exists. Many people see God, not as a deity who judges them, but as an unknowable power which encompasses everything, and is both immanent (inside us) and transcendent (outside us). Some people call everything that exists nature. Taoists speak of Tao.

The great Tao flows everywhere, both to the left and to the right.
The ten thousand things depend upon it; it holds nothing back.
It fulfils its purpose silently and makes no claim.[2]

We can name and describe everything that exists in whatever way suits us best – as God, or the Life Force, Tao or Nature. Our comprehension of it increases our understanding of our daily life, and our mindfulness of our daily life increases our understanding of everything that exists. Enlightenment is not a sudden switching on of a light: it is a gradually increasing brightness.

We can look at our world and say, 'It's nothing but . . .', or we can say, 'It's not this, but something more', or we can say, 'It is'. If we say that the world is nothing but politics or nuclear particles, then we have made our world a barren, lifeless place and ourselves barren, uninspired people. If we say that this world is unimportant and that what matters is something that transcends it, heaven, or paradise, or some spiritual realm, then we are dissatisfied and irritated with our world, and so, at best, we ignore it, and, at worst, destroy it through selfishness, or thoughtlessness or malice. But if we say, 'It is', then our world comes to us fresh each day, full of abundant life and endless charm.

We all know that beyond and within ourselves and our mundane world lies a reality which is awesome, mysterious and unknowable except in those rare moments when it reveals itself to us. If we deny that it is there, we deprive ourselves of a rich and vibrant nourishment, and so we become meagre and limited people, mere caricatures of what we might have been. If we recognise this reality but insist that we know exactly what it is, if we see it in terms of some fairy story where the good are invariably rewarded and protected and the bad punished, then we have to spend our lives denying our perceptions and lying to ourselves about our experiences, forever engaged in a game of make-believe. But if we can face and acknowledge the awesome mystery, then we shall know great fear and uncertainty, but we shall also know, in rare, life-sustaining moments, the greatest joy, wisdom and delight. These moments make the rest of life worthwhile.

NOTES

Preface to the third edition

1. Terry Lynch, *Beyond Prozac: Healing Mental Suffering without drugs*, Marino Books, Dublin, 2002, pp. 111, 112.
2. Ibid., p. 302.
3. Dorothy Rowe, *Beyond Fear*, second edition, HarperCollins, London, 2002.
4. *Postnatal Depression: Facing the Paradox of Loss, Happiness and Motherhood*, Wiley, Chichester, 2001.
5. Terry Lynch, op. cit., p. 116.
6. Gwyneth Lewis, *Sunbathing in the Rain: A Cheerful Book about Depression*, HarperCollins, London, 2002, p. xiii.

1. The prison

1. Dorothy Rowe, *Choosing Not Losing*, Wiley, Chichester, 1978.
2. Andrew Solomon, *The Noonday Demon*, Vintage, London, 2002, p. 18.

2. Inside the prison

1. D.H. Lawrence, 'The Hands of God' in *The Ship of Death and Other Poems*, Faber, London, 1952, p. 60.
2. Fleur Adcock, 'Things' in *The Inner Harbour*, Oxford University Press, 1979.
3. Gerard M. Hopkins, *Poems*, Oxford University Press, 1948, p. 110.
4. Gerald Priestland in *Listener*, October 1980, p. 538.
5. Colin Smith, 'One-eyed Gateman Guards the Tombs of El-Alamein Dead', *Observer*, 8 November 1981, p. 14.
6. Philip Toynbee, *Part of a Journey*, Collins, London, 1981, p. 44.

3. How to build your prison

1. David Healy, *Psychopharmacology and the Government of the Self*, *http://www.pharmapolitics.com/feb2healy.html* 24/01/02.
2. David Healy, *Psychiatric Drugs Explained*, third edition, Churchill-Livingstone, Edinburgh, 2002, p. 53.
3. P.J. Cowen, 'Cortisol, Serotonin and Depression: All Stressed Out?', *The British Journal of Psychiatry*, vol. 180, p. 99, February 2002.
4. Andrew Solomon, *The Noonday Demon*, Vintage, London, 2002, p. 22.
5. Craig Newnes, 'Brainwashed', *Guardian*, 1 January 2002.
6. See Chapter 2 in Dorothy Rowe, *Friends and Enemies*, HarperCollins, London, 2001, pp. 41–110.
7. Dorothy Rowe, *Choosing Not Losing*, Wiley, Chichester, 1978, p. 241.
8. Ibid., p. 237
9. Ibid., p. 238.
10. Ibid, p. 239.
11. Dorothy Rowe, *The Courage to Live*, Wiley, Chichester, 1982, p. 33.
12. Ibid., p. 65.
13. *Choosing Not Losing*, p. 217.
14. Julie Burchill, *Guardian*, 5 June 2002.
15. Tim Lott, *White City Blue*, Viking, London, 1999.
16. William Styron, *Darkness Visible*, Vintage, London, 2001, p. 39.
17. Ibid., p. 40.
18. Gwyneth Lewis, *Sunbathing in the Rain: A Cheerful Book about Depression*, HarperCollins, 2002, p. 192.
19. Jules Feiffer cartoon, *Observer* magazine, 20 February 1977.
20. 'Parkinson', BBC1, 4 May 2002.
21. Andrew Solomon, op. cit., p. 39.
22. Ibid., p. 282.
23. Ibid., p. 98.
24. Ibid., p. 326.
25. Ibid., p. 431.
26. George Bernard Shaw, *Major Barbara*, Constable, London, 1947, p. 334.
27. Theodore Mischel (ed.), *Understanding Other Persons*, Basil Blackwell, Oxford, 1974.
28. *Friends and Enemies*, pp. 385–6.
29. Alan Paton, 'The Challenge of Fear', *Saturday Review*, 9 September 1967. 'In one sense, the opposite of fear is courage, but in the dynamic sense the opposite of fear is love, whether it be love of man or love of justice.'
30. William Wordsworth, 'The Affliction of Margaret' (1804), *The*

Poetical Works of Wordsworth, Oxford University Press, London, 1960, p. 93.

31. European Values Study Group Results quoted by Ted Gorton in 'Belief in Britain', *Listener*, 17 and 24 December 1981, p. 742. 'Belief in God is high, at 76%, but regular church attendance, at 14%, is the lowest in Europe. In religious matters, the belief in the adjuncts of Christianity is low, particularly in the unpleasant areas of faith. Thus 30% believe in the devil and in hell. This rises to a 45% belief in life after death, and to an optimistic 57% for the notion of heaven. One of the most amazing claims is that 27% of British people believe in reincarnation. Sin is accepted as a reality by 69%. Perhaps not surprisingly, the highest figure for this is in Northern Ireland (91%).'

32. M. Argyle and B. Beit-Hallahmi, *The Social Psychology of Religion*, Routledge & Kegan Paul, London, 1975.

33. See Preface and Conclusions of *The Courage to Live*.

34. E. Slater and M. Roth, *Clinical Psychiatry*, Baillière, Tindall & Cassell, London, p. 247.

35. Gerald Priestland, personal communication quoted in *The Courage to Live*, p. 201.

36. Simon King-Spooner and Craig Newnes (eds), *Spirituality and Psychotherapy*, PCCS Books, Ross-on-Wye, 2001.

37. A fuller account of this is given in *The Courage to Live*.

38. Letter to *Observer*, Sunday 5 April 1981.

39. Shaul Rosenblatt, *London Jewish News*, 27 July 2001.

40. Cathy Comerford, *Guardian*, 7 February 2002.

41. *The Courage to Live*, p. 110.

42. Ibid., p. 67.

43. Ibid., p. 14.

44. C.S. Lewis, *A Grief Observed*, Faber, London, 1961, p. 61.

45. Gerard Manley Hopkins, *Poems*, Oxford University Press, 1948, p. 113.

46. 'Village Mourns Eight Lost Heroes', *Guardian*, Monday 21 December 1981.

47. Victoria Brittain, 'Next Year Seventeen Million Babies Are Doomed to Die', *Guardian Third World Review*, Friday 18 December 1981, p. 7.

48. Cf. the words of Bertrand Russell. 'Those whose lives are fruitful to themselves, to their friends, or to the world are inspired by hope and sustained by joy; they see in imagination the things that might be and the way in which they are able to be brought into existence. In their private relations they are not preoccupied with anxiety lest they should lose such affection and respect as they receive: they are engaged in giving affection and respect freely, and the reward comes of itself without their

seeking. In their work they are not haunted by jealousy of competitors, but are concerned with the actual matter that has to be done. In politics, they do not spend time and passion defending unjust privileges of their class or nation, but they aim at making the world as a whole happier, less cruel, less full of conflict between rival greeds, and more full of human beings whose growth has not been dwarfed and stunted by oppression.' *Proposed Roads to Freedom – Anarchy, Socialism and Syndicalism*, Henry Holt, New York, 1919, pp. 186–7.

49. That science has now made it possible for the human race to destroy itself and most other forms of life on this planet is a well-publicised fact that should concern everyone. There are other scientific discoveries, less well publicised, which raise major moral issues – for instance the techniques for creating foetuses in the test-tube, for preserving such foetuses in a frozen state and for producing clones from single eggs. Science creates anxiety not only through its practical results but also through its theory. The idea that the universe's expansion and contraction will mean the eventual destruction of our planet does not make scientists feel happy (see Steven Weinberg, *The First Three Minutes: A Modern View of the Origin of the Universe*, Scientific Book Club, London, 1977) since such an end, even millions of years hence, means an end to all human achievement. Even the fundamental concept of an infinite as against a finite universe can be a cause of anxiety. Tony *(The Courage to Live*, p. 14) said, 'A Person is a Being capable of living the life of the universe, it would be difficult to get close to. We're talking in terms of infinity. I don't know what infinity is but it scares hell out of me. There's no way I can cope thinking about an infinite God. One of the virtues of death is that it will end it. Death actually has a lot of things going for it. I'm not trying to be perverse but I do find the thought of some people and infinity more than I can bear.'

Gareth B. Matthews, in his *Philosophy and the Young Child* (Harvard University Press, Cambridge, MA, 1980, pp. 34–5) quotes Michael, aged seven, who had pondered on this problem of infinity. He said, 'I don't like to (think) about the universe without an end. It gives me a funny feeling in my stomach. If the universe goes on forever there is no place for God to live who made it . . . It's nice to know you're *here*. It is not nice to know about nothing. I hope (the universe) doesn't go on and on forever. I don't like the idea of it going on forever because it's obvious it can't be anywhere.'

50. European Values Study Group, op. cit.
51. *The Courage to Live*, p. 118.
52. See Mr G. in *The Courage to Live*, p. 143.

53. Ibid., p. 126ff.
54. *Choosing Not Losing*, p. 96.
55. *The Courage to Live*, p. 127.
56. Ibid., pp. 86, 84.
57. Jacky Gillott, 'Depression', *Cosmopolitan*, May 1976, pp. 116, 118.
58. *Guardian*, 14 February 2002.
59. Tim Lott, *The Scent of Dried Roses*, Viking, London, 1996, p. 265.
60. Ibid., p. 266.
61. Epictetus, *Discourses as reported by Arrian*, trans. W.A. Oldfeather, Loeb Library.
62. George Brown and Tirrel Harris, *Social Origins of Depression*, Tavistock, London, 1978.
63. Alan Watts, *The Way of Zen*, Penguin Books, Harmondsworth, 1978, p. 26.
64. Connie Bensley, 'April', in *Progress Report*, Harry Chambers/ Peterloo Poets, Cornwall, 1981, p. 10.
65. Connie Bensley, 'Technique', Ibid, p. 53.
66. Robert Lowell, *Day by Day*, Faber, 1978.
67. Philip Toynbee, *Part of a Journey*, Collins, London, 1981, pp. 72, 238, 247, 257.
68. Alan Watts, op. cit., p. 72.
69. *Choosing Not Losing*, p. 230.
70. As the psychoanalysts would say, every fear contains a wish.
71. Philip Toynbee, op cit., pp. 87, 88, 90, 91, 99, 100, 101.
72. Ibid., p. 85.
73. *Choosing Not Losing*, p. 72.
74. Ibid., p. 123.
75. Ibid., p. 293.
76. *The Courage to Live*, p. 171.
77. Ibid., p. 140.
78. Ibid., p. 226.
79. See Tony's story in *The Courage to Live*.
80. Matthew 7:1, 2.
81. Matthew 18:22.
82. Matthew 5:44.
83. Matthew 18:21 to 35.
84. Matthew 6:12, 14, 15.
85. Matthew 10:34.
86. 'All manner of sin and blasphemy shall be forgiven unto men; but the blasphemy against the Holy Ghost shall not be forgiven unto men. And whosoever speaketh a word against the Son of Man, it shall be forgiven him, but whosoever speaketh against the Holy Ghost, it shall not be forgiven him, neither in this world, neither in the world to come.' Matthew 12:31, 32.

87. *The Courage to Live*, p. 275.
88. *Choosing Not Losing*, p. 299.
89. Ibid., p. 61.
90. Ibid., p. 236.
91. *The Courage to Live*, p. 265.
92. See Ronald Eyre, *On the Long Search*, Collins, London, 1979, p. 83. Eyre wrote, 'The most useful thumbnail definition of *dukkha* that I know came from a Buddhist monk in California (though it may not have started with him): "*Dukkha*," he said, "is the attempt to make reality repeatable." The sentence itself is very repeatable and each time I spin it round it really seems to dig deeper and deeper.'
93. *Choosing Not Losing*, p. 308.
94. Ibid., p. 308.

4. The depression story

1. See Dorothy Rowe, *Beyond Fear*, second edition, HarperCollins, London, 2002.
2. Gwyneth Lewis, *Sunbathing in the Rain: A Cheerful Book about Depression*, HarperCollins, London, 2002, p. 21.
3. Ibid., p. 199.
4. Ibid., p. 201.
5. William Styron, *Darkness Visible*, Vintage, London, 2001, p. 44.
6. Andrew Solomon, *The Noonday Demon*, Vintage, London, 2002, p. 50.

5. Why not leave the prison?

1. D. Rowe, 'Poor Prognosis in a Case of Depression as Predicted by the Repertory Grid', *British Journal of Psychiatry*, vol. 118, pp. 297–300, 1971.
2. See Sheldon Kopp, *The End of Innocence – Facing Life without Illusions*, Bantam Books, New York, 1981.

6. Why I won't leave the prison

1. Melvyn Bragg, 'Writers of the Lost Ark', *Punch*, November 1981, p. 817.
2. C.G. Jung, 'Psychotherapy', *Collected Works*, trans. R.F.C. Hull, Routledge & Kegan Paul, London, 1960.
3. T.S. Eliot, *The Elder Statesman*, Faber, London, 1958, p. 44.
4. Dorothy Rowe, *Choosing Not Losing*, Wiley, Chichester, 1978, p. 225.
5. Antonia Bifulco and Patricia Moran, *Wednesday's Child: Research into Women's Experience of Neglect and Abuse in*

Childhood, and Adult Depression, Routledge, London, 1998, p. 55.

6. Alan Watts, *The Way of Zen*, Penguin, Harmondsworth, 1978, p. 68.

7. If you want to find your way out of your depression and within a Christian context you may find the books by Harry Williams extremely helpful. See *Tensions, Necessary Conflicts in Life and Love*, Mitchell Beazley, London, 1976.

8. Louis MacNeice, 'Entirely', *Collected Works*, Faber, London, 1966.

9. Lao Tsu, *Tao Te Ching*, trans. Gia-Fu Teng and Jane English, Wildwood House, London, 1973.

10. George Brown and Tirril Harris, *Social Origins of Depression*, Tavistock, London, 1978.

11. Simone Hatterstone, 'This Is a Setup', *Guardian*, 4 March 2002.

12. Ibid.

13. Andrew Solomon, *The Noonday Demon*, Vintage, London, 2002, p. 40.

14. 'You've Got to Learn' Charles Aznavour, M. Stellman, arr.Horace Ott, Ludlow Music Inc., Album 'I Put a Spell on You', Philips (US) PHMS (S) 2(6)00–172, 1965.

15. Connie Bensley, 'Willpower', in *Progress Report*, Harry Chambers/Peterloo Poets, Cornwall, 1981, p. 62.

16. See Chapter 8 'Suffering and Change' in Dorothy Rowe, *The Courage to Live*, Wiley, Chichester, 1982, pp. 244–80.

17. See Jill, pp. 132ff, and Felicity, pp. 116f, 176, in *The Courage to Live*.

18. John Milton, *Paradise Lost*.

7. Outside the wall: living with a depressed person

1. William Styron, *Darkness Visible*, Vintage, London, 2001, p. 56.

2. Michael Wynne, *The People Are Friendly*, Jerwood New Playwrights, London, 2002, p. 112.

3. William Styron, op. cit., pp. 44, 14.

4. Dorothy Rowe, *The Courage to Live*, Wiley, Chichester, 1982, p. 253.

5. Dorothy Rowe, *Choosing Not Losing*, Wiley, Chichester, 1978, pp. 225–50.

6. Jill Tweedie, *In the Name of Love*, Jonathan Cape, London, 1979, pp. 106, 159–60.

7. George Brown and Tirril Harris, *Social Origins of Depression*, Tavistock, London, 1978.

8. Andrew Solomon, *The Noonday Demon*, Vintage, London, 2002, p. 436.

9. Gwyneth Lewis, *Sunbathing in the Rain: A Cheerful Book about Depression*, HarperCollins, London, 2002, p. xviii.
10. Ibid., p. 139.
11. Ibid., p. 141.
12. Ibid., p. 140.
13. Ibid., p. 139.
14. Ibid., p. 141.

8. Suppose I did want to leave the prison, what should I do?

1. Lao Tsu, *Tao Te Ching*, trans. Gia-Fu Teng and Jane English, Wildwood House, London, 1973.
2. Vicky Rippere, 'Behavioural Treatment of Depression in Historical Perspective', in S. Rachman (ed.), *Contributions to Medical Psychology*, vol. 2, Pergamon Press, Oxford, 1980, pp. 31–54.
3. Judith Gray in her study, 'The Effect of the Doctor's Sex on the Doctor–Patient Relationship', *Journal of the Royal College of General Practitioners*, vol. 32, pp. 167–9, 1982, found that 'Communication is easier, more time is given, drugs are less frequently dispensed and women patients are treated more seriously if the doctor is a woman.' There is no doubt that some women have quite severe symptoms premenstrually and in the menopause. While most doctors agree that this is so, not all doctors agree on the appropriate treatment. Since being depressed never has one single cause but a whole complex of causes, premenstrual tension or the menopause cannot be the sole cause of a woman's depression but they can certainly make it a great deal worse, so if you are aware that you feel more depressed and irritable in the week before your period or that your depression and the menopause coincide, you must get your doctor to help you deal with these menstrual changes.
4. Gerard Manley Hopkins, *Poems*, Oxford University Press, London, 1948, p. 110.
5. Gwyneth Lewis, *Sunbathing in the Rain: A Cheerful Book about Depression*, HarperCollins, London, 2002, p. xix.
6. Ibid., p. 73.
7. Susan Greenfield, *The Private Life of the Brain*, Allen Lane The Penguin Press, London, 2000.
8. Ian C. Reid and Caroline A. Stewart, 'How Antidepressants Work', *British Journal of Psychiatry*, vol. 178, pp. 299–303, 2001.
9. Jerome Burne, 'Make-believe Medicine', *Guardian* 6 June 2002.
10. Ibid.
11. David Healy, *Psychiatric Drugs Explained*, third edition, Churchill Livingstone, Edinburgh, 2002.

12. Ibid., p. 77.
13. William Skidelsky, 'Jagged Little Pills', *Guardian*, 14 February 2002.
14. *Guardian*, 27 July 2002.
15. David Healy, op. cit., p. 29.
16. Shameen Mir and David Taylor, 'Serotonin Syndrome' *Psychiatric Bulletin*, vol. 23, pp. 742–7.
17. Lawrence Le Shan, *How to Meditate: A Guide to Self Discovery*, Bantam Books, New York, 1974.
18. Krishnamurti, *The Second Penguin Krishnamurti Reader*, quoted by J.M. Cohen and J.F. Phipps in *The Common Experience*, Rider, London, 1979, p. 19.
19. See Daniel Goleman, *The Varieties of the Meditative Experience*, Rider, London, 1977, for an account of the different 'Meditation Paths' developed from different religious traditions. Goleman shows that the similarities outweigh the differences, as did Aldous Huxley in *The Perennial Philosophy*, Chatto & Windus, London, 1946, and Cohen and Phipps, in *The Common Experience*.
20. See Alan Watts, *Psychotherapy East and West*, Ballantine Books, New York, 1968.
21. See Eugen Herrigel, *Zen in the Art of Archery*, and *Zen in the Art of Flower Arranging*, and David Brandon, *Zen in the Art of Helping*, all published by Routledge & Kegan Paul. There is a series of books entitled *Zen and the Art of . . .*, Zen practices adapted for sports like running and tennis, which have, from all reports, brought remarkable changes to the practitioners of these sports. The message of these books is 'Do not try; just be'.
22. Gwyneth Lewis, op. cit., pp. xiv, xv.
23. Dorothy Rowe, *The Courage to Live*, Wiley, Chichester, 1982, pp. 192–3.
24. Jeffrey Russell, *The Devil. Perceptions of Evil from Antiquity to Primitive Christianity* and *Satan. The Early Christian Tradition*, Cornell University Press, Ithaca, 1977 and 1981.
25. Jeffrey Russell, personal communication, 1982.
26. Sheldon Kopp, *The End of Innocence – Facing Life without Illusions*, Bantam Books, New York, 1981, p. 45.
27. Sri-Ramamurti in *Seeking the Master* by Muz Murray, Neville Spearman, Jersey, 1980, p. 12.
28. Joseph Needham in *On the Long Search* (based on the BBC series on world religions, 'The Long Search', by Ronald Eyre), Fount Paperbacks, London, 1979, p. 272.
29. Tony Lewis, 'The Struggle to Keep the Mind's Eye Open' and 'Down But Not Out', *Guardian*, 4 and 5 May 1982.
30. Carol Parris, 'I Find Talking to My Friends Can Be a Lot Easier Than Talking to My Husband', *Guardian*, 7 August 1982.

31. Sheldon Kopp, *If You Meet the Buddha on the Road, Kill Him*, Science and Behaviour Books, Palo Alto, CA, 1972, p. 26.
32. Jill Tweedie, 'The Vision of Life Seen in Depression Has the Truth in it, the Bare-boned Skeletal Truth', *Guardian*, 17 April 1982.
33. T.S. Eliot, 'Little Gidding', in *Four Quartets*, Faber, London, 1974, p. 54.
34. H.A. Williams, *Tensions, Necessary Conflicts in Life and Love*, Mitchell Beazley, London, 1976, pp. 111–12.
35. Dorothy Rowe, *Beyond Fear*, second edition, HarperCollins, London, p. 380.
36. Sam Forshall and David Nutt, 'Maintenance Pharmocotherapy in Unipolar Depression', *Psychiatric Bulletin*, 23, pp. 370–3, 1999.
37. Robert Hirschfeld, 'Clinical Importance of Long-term Antidepressant Treatment', *British Journal of Psychiatry*, Supplement 42, vol. 179, pp. 4–8, 2002.
38. Lucy Johnstone, *Users and Abusers of Psychiatry*, second edition, Routledge, London, 2000, p. 189.
39. Terry Lynch, *Beyond Prozac: Healing Mental Suffering without Drugs*, Marino Books, Dublin, 2002, p. 43.
40. *The Diagnostic and Statistical Manual*, fourth edition, American Psychiatric Association, Washington, DC, 1994, pp.794–5.
41. A report issued by the Department of Health in October, 1999, showed that 2,800 people – two-thirds of them women – were given ECT in the first three months of that year. Robert Kendall, then President of the Royal College of Psychiatrists, explained that women were more likely to be given ECT because more women than men got depressed, and that older women were given ECT because they were more prone to the side effects of drugs. *Guardian*, 2 October 1999.
42. Gwyneth Lewis, op. cit., pp. 6–7.
43. Fellowship of Depressives Anonymous, 36 Chestnut Avenue, Beverley HU17 9QU.
44. Depression Alliance, PO Box 1022, London SE1 7QB.
45. Depressed Anonymous, Box 17471, Louisville, Kentucky 40217, USA, http://www.depressedanon.com
46. Sheila Ernst and Lucy Goodison, *In Our Own Hands, A Book of Self Help Therapy*, The Women's Press, London, 1981.
47. Rainer Maria Rilke, 'For Wolf Graf von Kalckreuth' in *Requiem and Other Poems*, trans. J.B. Leishman, Hogarth Press, London, 1957, pp. 137–41.
48. Gwyneth Lewis, op. cit., p. 50.
49. Ibid., p. 96.

50. Sheldon Kopp, dedication in *If You Meet the Buddha on the Road, Kill Him*.
51. For a detailed account of extraverts and introverts see Dorothy Rowe, *The Successful Self*, HarperCollins, London, 1989.
52. Gwyneth Lewis, op. cit., p. 45.
53. Dorothy Rowe, *Breaking the Bonds*, HarperCollins, London, 1991, pp. 303–24.
54. See Margaret's story, ibid., pp. 187–9.
55. Gwyneth Lewis, op. cit., pp. 177, 213.
56. Ibid., p. 213.
57. Dorothy Rowe, *Time on Our Side: Growing in Wisdom, Not Growing Old*, HarperCollins, London, 1994.
58. Philip Toynbee, *Part of a Journey*, Collins, London, 1981, p. 66.
59. Fenelon, quoted by Aldous Huxley in *The Perennial Philosophy*, Chatto & Windus, London, 1946, p. 292.
60. Lao Tsu, op. cit.
61. Philip Toynbee, op. cit., p. 13.

9. Leaving the prison

1. Philip Toynbee, *Part of a Journey*, Collins, London, 1981, pp. 56, 65, 337.
2. Jill Tweedie, *Guardian*, 12 April 1982. The optical illusions which Jill referred to are:

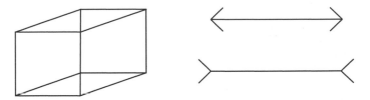

These show how we create our reality with our eyes, and how we can change reality. We can change reality, too, with our words. Is this glass half full or half empty?

3. Dorothy Rowe, *Breaking the Bonds*, HarperCollins, London, 1991.

10. The prison vanishes

1. T.S. Eliot, 'Little Gidding', in *Four Quartets*, Faber, London, 1974.
2. Lao Tsu, *Tao Te Ching*, trans. Gia-Fu Teng and Jane English, Wildwood House, London, 1973.

INDEX